A YEAR IN PEMBROKESHIRE

Jamie Owen and David Wilson

GRAFFEG

A Year in Pembrokeshire
Published in Great Britain in 2018
by Graffeg Limited

Graffeg Limited, 24 Stradey Park Business Centre,
Mwrwg Road, Llangennech, Llanelli,
Carmarthenshire SA14 8YP Wales UK
Tel 01554 824000 www.graffeg.com

A CIP Catalogue record for this book is available from the British Library.

The publisher gratefully acknowledges the financial support of this book by the Welsh Books Council
www.gwales.com

ISBN 9781912213658

1 2 3 4 5 6 7 8 9

Contents

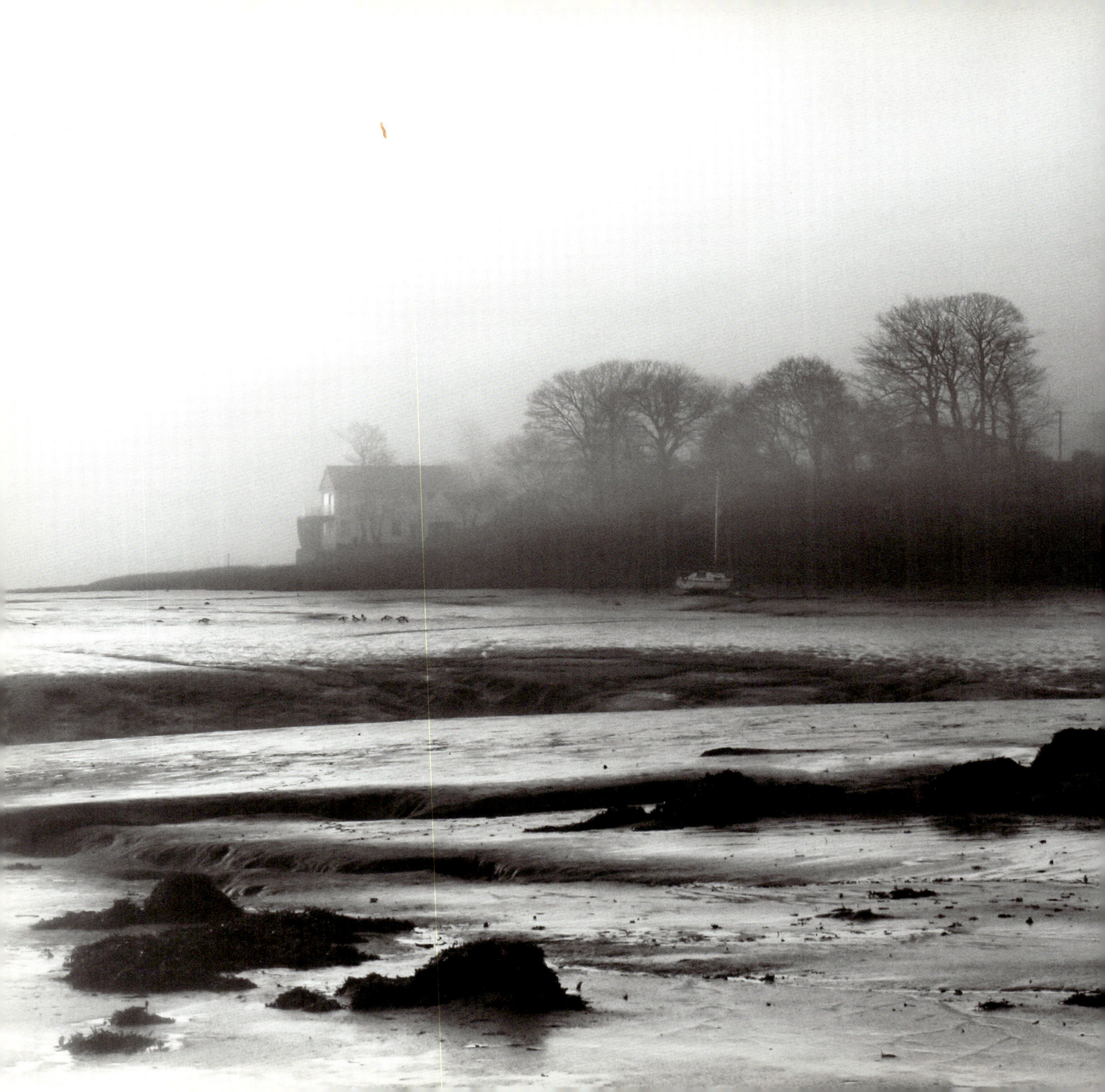

Foreword by Huw Edwards

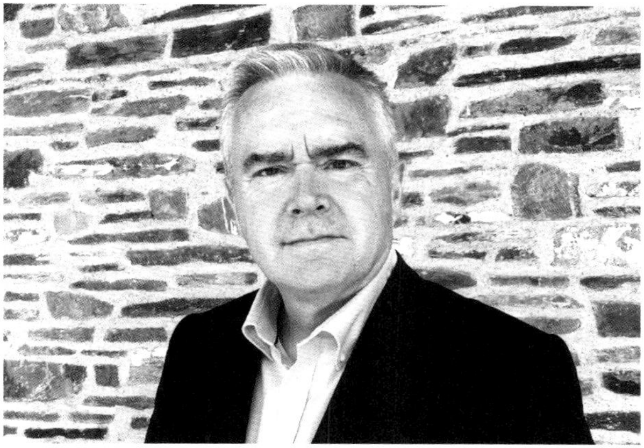

Many of us like to think we know our country like the back of our hands. Lots of us have enjoyed seaside holidays in Tenby or Saundersfoot. But perhaps few of us really know the land that lies beyond the beach or over the hill from the well-trodden paths of those famous picture postcard destinations. It always takes insiders to get the real story. *A Year in Pembrokeshire* is the inside story of two people's passion for Pembrokeshire and some of its less well-known corners.

You'll find treasures here like the Gwaun Valley's celebration of the old new year, Hen Galan, a sailing voyage on the hidden waterway of the upper reaches of the River Cleddau and a walk in the Preseli Hills – all so often ignored by beach-bound visitors.

David Wilson has become one of Wales' most interesting photographers and his stunning images have captured the county he loves. You only achieve this kind of work when you know what to look for and wait patiently for the light and shade to be just right. Jamie Owen has spent his life reporting on the wider canvas of Wales, but his true passion is his native Pembrokeshire. Together they have travelled the county over twelve months, camera and notebook in hand. Their talents combined have produced a hymn of praise to the place they both call home.

A Year in Pembrokeshire is a wonderful celebration of a part of Wales that has been at the crossroads of history for thousands of years. It remains a fascinating and beguiling corner of Britain and this book beautifully captures the people and places that make it so special.

Huw Edwards,
BBC News

Introduction by Jamie Owen and David Wilson

Pembrokeshire is, in some ways, a microcosm of Wales – the north is agricultural and welsh-speaking, the south is more urban, industrial and anglicised. I was born in the south and now live in the north, and like a parent choosing between children, I love them both equally. But they are very different communities. I came from a family that was fiercely proud of its roots – this was the 1970s and the era local government reorganisation saw Pembrokeshire deleted from the map. It heightened a sense of who we were and where we were from. My father loaned me his copy of Richard Fenton's *A Historical Tour through Pembrokeshire* when I was a boy. I devoured its yellowing pages of travels on horseback. The peeling faded leather volume is among my most prized possessions and it is my constant companion on my travels in Pembrokeshire.

Metropolitan media leads us to think that Britain is a homogenised society where everyone does much the same thing as everyone else. In Pembrokeshire you'll still find an independence of spirit that ignores the crowd and has its own ways. This is a community that is proud to be distinctive and different.

There are none so ardent as the exile and I have spent my adult life leaving and returning to Pembrokeshire. Its hold over me is as strong as ever.

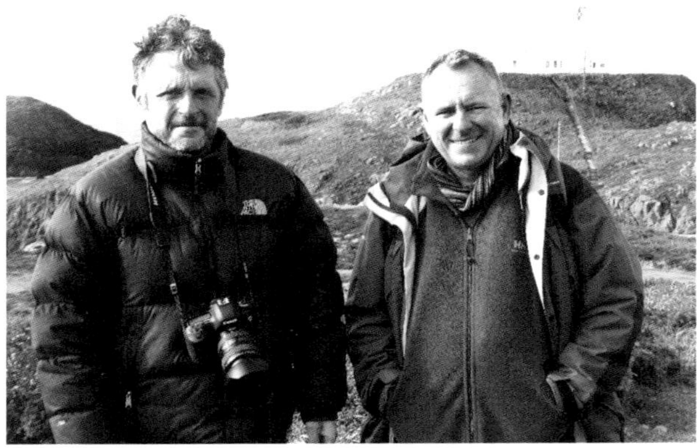

David Wilson and Jamie Owen, Strumble Head

In a noisy, digital world, it offers the peace and stillness that so many of us yearn for.

This is the book I always wanted to write. I've wanted to work with David Wilson for many years and at last we've managed it. To have spent a year in Pembrokeshire, travelling its lanes with someone who is as passionate as me in capturing its spirit has been a joy. This is a love story in prose and pictures.

Jamie Owen

Just over ten years ago, I was given a book of photography called *An English Eye: The Photographs of James Ravilious*. In the 1970s and 80s, Ravilious documented rural communities in north Devon on the cusp of change. He photographed farms, village fairs, church tea parties, and the minutiae of rural life, recording what he sensed was a disappearing culture. It instantly became my most precious photographic book.

The notion of 'a sense of place', so beautifully evoked in Ravilious' book, is difficult to define – it is a combination of many elements; environment and landscape, people and community, customs and celebrations. Ravilious' ability to capture the essence of those rural communities has long been an inspiration to me. And so, when the opportunity arose to document that elusive notion of 'a sense of place' in Pembrokeshire, I was thrilled. Here was the book I had long wanted to photograph.

For Jamie Owen and I, who were both born and brought up in Pembrokeshire, the idea for the book grew from the shared sense that some ways of life are finding their foothold increasingly precarious in a world that speeds up and becomes ever-more uniform with each passing year.

But this is no lament to a dying way of life. It is a celebration of the vibrancy and resilience of diverse local communities within our midst. I would hope that in 50 or even 100 years' time, people will come across this book and view what seems to us now as ordinary, traditional lives, as something unique and special, which of course they are.

David Wilson

In Pembrokeshire you'll still find an independence of spirit that ignores the crowd and has its own ways. This is a community that is proud to be distinctive and different.

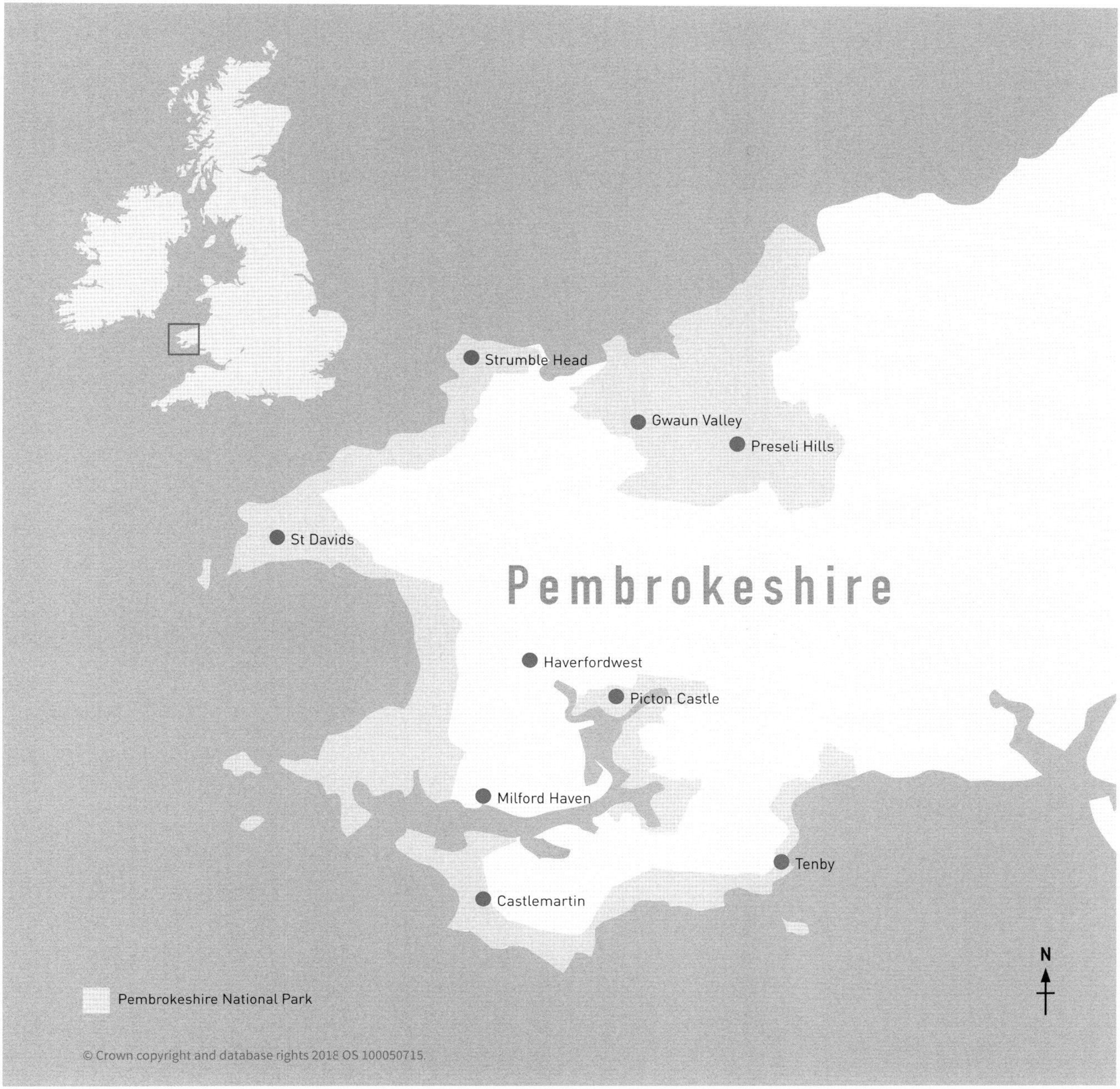
Strumble Head
Gwaun Valley
Preseli Hills
St Davids
Pembrokeshire
Haverfordwest
Picton Castle
Milford Haven
Tenby
Castlemartin
N
Pembrokeshire National Park
© Crown copyright and database rights 2018 OS 100050715.

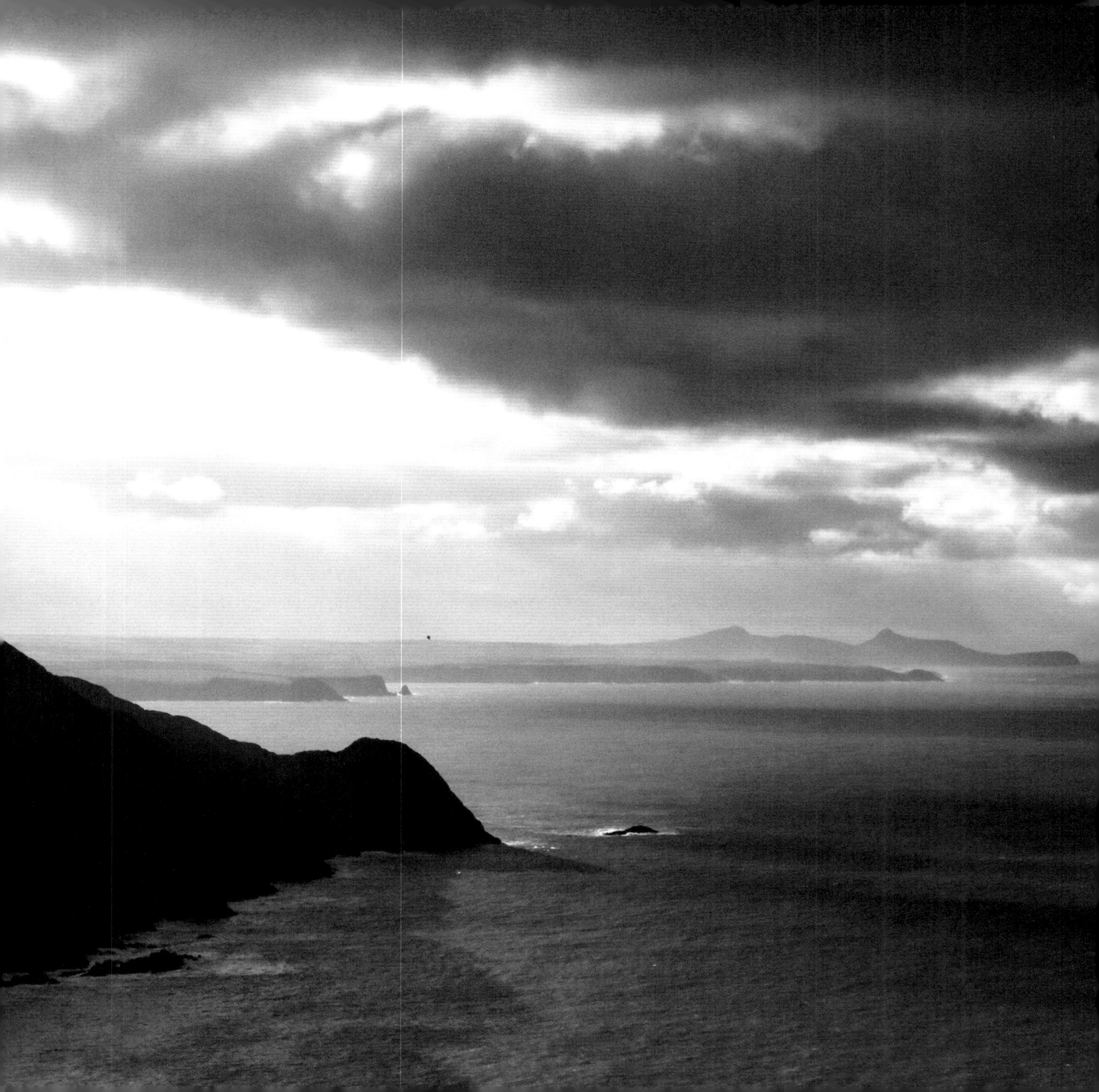

Strumble Head
Walking the Coast

Britain has been battered by storms for days. Thousands of homes are without electricity. Scotland is battling snow. February might not seem the best month to be walking on the edge of the cliffs of the Pembrokeshire Coast Path, but in the calm after the storm, today offers a brief window of sunshine and blue sky. The coast will be deserted and mine alone to enjoy. In a month or two, this route will be busy with wild-flower lovers and dolphin spotters. Their warmer walks will be carpeted with spring colours. My journey will be enjoyed in monochrome, except for my face and hands, red from windburn. This is a solitary and selfish expedition. I will be spoilt with the generosity of a bleak landscape that is almost empty.

Gale force winds cancelled yesterday's ferry. On the tarmac below in Fishguard harbour, a day's worth of delayed Ireland-bound road traffic waits for the ship from Rosslare. Even in the age of the internet and mobile phones, a good storm returns travelling to its ancient uncertainties – sitting in a harbour watching for a break in the weather, timetables forgotten, waiting for high water, calmer waves and the skies to lighten.

At first light, the previous day's rolling Irish Sea has given way to a shimmering, Mediterranean-like stillness, the early sun flashing off the water.

Fishguard's harbour was blasted out of rock from the hillside to make a long protective arm of a breakwater reaching into the sea. When it was opened, this was to be the terminus of the Great Western Railway, intended as Pembrokeshire's main seaport, replacing Neyland in the south of the county. The Great Western Railway ordered three new steamers for its service to Rosslare. It was an auspicious start to a bold ambition – a busy port servicing the world's sea traffic – but it never really gathered momentum. Today, towns like Fishguard, Pembroke Dock and Holyhead seem to have lost their early drive. Few travellers linger around ports and spend their money; instead they speed on their way, leaving Pembrokeshire's harbours in their mirrors. The small stores and pubs of Fishguard, once bustling with customers, are losing the struggle with out-of-town retail and the rise of internet shopping.

The breakwater's construction in Fishguard Harbour led to unanticipated silting and the prospect of future

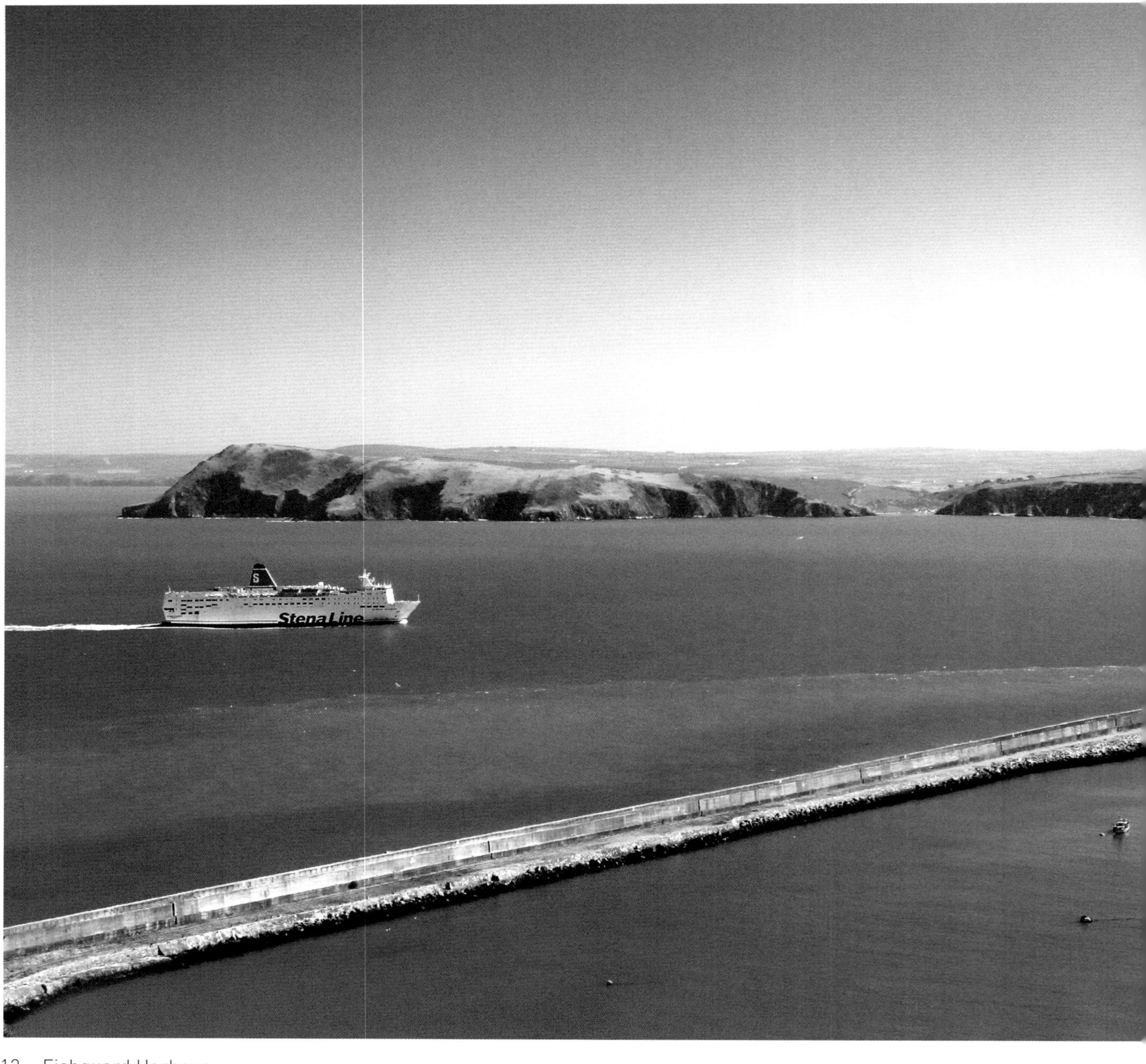
Stena Line

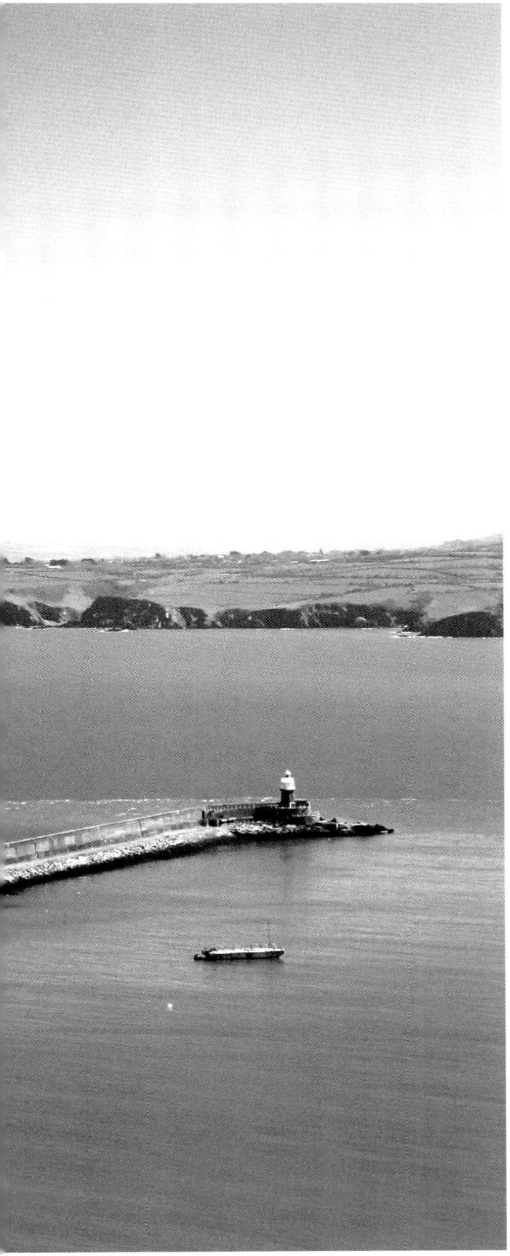

visits from larger liners was abandoned. Harbour Village, the start of my walk, was originally built to house workers during its construction. The men who lived in the houses beside me once walked down the hill to build the huge wall of stone that would outlast their lives.

This is also home to an important chapter in the story of air travel; the first successful flight from Britain to Ireland was made from Harbour Village in 1912 by Denys Corbett Wilson, flying a Bleriot XI. The flight lasted 1 hour 40 minutes and landed near Enniscorthy in Ireland.

Strumble Head still plays a significant part in contemporary flight. It is home to a clever bit of kit called a VHF omnidirectional radio range (VOR) – a short-range radio navigation system enabling aircraft to know their position and stay on course by receiving radio signals transmitted by a network of fixed ground radio beacons. Strumble VOR is a way-point in many transatlantic flights.

My navigational plan, with my feet firmly on the ground, is to leave Fishguard and Goodwick behind me and walk the coast path around Strumble Head. This is part of the Pembrokeshire Coast Path, although I won't be tackling its full 186 miles. The days are still short and cold, so I'm planning to walk just eight.

There's good reason to choose this stretch of Pembrokeshire for a brisk winter's walk – Strumble Head is one of the best sites in Britain to view porpoise and seals. They can often be spotted in the water beneath the lighthouse at Strumble, though today will be too cold to hang around waiting for a glimpse.

This coast has wrecked plenty of ships, resulting in the construction of the lighthouse. Among their number, a French shipwreck, possibly from the last invasion of Britain, lies beneath the waves, and Calburga, wrecked in 1915, was one of Canada's last square-rigged sailing ships.

Past Crincoed Point and Pen Anglas now and the muted sound of a chugging inboard diesel engine floats over a quiet cliff, before a day-boat comes into view. The fisherman standing at the tiller wears bright yellow oilskins, the same colour as the gorse beside the coast path. He'll have been stuck in harbour for the best part of a week in this bad weather. A better day beckons.

I'd expected the path to be a sea of mud after days of rain but the wind has dried the earth. Spring is approaching and soon the clocks go forward. The few small trees inland to my left, bent from the wind, are still skeletal and are weeks from bursting into bud.

Anglas Bay, Porth Maen and Maen Jaspis fall behind me. Ciliau Moor holds a week's worth of rain in its deceptive grass, which squelches sponge-like beneath my boots. Even the stepping-stones, so kindly laid, now struggle to keep their heads above water. There's a dog barking at Ciliau Farm, but no one is at home.

A brief detour from the cliffs for a few minutes, to head one field inland, offers the chance to see Llanwnda.

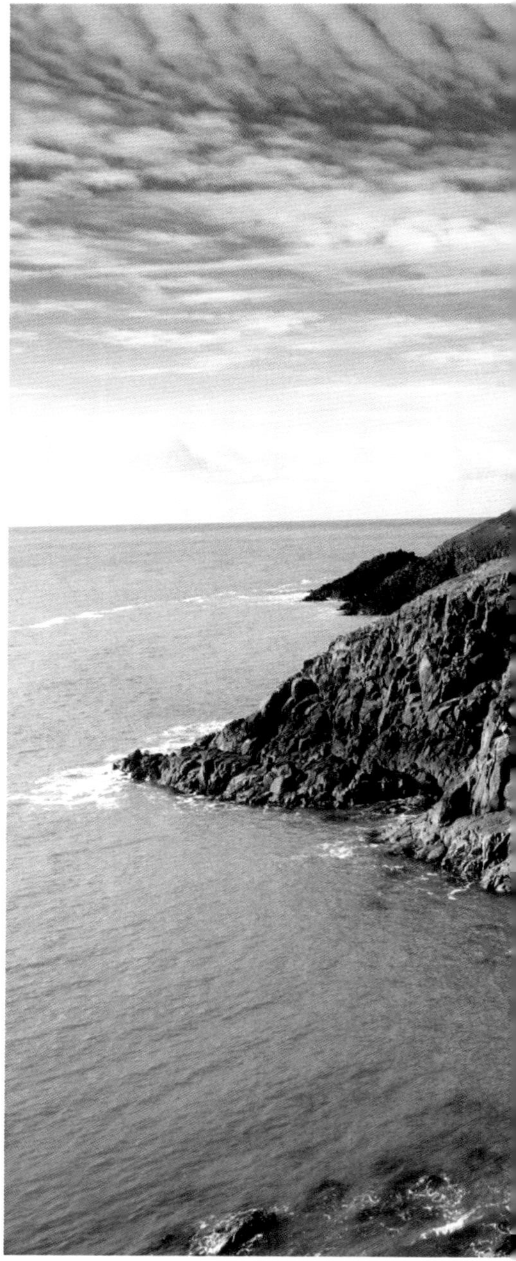

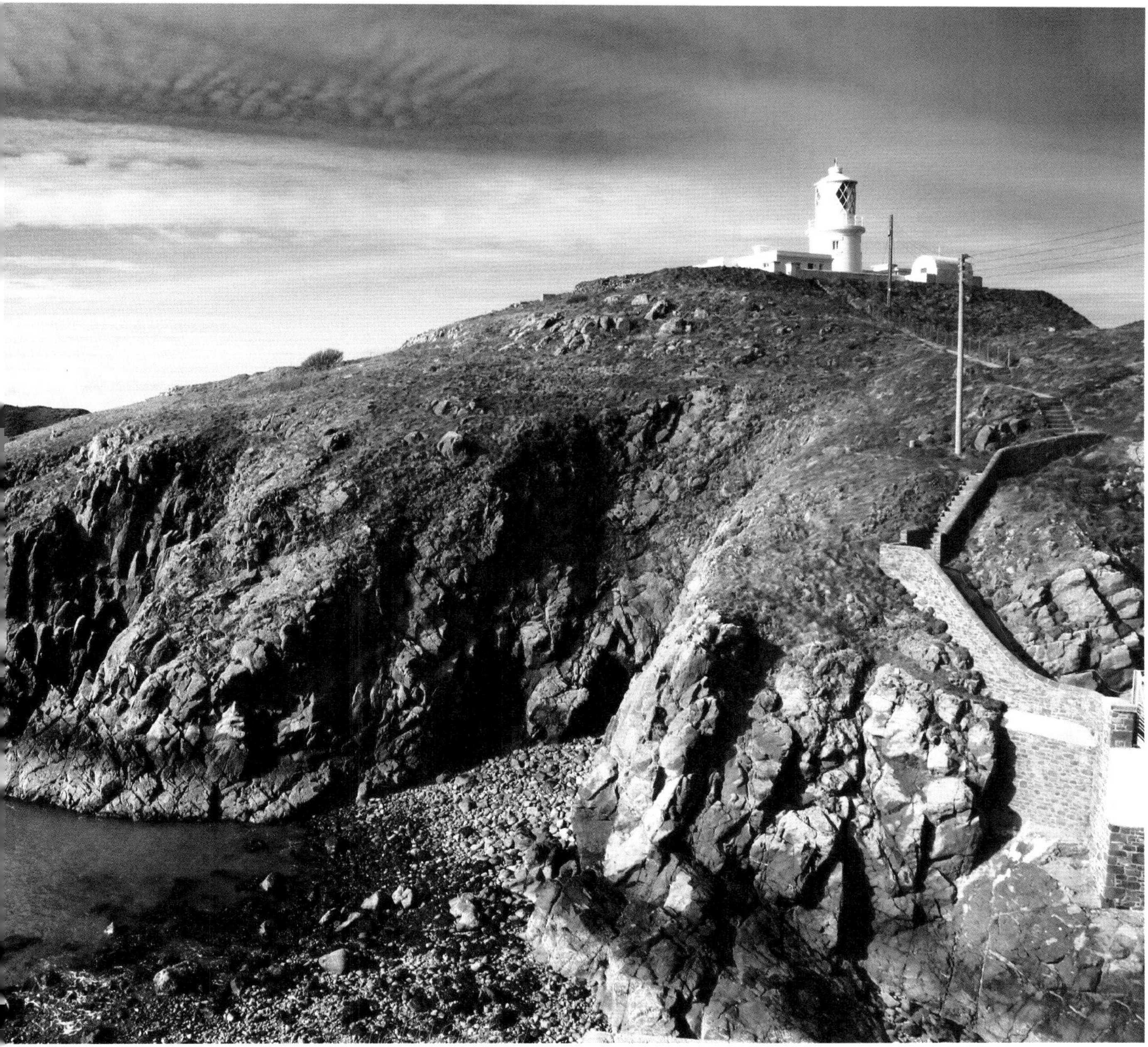

Strumble Head lighthouse

Hunched low to shelter from the storms, St Gwyndaf's sits within the walled churchyard in the centre of Llanwnda. The fabric is essentially a medieval parish church, but was restored in the 1880s.

A short walk back towards the cliffs and the coast path, where a rope and some swings have been suspended from the trees – a playground dangling over the stream.

Past Aber Felin now and the headland Carregwastad, then the memorial stone to mark the last invasion of Britain in 1797. It's strange to stand here on this quietest of deserted mornings and think that on another distant day, in a long forgotten February, an invasion began here. It takes me a few moments to realise that the hissing sound just inches from my boots is an adder, disturbed from hibernation under the stones and now moving slowly into the nearby bush. Its dark zigzag gradually disappears but its lethargy suggests it's not as nervous as I am.

The fading words carved into the memorial stone recall the Battle of Fishguard – the military invasion of mainland Great Britain by revolutionary France. Local tradition has it that the rag-tag French rabble got drunk and were rounded up by Pembrokeshire women dressed as men carrying pitchforks – the perfect ingredients for tabloid legend, or at least one of the many versions of history.

There isn't another soul on my walk – no one else in either direction, although I am never alone. Welsh mountain sheep and black cattle look up from their grazing behind fences and stone walls to spy their momentary companion before continuing their all-day breakfast.

The National Park has reintroduced Welsh mountain ponies to Strumble Head. They help to tread down the bracken and improve the biodiversity of the landscape and are usually inquisitive and friendly. Mares with foals can be unpredictable, but the pair I encounter are obviously used to greeting walkers and receiving food too. They walk with me for more than half a mile before a kissing gate parts us.

The white hulk of the Irish ferry emerges and makes its way towards Fishguard. It's proceeding dead slow and biding its time for high water on the Pembrokeshire coast.

Penrhyn is a squat little cottage that clings to the edge of the coast path. Like so many houses built near the sea, it faces away from the view with its back to the prevailing wind. When it was originally built, the best protection against a storm was stone walls, and so the living rooms are on the leeward side of the building, looking inland. The kitchen and bathroom have the best sea-facing views. This morning its occupants can look across the Irish Sea for miles.

After rambling along the coast path for more than an hour, at last some other walkers are heading towards me, four walkers with dogs making for Fishguard. They are in Pembrokeshire for the weekend, enjoying the one dry sunny day of their holiday.

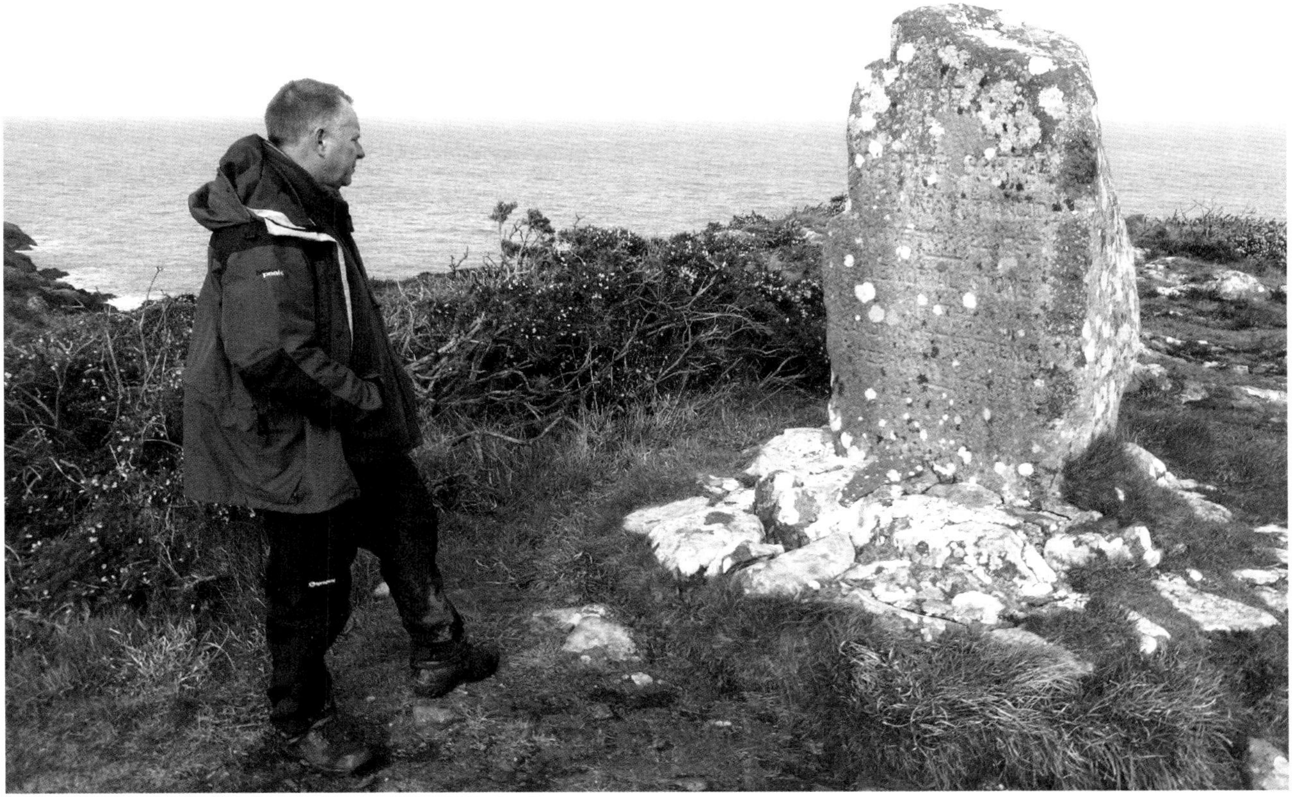

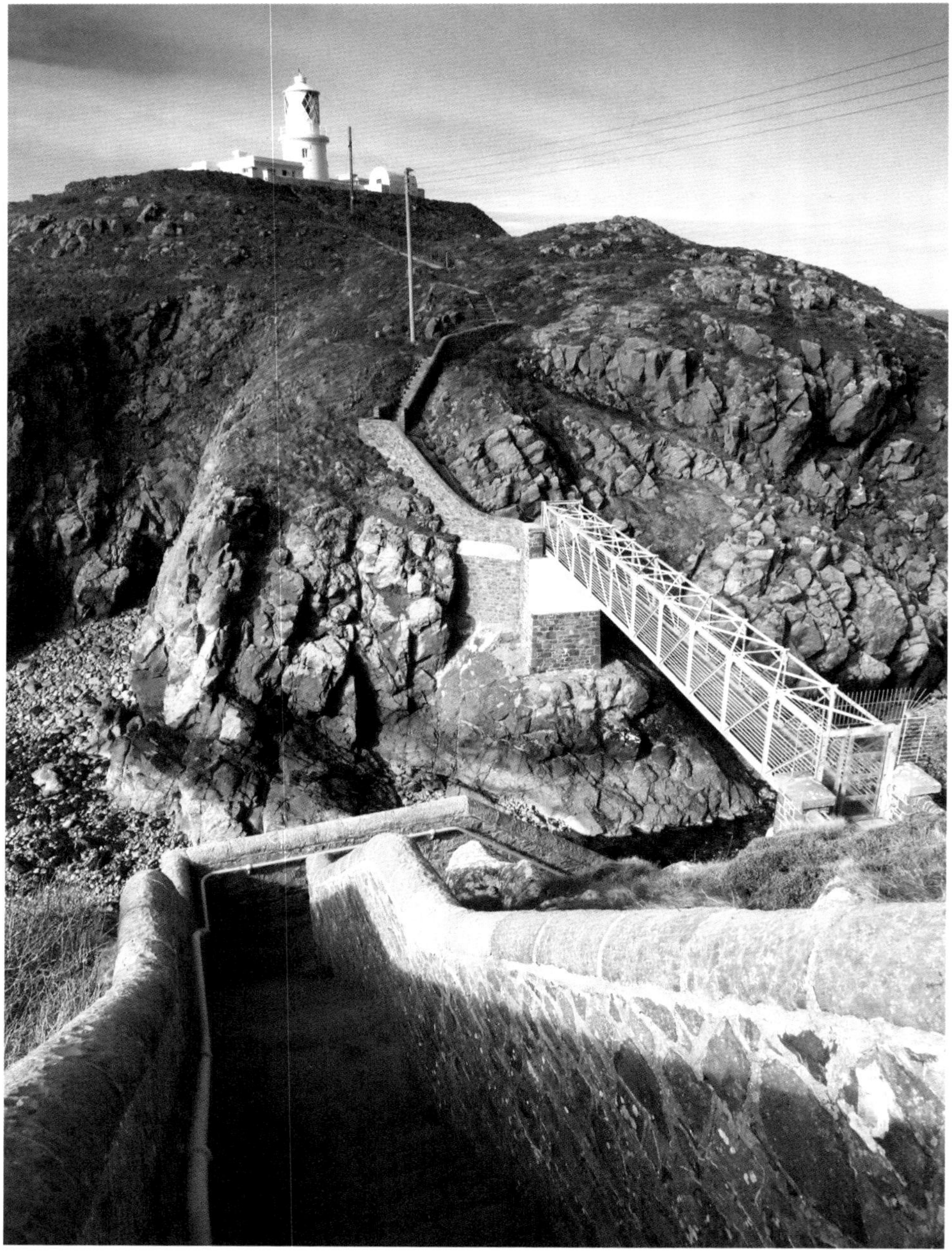

Strumble Head Lighthouse sits not on the highest point of the landscape but on the edge of the cliff. Its sterile white paint is in stark contrast to the intense blue of the sea and the faded baize tapestry of surrounding fields. The small car park provides the perfect place to sit and watch the ocean. A few families leave their cars and wrap up against the cold for a short wander before clambering back into their vehicles.

The present lighthouse was constructed in 1908 and was one of the last lighthouses to be built in Britain. Inside its castle-like stone tower the original lantern sits on a mercury bath. The lighthouse was fully electrified in 1965 and the lighthouse keepers are long gone. This is now a fully automated lighthouse operated from Trinity House Operations Control Centre in Harwich. A plaque in the lantern-room is inscribed with a verse from Psalm 127:

Except the Lord build the house,
They labour in vain that build it:
Except the Lord keep the city,
the watchman waketh but in vain.

An electric fog signal was installed at the lighthouse in 1969. Before this, mariners listened out for a warning system that used explosive signal charges. It couldn't have been much fun living on Strumble Head when the explosives were going off in deep fog.

The present lighthouse was constructed in 1908 and was one of the last lighthouses to be built in Britain.

In an age of sophisticated satellite navigation systems and ferryboats that can almost dock themselves, the lighthouse might seem an anachronism. But when electrical systems fail on ships, it's comforting to know that the light still shines on the cliffs on one of the most dangerous stretches of water in the country.

Throughout the ages people have always held islands and peninsulas in reverence. Saints, warriors, painters and thinkers have continually headed for these thin stretches of land that reach into the sea. The Ordnance Survey map shows Strumble Head littered with standing stones and ruined forts. These days Strumble is a favourite destination to reconnect with the natural world through walking, bird watching or seal spotting. Most days you'll see waterproofed worshippers paying homage. But relatively recently, in 1904, Strumble Head was witness to a religious revival at Harmony Baptist Church. A contemporary source gives this account:

'The revival has taken deep root at Harmony, and for some time past prayer meetings have been held nightly, at which some remarkable scenes of conversion have been witnessed. This reached a grand culmination on Saturday afternoon and Sunday morning last when forty converts were baptised in the baptistry...six of the converts were baptised on Saturday afternoon, and the remaining 34 were baptised on Sunday morning. A more suitable day for the performance of this rite could hardly have been desired. True, there was a keen wind blowing, but there was a freshness in the air which invigorated

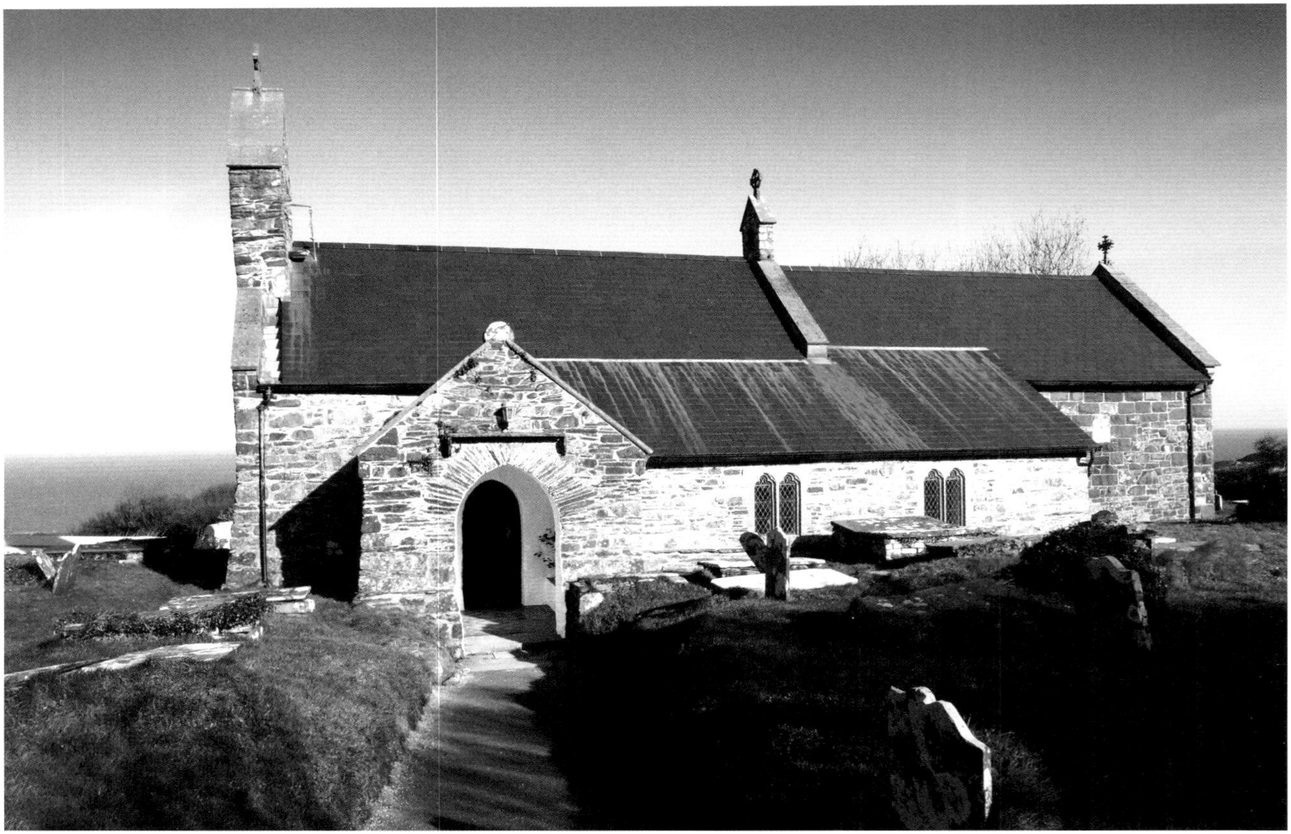

 St Gwyndaf's Church, Llanwnda

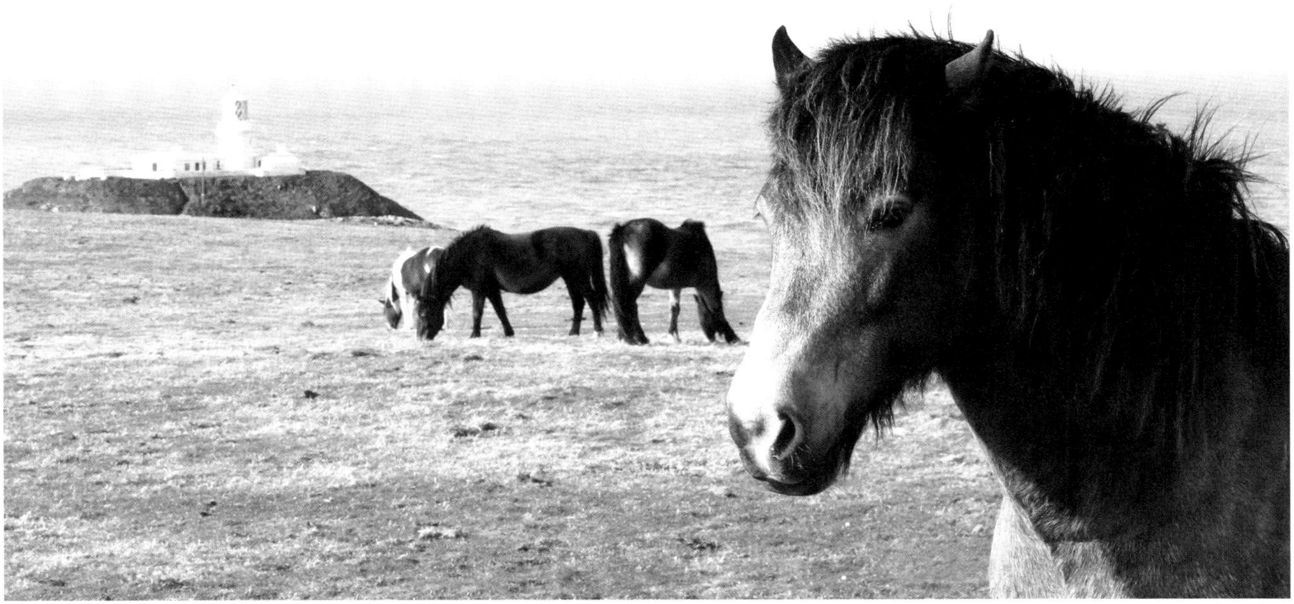

one, and under these pleasant conditions it was not surprising to find hundreds of people assembling at the place of Baptism to witness the ceremony. At the baptistry the service was introduced by the Rev W Rees...wading into the water waist deep.'

Garn Fawr is a towering, constant presence in my final miles. They chose wisely when they staked out locations for Iron Age forts – from the top of Garn Fawr you can see for miles in every direction. Today even the lighthouse seems dwarfed. The ramparts have lasted well over 2000 years. The fort was chosen for a First World War lookout point. There is no noise today other than the sound of the sea and birdsong, but 440 million years ago volcanoes shook Pembrokeshire. Garn Fawr is a prehistoric relic from that time, along with Garn Fechan and Garn Gilfach.

Pwll Deri is home to surely one of the prettiest youth hostels in Britain. For the price of a round of drinks you can stay here on the edge of the cliff staring out at one of the most mesmeric locations in Wales. A memorial stone nearby commemorates the poet Dewi Emrys, whose poem *Pwllderi* was written in Pembrokeshire dialect:

'a thina'r meddilie sy'n dwad ichi
pan foch chi'n ishte uwchben Pwllderi'

'and these are the thoughts that come to you
when you sit above Pwllderi'

Dewi won the Chair at the National Eisteddfod on four occasions and infamously pawned his 1926 Eisteddfod Crown in Swansea.

Wherever you look on this peninsula you'll see a perfect landscape or seascape that has inspired countless poets and painters. The artist John Piper made his home here with his wife, Myfanwy Evans. For a young man who lost a brother in the First World War and made his name sketching the ruins of bombed out cities during the Second, Strumble Head was a simple escape.

Myfanwy was born into a Welsh family in London and was awarded a scholarship to Oxford. Later she became an art critic and opera librettist. She regularly collaborated with the composer Benjamin Britten on his operas and also with composer Alun Hoddinott on most of his operatic works. She was a friend of the poet John Betjeman, who wrote several poems about her, including *Myfanwy* and *Myfanwy at Oxford*.

At the start of the Second World War, Piper volunteered to work interpreting aerial reconnaissance photographs for the RAF but was persuaded to work as an official war artist instead, leading him to ask to be allowed to paint bombed churches in 1940. He'd visit bombed cities as soon as possible following an air raid and arrived in Coventry the morning after the attack of 1940 that resulted in 1000 casualties and the destruction of the medieval cathedral. In the 1960s and 1970s his cottage on Strumble Head was his haven and inspiration.

The artist John Piper made his home here with his wife, Myfanwy Evans.

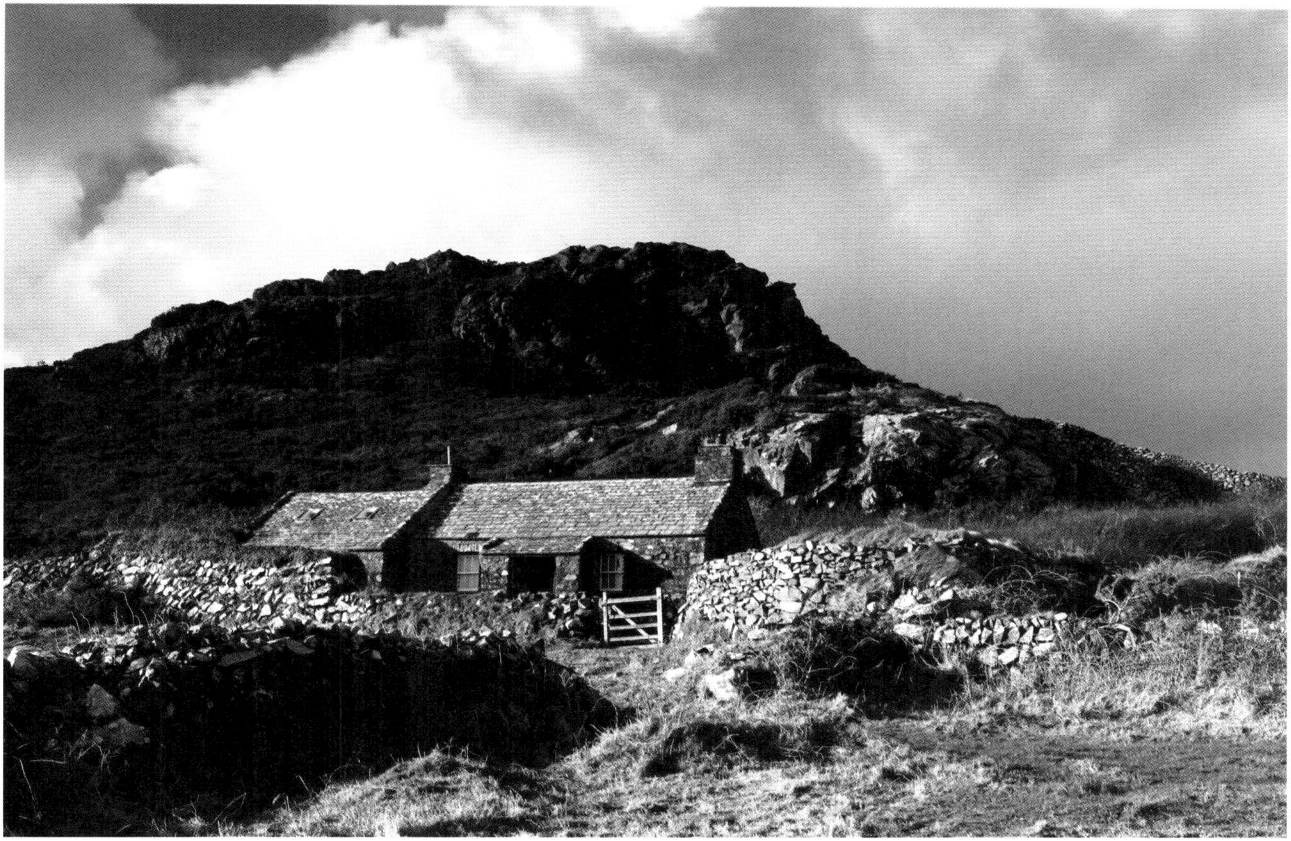

John Piper's cottage beneath Garn Fawr

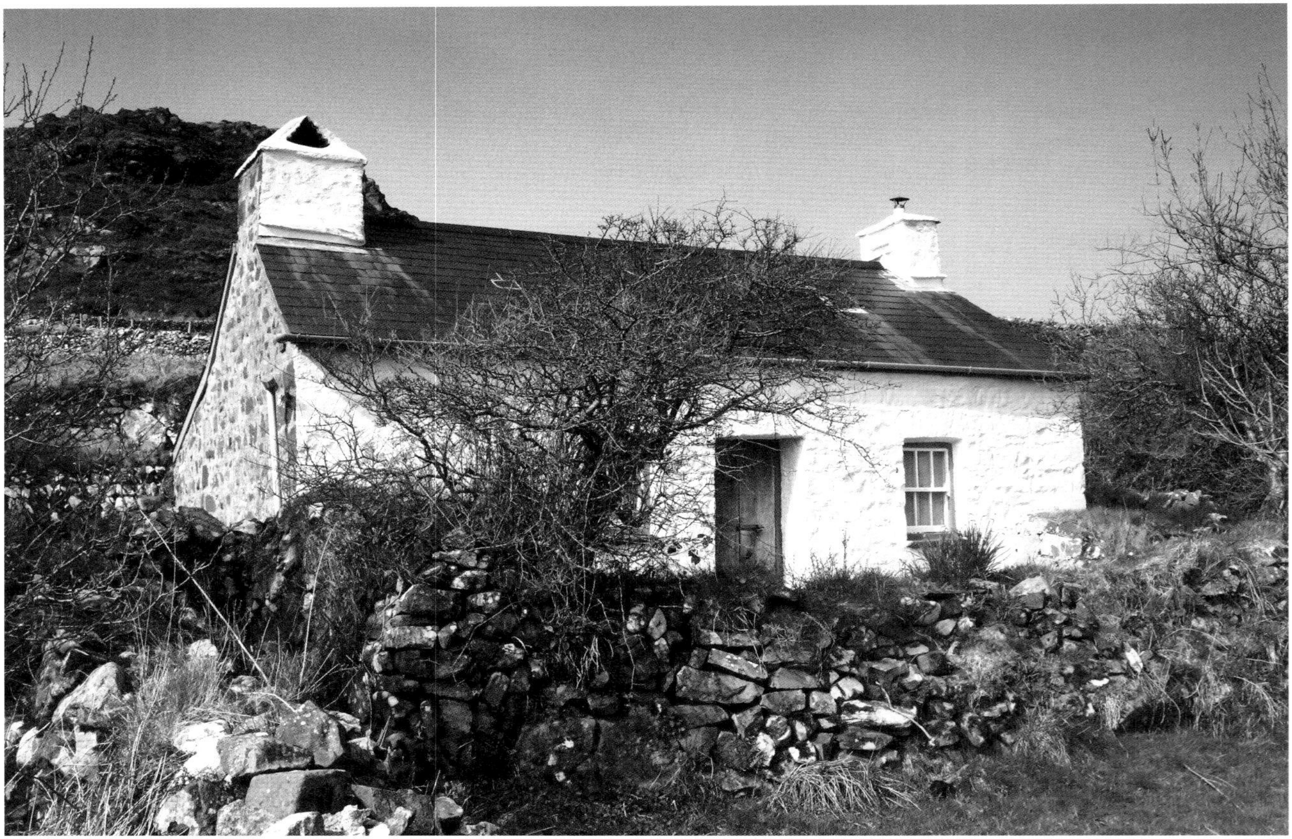

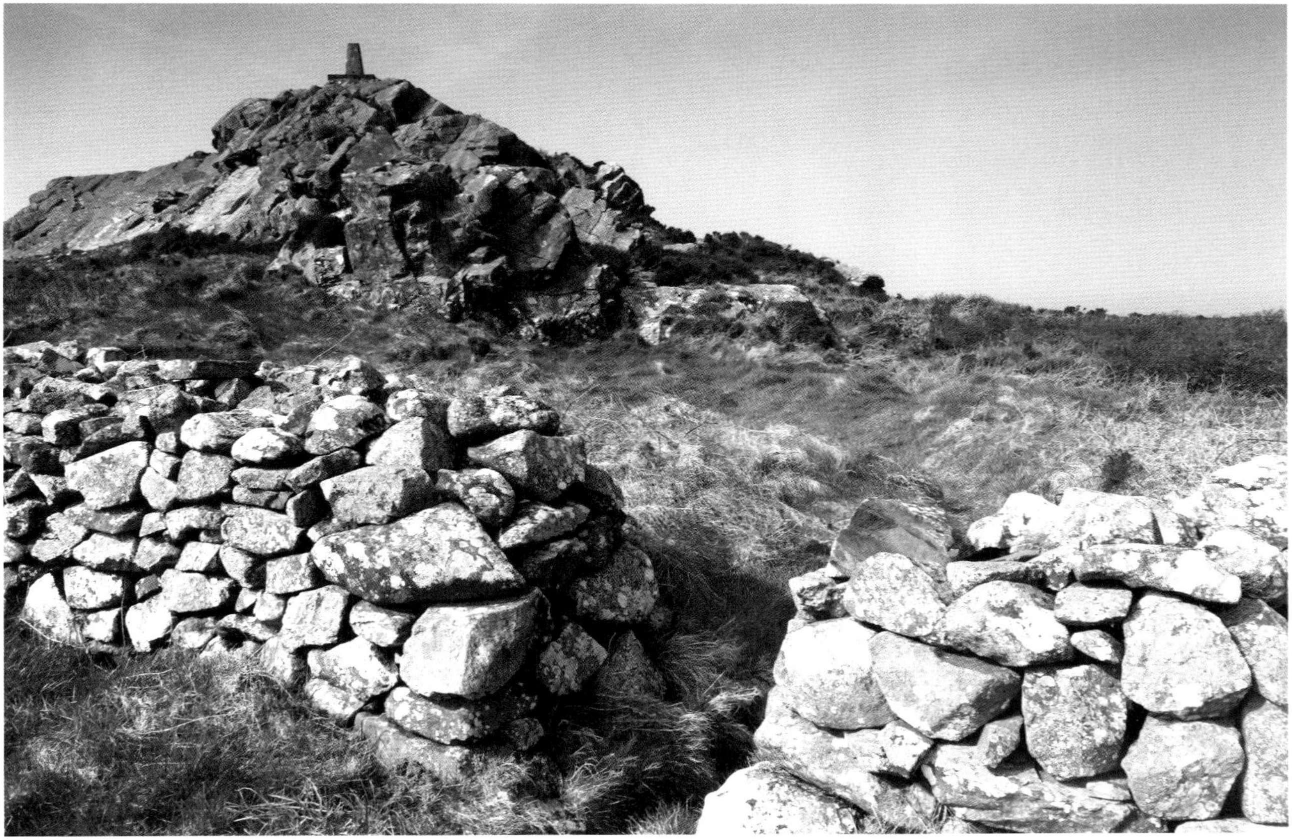

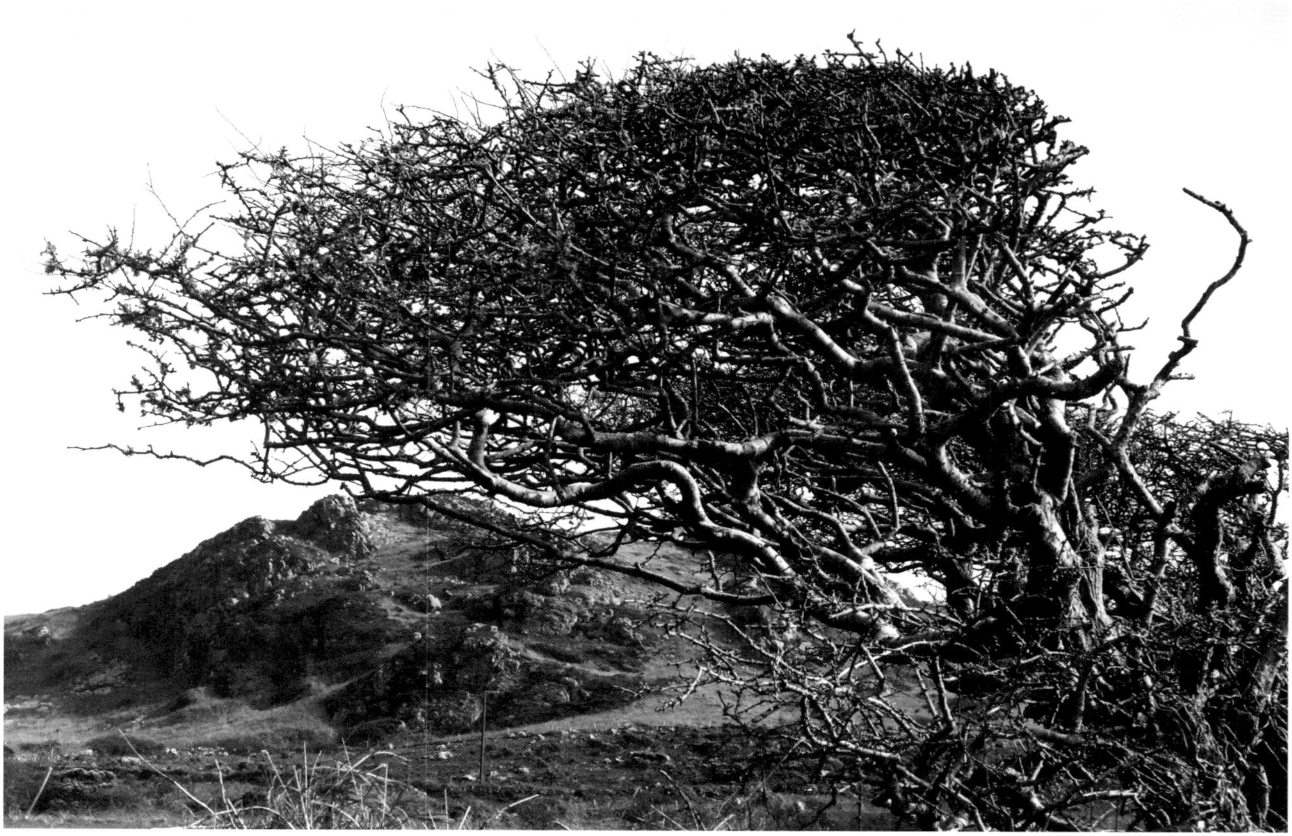

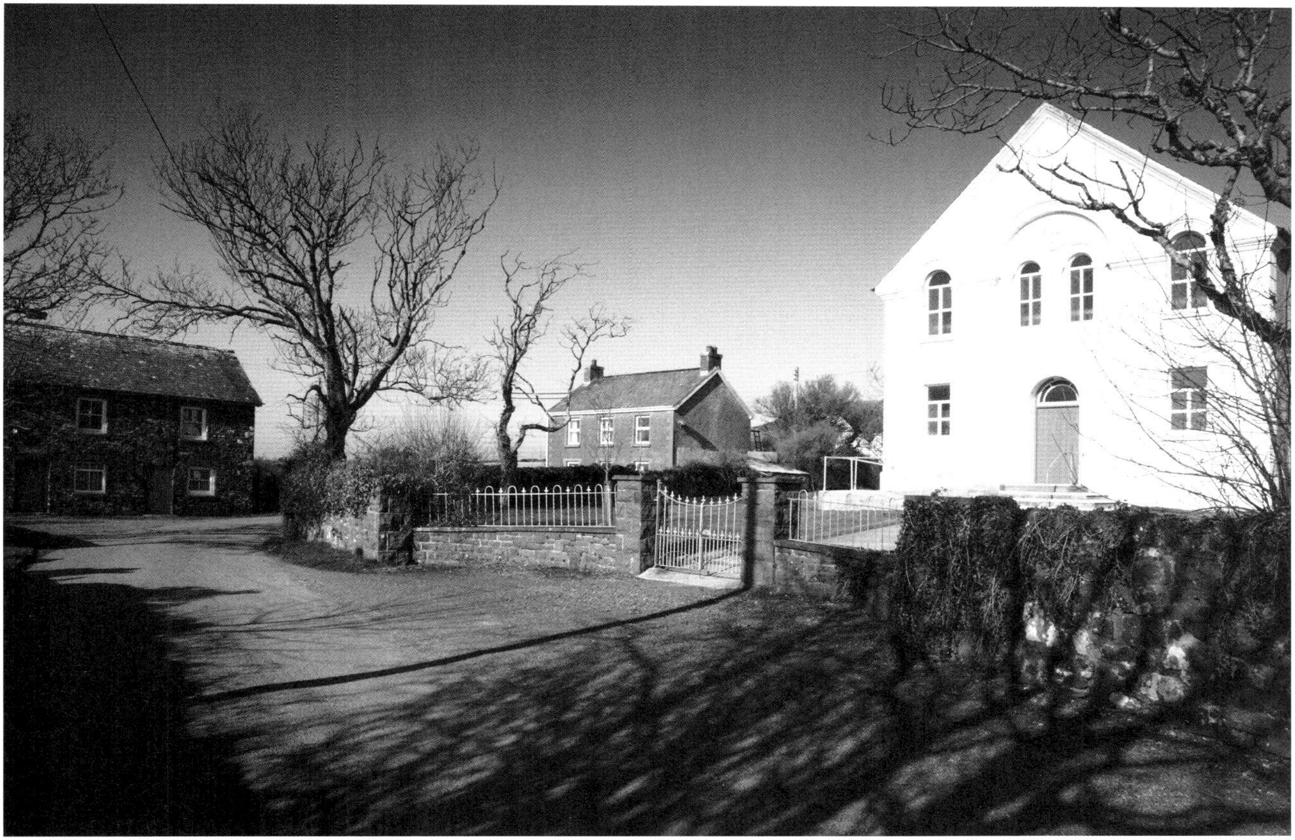

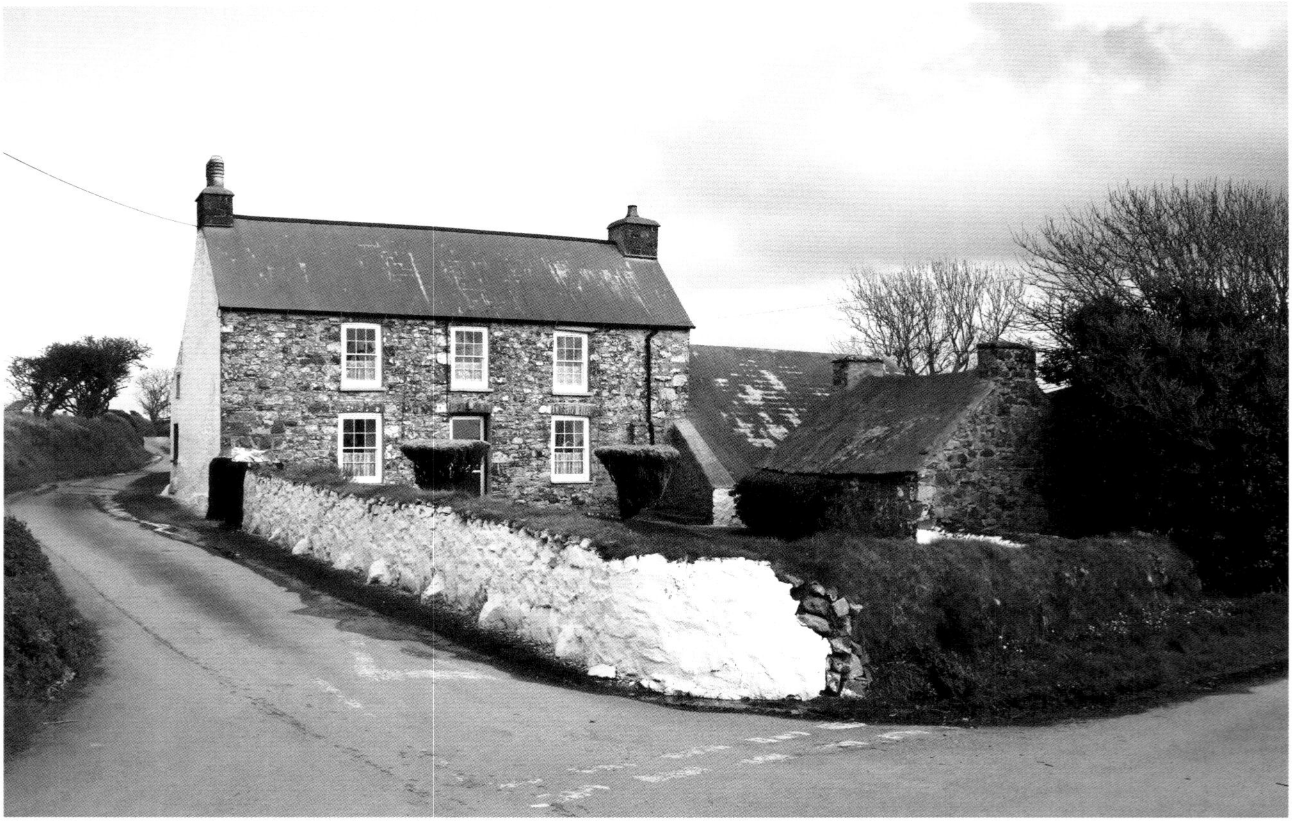

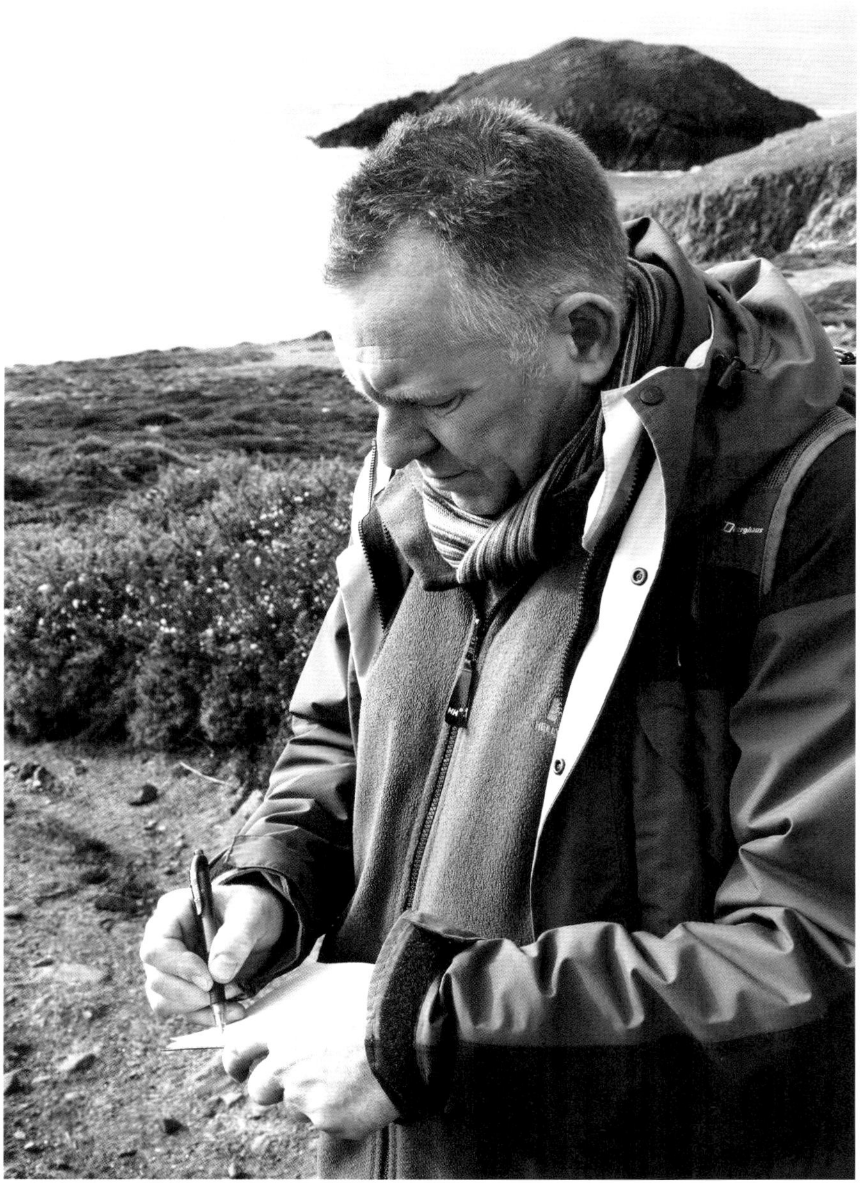

Jamie Owen, Strumble Head

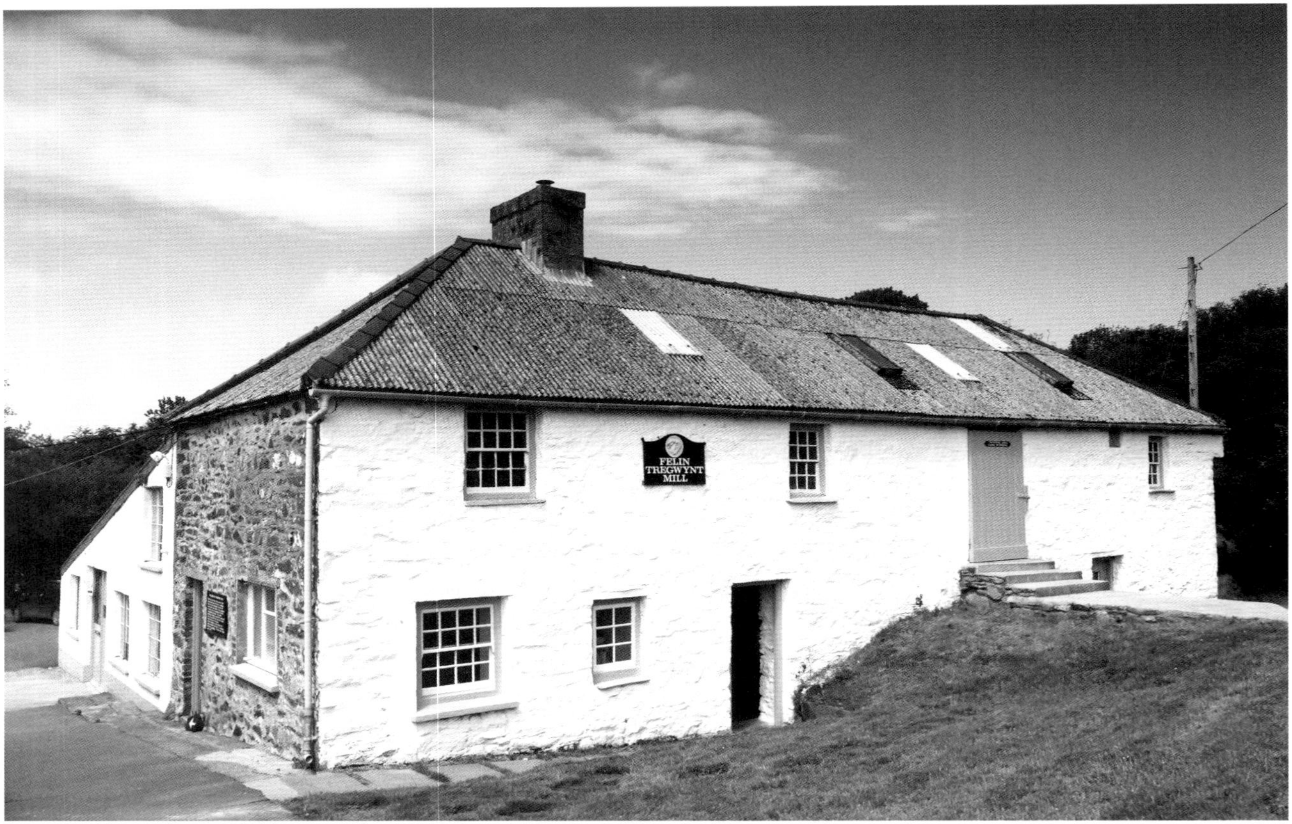
FELIN
TREGWYNT
MILL

My feet are tired and I'm in need of a hot drink. The last few miles are in sight. My final destination on my coast path walk is Melin Tregwynt Woollen Mill and in particular its tea shop.

Behind the entrance to the looms, where the tourists watch the weaving, worn stone steps lead to a first floor storeroom. Stretching the length of a cricket pitch, boxes of yarn of every colour imaginable wait patiently to be turned into cloth. Even in their individual, bright colours, before they are combined to make rugs and clothes, they invite caressing. The rolls of material are labelled with exotic names: Red Venetian, Peony, Light Blue, Silvery Grey, Viola, King Fisher, Dark Apple, Pineapple, Mustard and Brandy will soon lose their single status and be married many times over with the myriad of combinations that the designers choose.

Melin Tregwynt is half a mile or so from the Coast Path. There's been a mill here since 1819, originally for corn and converted to a woollen mill later in the 19th century. The business thrived in the 1960s and 1970s and survived the recession that forced many Welsh mills to close during the 1980s. Its workers have been taking fleeces from sheep on surrounding farms and spinning them into cloth and blankets for generations, but this isn't some twee folksy throwback. The founder's grandson entered the business and started to develop foreign trade. Pembrokeshire's businesses once built their fortunes on the ocean, and now it's the internet that allows them to export overseas.

These days you'll find Melin Tregwynt exporting internationally, with their goods available in the United States, Japan and the Middle East. Strumble Head might be a long way from anywhere, but this is a thriving operation with its sights firmly set on the global market. Far from being located in the back of beyond, the business is sitting beside the high seas and its customers are all over the world.

Melin Tregwynt is half a mile or so from the Coast Path.

Another sign of the mill's modernisation is apparent as the whitewashed stone building is shrouded in scaffolding – they are installing solar panels to generate electricity for the looms and the builders are tidying up at the end of the day.

The mill was previously powered by water from the stream. Unusually, the water wheel is inside the building rather than outside and no longer powers the machinery, though there are plans to use hydro-power here once more.

A handful of customers enjoy afternoon tea in the shop, some of them clutching their carrier bags from the adjacent store: a new blanket for a bed, a dressing gown, a handbag and a new purse peep out of their packaging. I join the queue for tea and cake, walking a little more slowly now after eight miles on a winter's day.

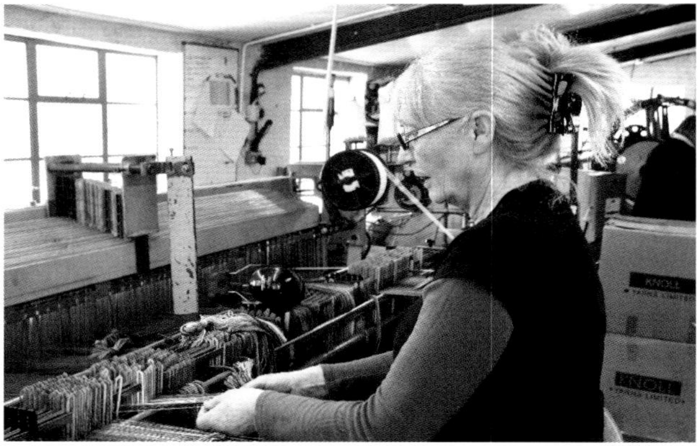
KNOLL
KNOLL
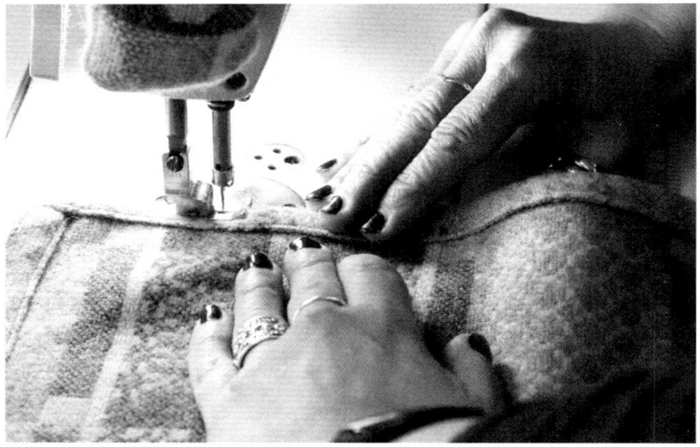
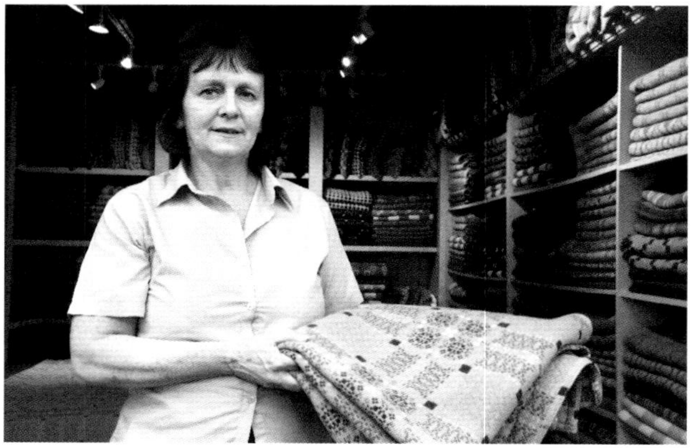
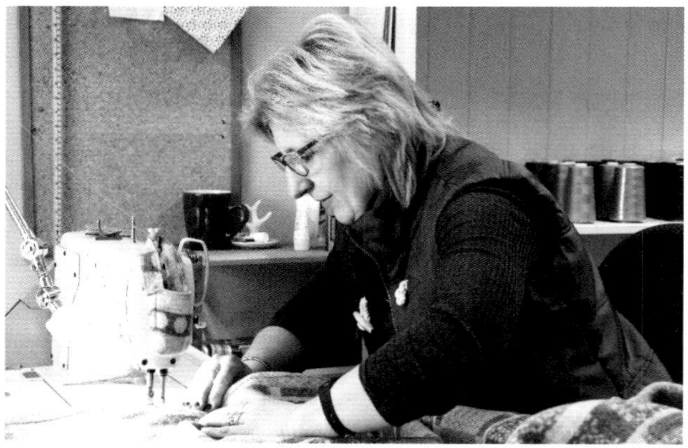

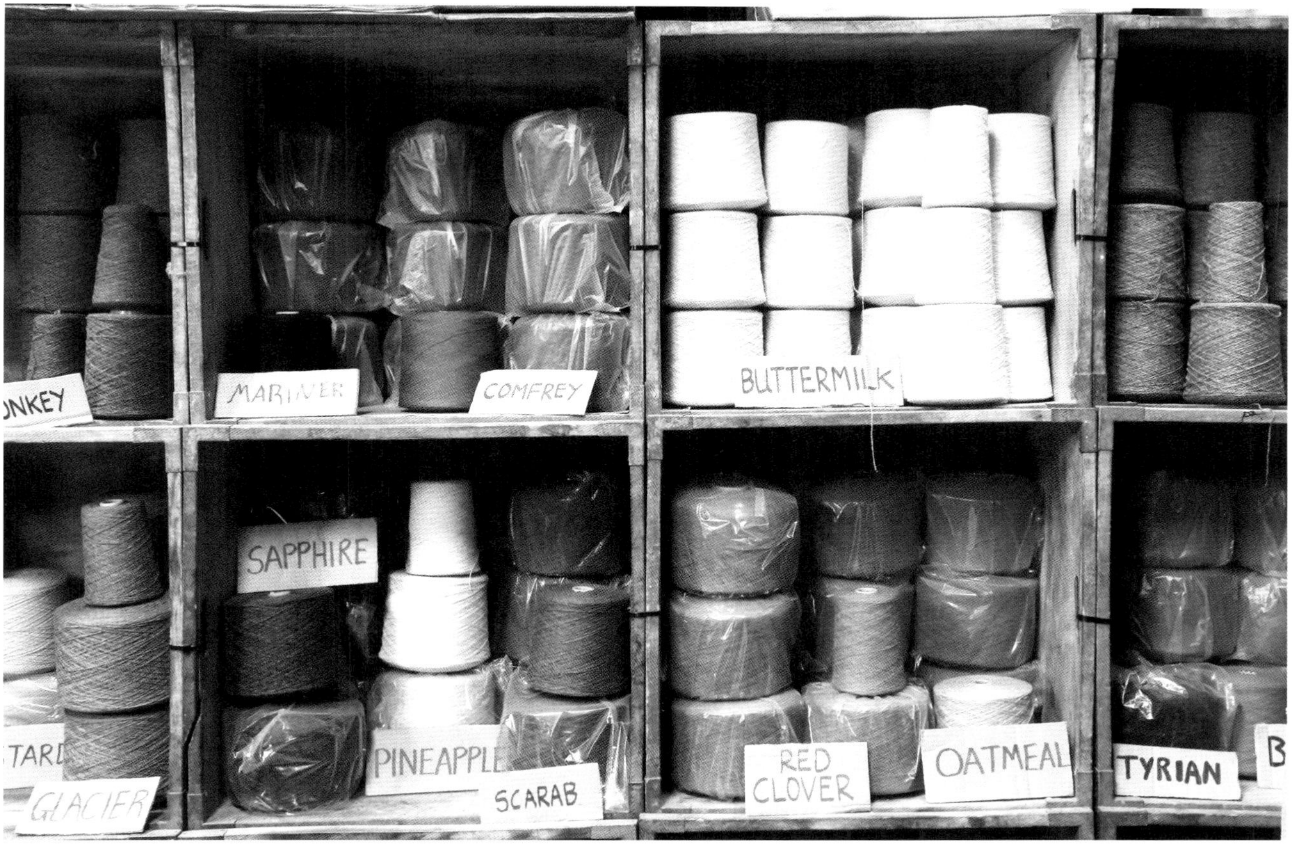
MARINER
COMFREY
BUTTERMILK
SAPPHIRE
PINEAPPLE
SCARAB
GLACIER
RED CLOVER
OATMEAL
TYRIAN

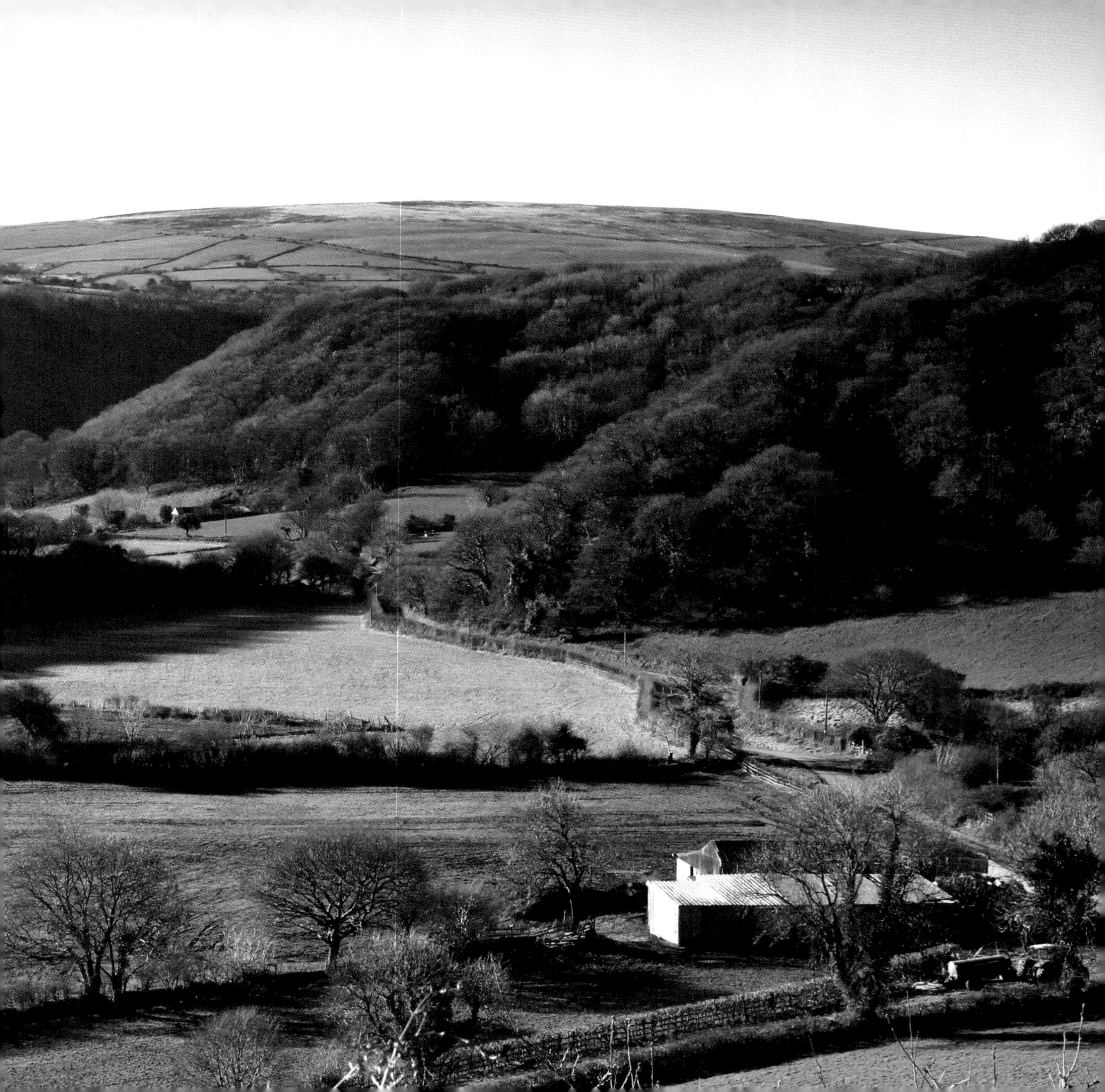

Hen Galan

New Year in the Gwaun Valley

It's early morning on the first day of a new year in the Gwaun Valley – so early that the mist, fast asleep on the valley floor, has yet to wake. The sun is slow to arrive here and will be early to leave. Even if you think you know Pembrokeshire, you would probably have to get lost to find the Gwaun Valley – its twisting lanes and hidden hamlets are a well-kept secret. Come here and you are entering a quieter life, away from the noise.

Today is 13 January and the start of Hen Galan, the celebrations to mark the New Year in the Gwaun Valley. Time passes slowly here. A tradition from an old calendar is about to be reborn with a new generation following in the footsteps of their ancestors. Young children will soon gather at their school before setting off around the houses of the Gwaun Valley, singing traditional Welsh songs. In return, householders provide *calennig* (gifts) of sweets and money. A day as magical as Christmas is about to unfold.

For the Romans, Janus, from whom the month of January is thought to have taken its name, was the god of new beginnings.

Observing the old calendar is not unique to the Gwaun Valley. Various Christian feast dates were used for the New Year in Europe during the Middle Ages, but in the 16th century European countries began officially making 1 January the start of the New Year. The Julian calendar was proposed by Caesar in 46 BC. It was the dominant calendar in the Roman world, until replaced by the Gregorian calendar in 1582 by Pope Gregory XIII.

Beneath blue sky and weak sunshine, two hill forts keep watch over a herd of mud-splattered black Welsh cattle, grazing silently beside the loud, twisting and full to the brim River Gwaun.

In Llanychllwydog School, built in the 1880s, Headteacher Mrs Meredydd Francis and her teaching assistant Nerys are preparing to welcome back the 25 children who have spent the early morning travelling around the farms of the Gwaun Valley, ushering in New Year. This is her third year in charge of a school that is responsible for pupils aged from 3 to 11. There are only two classrooms, their walls covered in the drawings and paintings of childhood. Lunch will be delivered from Puncheston School a few miles away and is eaten at the desks in the bigger classroom. Mrs Francis and her two staff are former pupils.

There is singing at the schoolroom door. The children complete a verse before the door is opened and they are admitted. In bobble hats, scarves and puffer jackets of every colour, they walk in quickly, rubbing their hands to warm themselves out of the bitter January cold. Their prize for singing is a coin each and lots of chocolates.

The etiquette for travelling around the Gwaun Valley celebrating Hen Galan is that children never knock at the door. They announce their presence by singing until someone greets them. For the children who are old enough to remember last year's Hen Galan, they say this will be better than Christmas.

Few schools could offer the attention and affection that this school showers upon its children. The Victorian building has been extended, its original construction too small for the 21st century. But the children bouncing back into their classroom radiate a happiness that emanates from a community where everyone knows one another.

Mrs Francis says that with such a wide age range taught together in two classes, the older pupils help the younger ones. Where other communities have battled and lost their small schools, post office, shop, pub or garage, here in the Gwaun Valley the community is resilient and the school is at its centre.

A walk in the Gwaun Valley is the perfect metaphor for a life well-lived. You might start your journey by first heading past the school gate. After a few yards, you'll see men building a fence on the farm, their sledge-hammer blows echoing around the hills. Then, the pub, the Dyffryn Arms, before finally, across the bridge and up the hill, the church and the graveyard.

The Dyffryn Arms is better known as Bessie's and has been run by Bessie Davies's family since 1845. The pub was originally called Llwyn Celyn (Holly Bush); you'll see the date carved in stone.

In winter, even on a special day like Hen Galan, entry is by the back door – as is the way in the country. Bessie is sitting beside the fire, wearing just one glove, the glove covering the hand that pours pints from the jug dipped in the barrel. Sunlight pouring through the window, Bessie receives her many visitors in the small bar that looks like a slightly austere front parlour. She is sometimes to be found behind the sliding serving hatch, although less often these days. A small bell invites customers to call for service. On the walls, the advertising posters as old as a century promote long-forgotten treats for customers. A framed 'Gilbey's Spey Royal Whisky' takes pride of place alongside a black and white photograph of Edward as Prince of Wales, who stares out, not altogether approvingly, before his abdication.

The etiquette for travelling around the Gwaun Valley celebrating Hen Galan is that children never knock at the door.

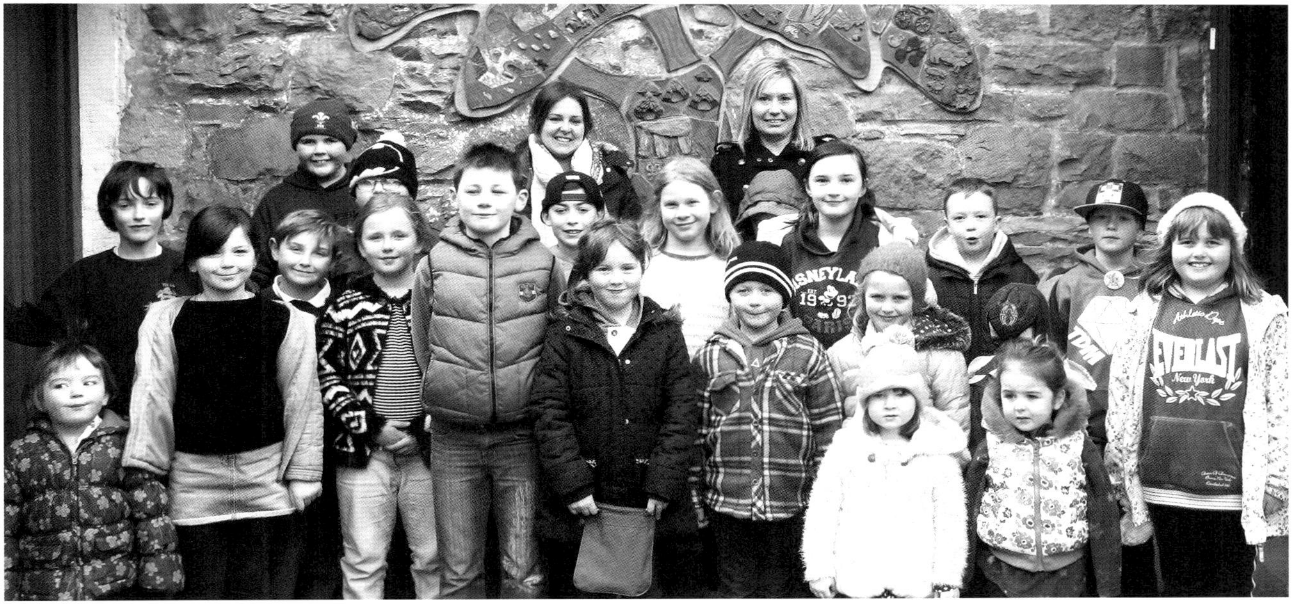
EVERLAST
New York
TDM

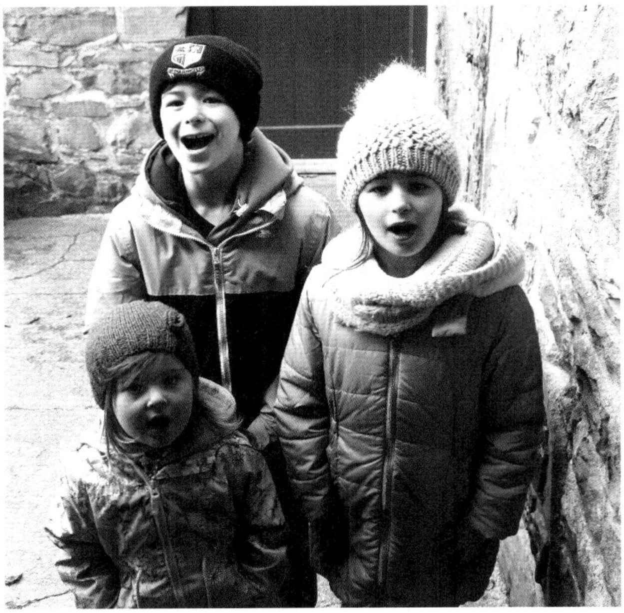

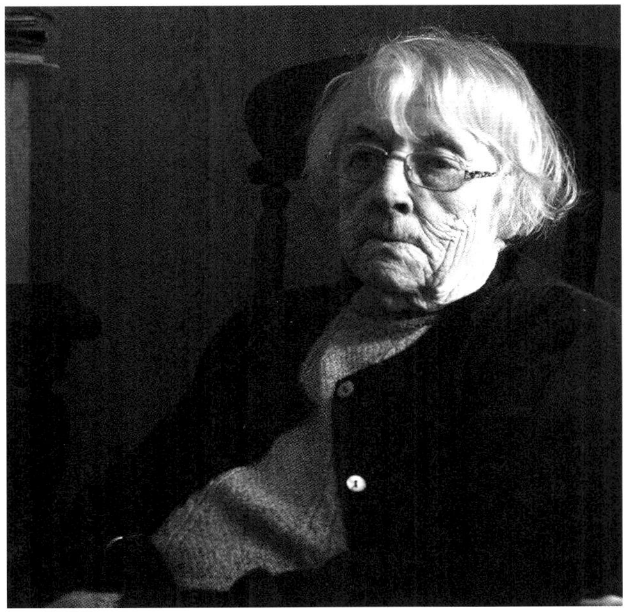

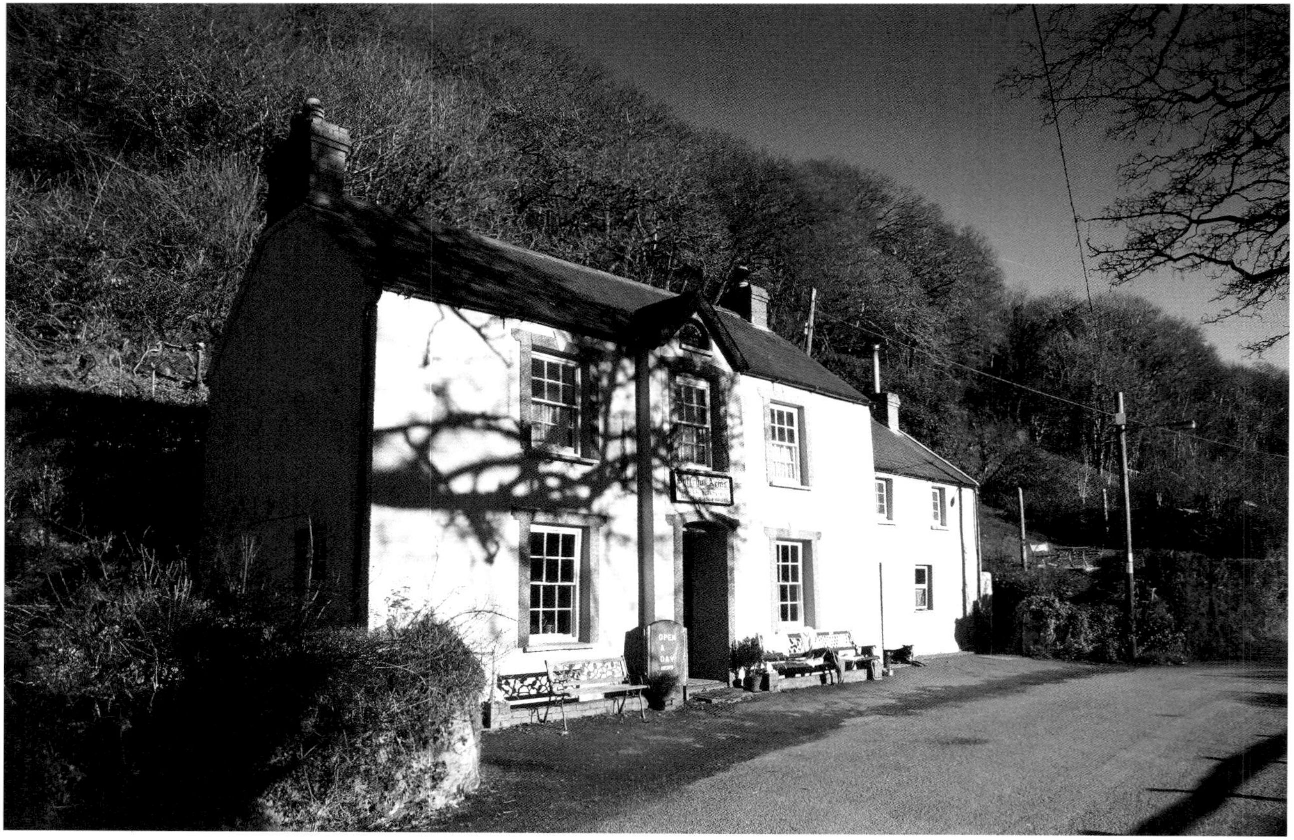

 Dyffryn Arms

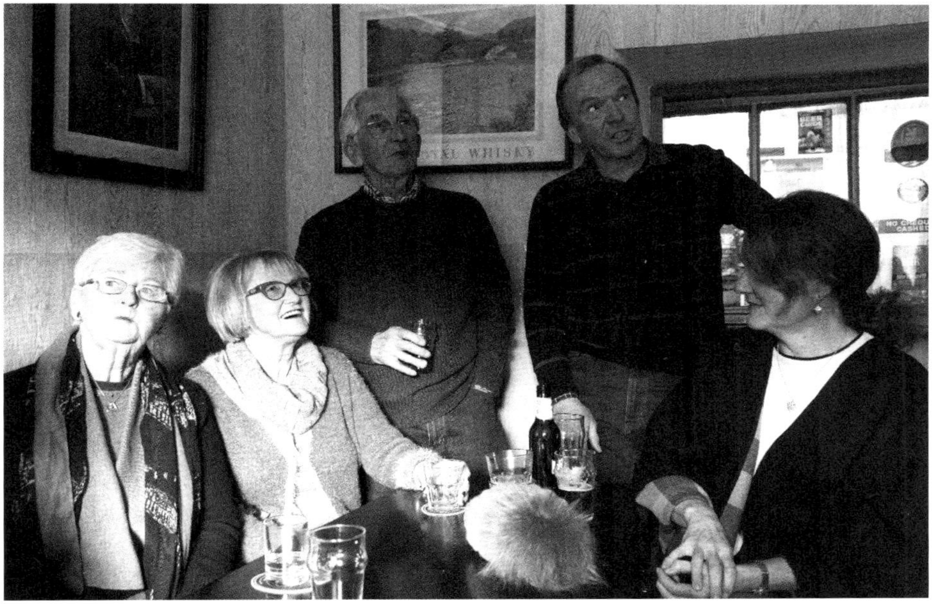
WHISKY

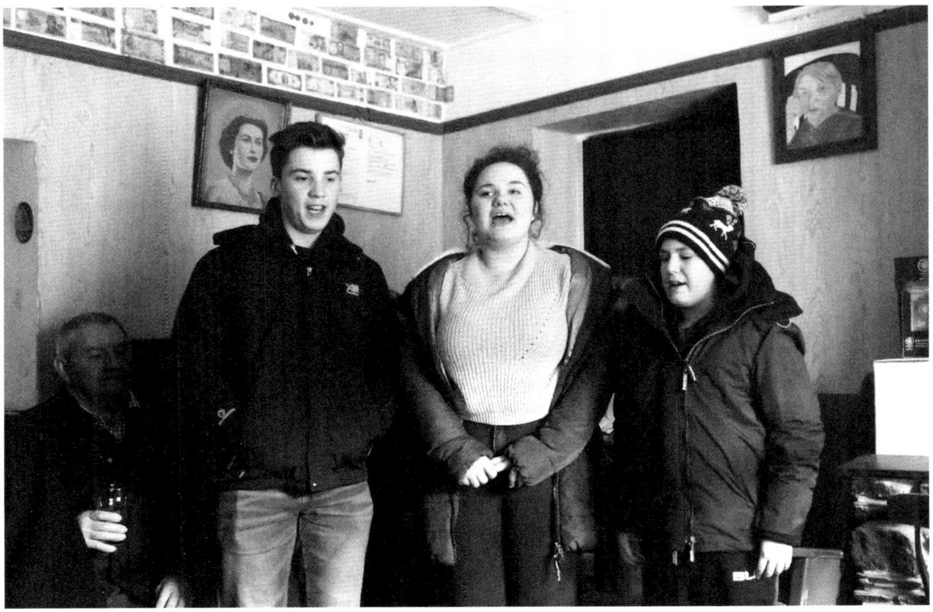

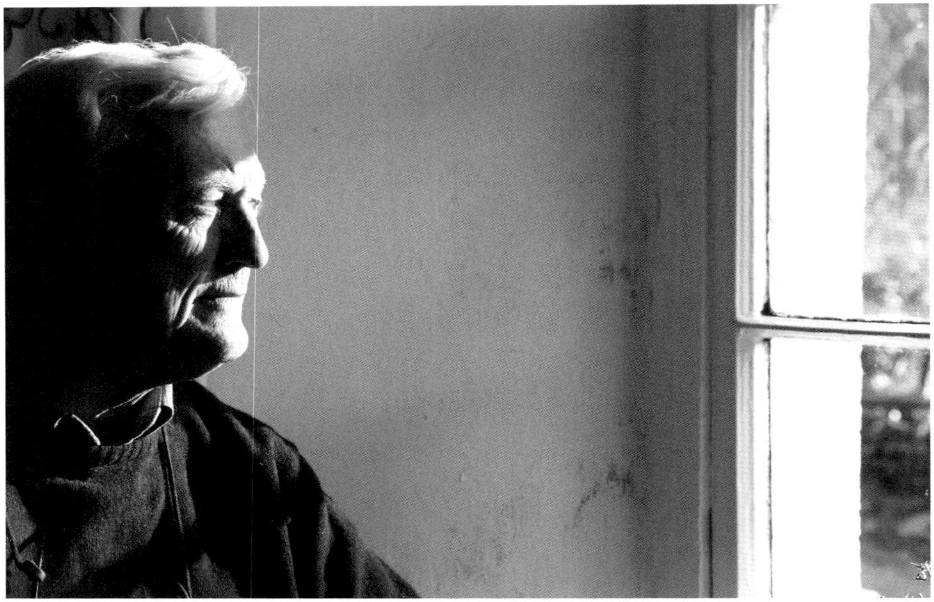

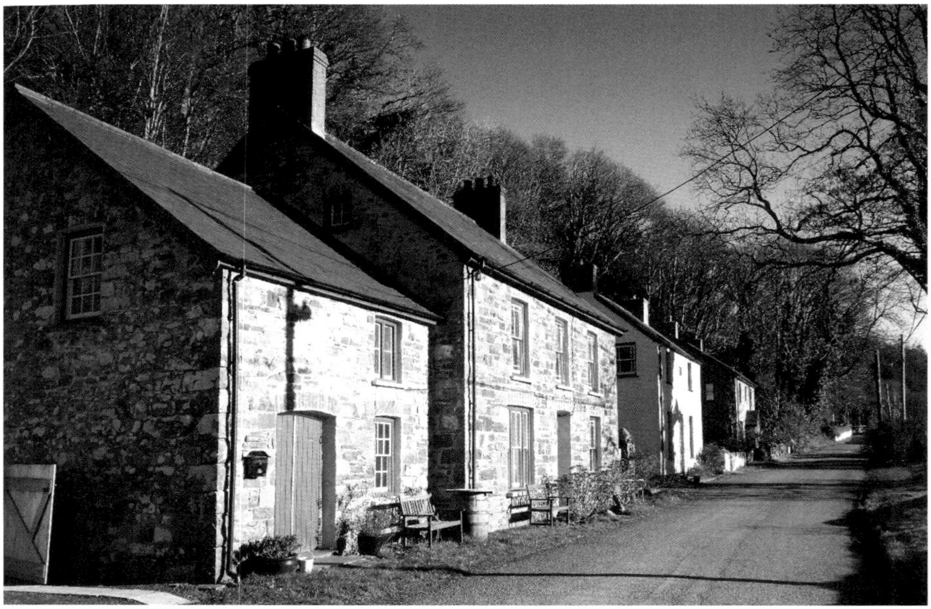

40 Eryl Davies, Hen Galan

Where the walls meet the ceiling, you'll see a cornice papered with currency – bank notes from around the world are pinned to the wallpaper. Despite the globe trotting generosity of the clientele's travels, the bar displays a sign, NO CHEQUES CASHED. Brown Victorian furniture of oak farmhouse chairs, a Pembroke table and an old box settle sit on the black and red quarry tile floor. The furniture has always been here, even when Bessie took over. Fashions have come and gone, but the fixtures and furnishings remain. The Alsatian cross, arthritic and half-blind, makes an unenthusiastic attempt to greet each guest at the door, but then thinks better of it and slumps back in front of the small fire.

There is no food for sale here. No menu. This is a pub where only beer and conversation are to be had, though you couldn't have a private conversation in Bessie's. The small front room cum bar is conducive to forcing strangers to become friends and quickly explain every detail of where you are from, what you do, and your business in these parts. In a fashion that would rarely happen anywhere else, soon the 12 lunchtime drinkers are all talking over each other like old friends. There's no television, no music, no jukebox or video games to interrupt.

One of Bessie's lunchtime drinkers has driven from Kent to mark the New Year in the Gwaun Valley. Eryl Davies is a veterinary surgeon who practices in the south east of England but grew up here 50 years ago. He's come back to mark Hen Galan for the first time in 40 years. Like many others in this community, he didn't speak English until he was seven. He says that the school, which propelled him through veterinary college, was the making of him. Its only downside was the lack of competitive sport. You can't easily raise two equally-matched rugby or football teams with just 25 pupils aged 3 to 11.

Eryl says that Hen Galan is a private affair to be celebrated between friends and families. The community isn't much taken with the press or the media descending to report on this Pembrokeshire custom. They have grown up with the tradition and it's in the blood. To them it is as ordinary as the rain, the January cold and the beauty of the trees.

Eryl was a boy actor in the original production of the film *Under Milk Wood*, filmed in nearby Lower Town, Fishguard. The producers wrote to the local schools looking for children who could speak Welsh and sing. They were paid £3/10 shillings a day. This was a small fortune in 1971, if you were a small boy and had nothing to spend it on. Eryl said that Richard Burton complained that his billet, a room in the Fishguard Bay Hotel, had no fridge. The boy actors were not troubled by such inconveniences. Eryl and the other children couldn't go to the premier of the film as they were too young for its adult rating.

Bessie's front room fills up with a car-load of four people visiting from the Vale of Glamorgan. There's an air of anticipation and excitement for the night still to come. The pub chatter, over half pints of bitter, suddenly quietens as distant singing comes closer. The children, who started their day at the school and have sung outside the farms and cottages along the road, have now reached the Dyffryn Arms. Bessie listens and then reaches into her bag for more coins and sweets for the singers now entering the warm bar.

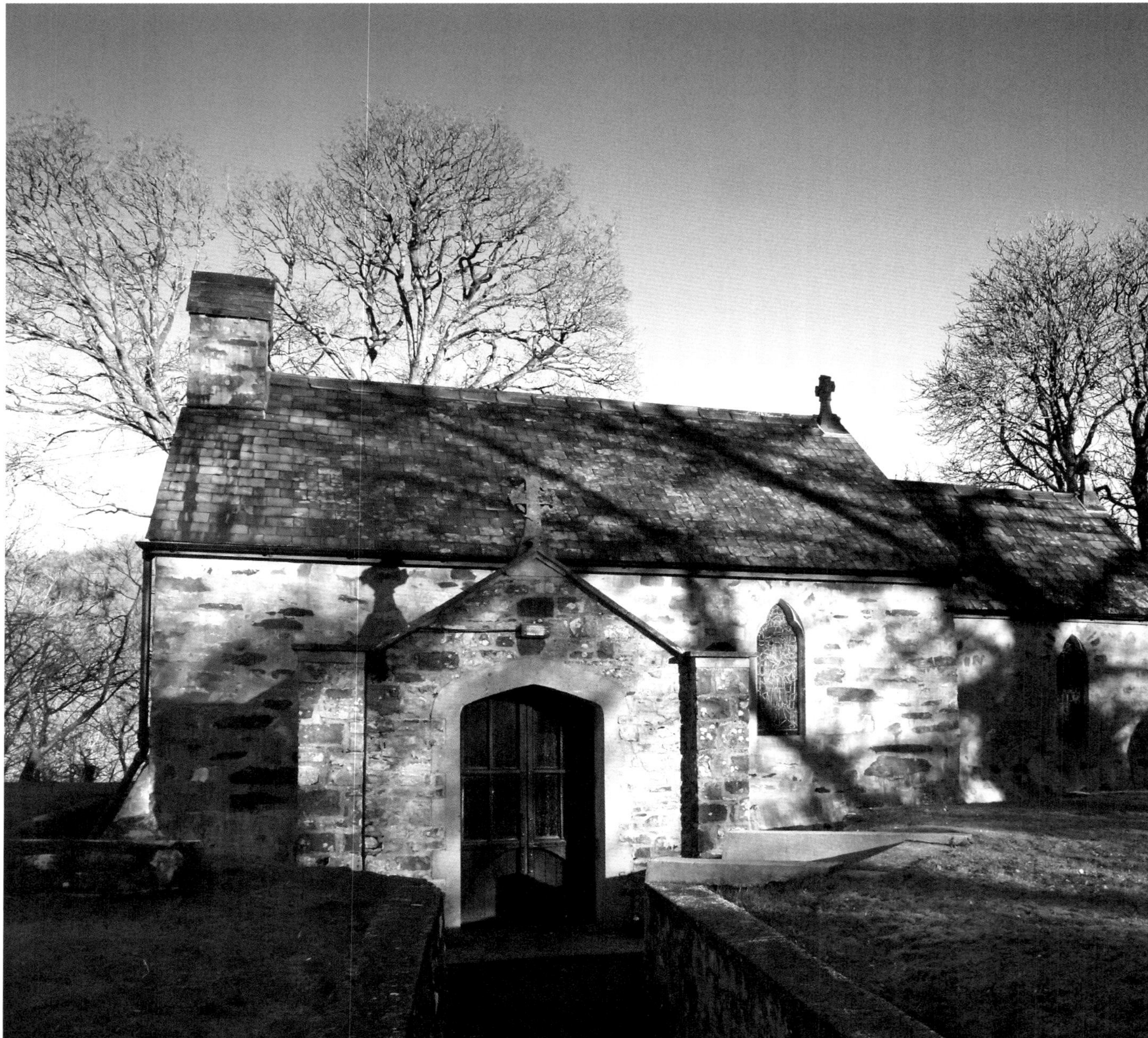

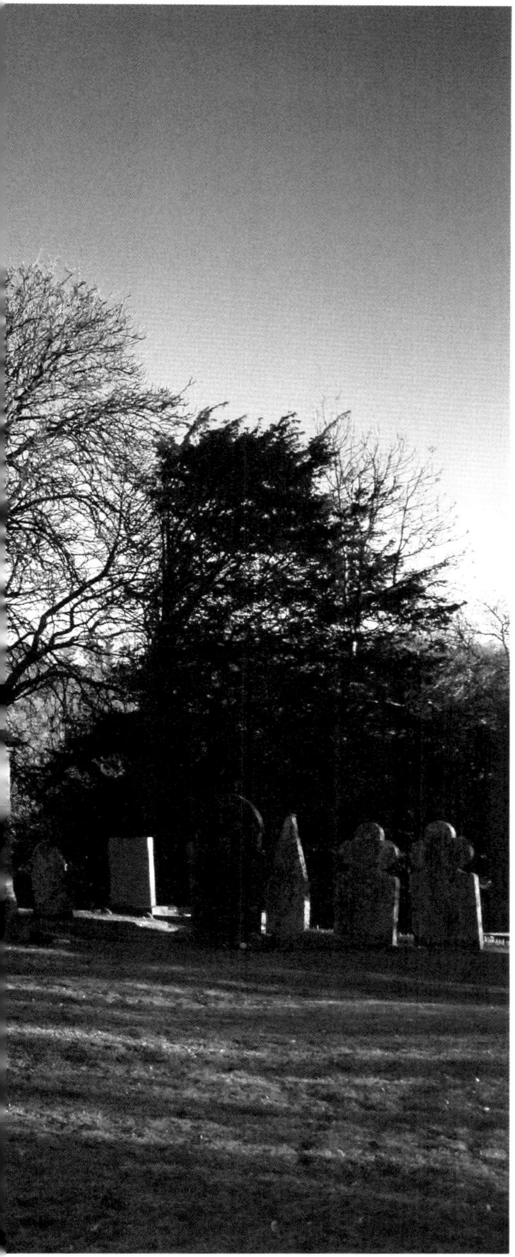

Richard Fenton rode through the Gwaun Valley two centuries ago writing his *A Historical Tour through Pembrokeshire*. He found:

'...woods that clothe the sides of its hills for eight or nine miles almost to meet, and the murmur of its stream to increase to a torrent roar. The angler and draftsman may find ample employ, the river abounding with salmon, sewen and trout.'

Anglers, draughtsmen and geology students might today be added to that list of visitors who will find reward in the Gwaun Valley. Students come here to study one of the most important meltwater channels from the last ice age in the British Isles, gathered in the vast sponge of the Preseli Hills. The valley's forest of moss-covered oak, beech, alder and willow is twisted and bare in bitter winter and still in shadow even at midday. Richard Fenton, who was writing at the turn of the 19th century, would find that little has changed in this part of the country since his excursions on horseback.

Walk up the hill and set in the grounds of Pontfaen House is St Brynach's Church, its door unlocked. The tiny church dates back to the saint himself, who settled here before going on to nearby Nevern. You'd be pushed to find a better kept church in Pembrokeshire; warm and light, the wood polished and the air thick with a bouquet of fresh flowers and candlewax. It wasn't always so. The church was first established here by St Brynach in 540 AD, but by 1858 the church was described by *Archeologica Cambrensis* as:

'Ruined...within the abandoned walls, and its font open to all the birds of heaven... the windows were broken, the roof had fallen in, the communion rails were

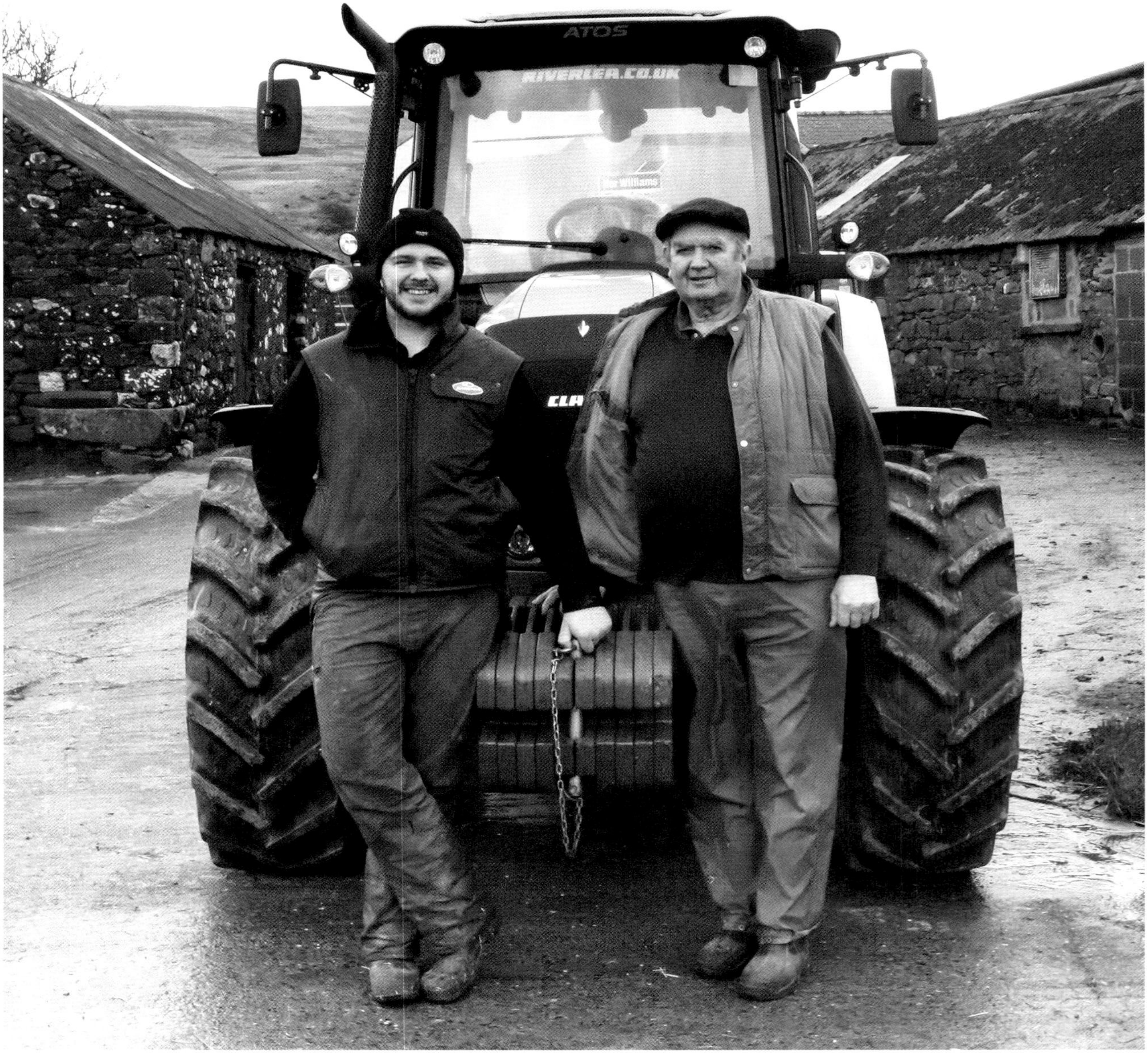

 Vivien Davies and grandson Llyr

broken, the font, a plain basin, was full of mud, and no service had been held in the church for some time.'

This would have been the end of St Brynach's Church, had it not been for the Arden family who bought the estate of Pontfaen. When Percy Arden saw the state of the church, he undertook to fund the restorations. St Brynach's reopened in 1904 and owes its fabric to his patronage.

Walk out of the valley, climb the hill and you'll come to Penlanwynt Farm, which hangs onto the upper slopes of Cerrig Lladron (Foel Eryr), the second highest mountain in the Preseli Hills. Mr and Mrs Vivian Davies farm beef and sheep on their 350 acres. Their long, rutted lane is lined by disorderly telegraph poles and a few brave ewes leaning into the wind. The skeletal oak trees, few as they are, are twisted in the gales and stunted in thin earth. This is the top of the world. From here everything else falls beneath us. On the distant road below, toy-like cars and far away farmsteads look like white matchboxes in the shivering white-green landscape.

The squat farmhouse hunkers into the hill and is built to withstand the blast from winter with thick walls and small windows. The table in the front room is laden with tins of chocolate, crisps and fruit. 'Christmas Day in my childhood meant nothing to me,' explains Vivian. 'It was old New Year when we had the goose.'

There is no organiser of Hen Galan, but if there is an unofficial historian, or its collective memory, it is Mrs Davies. Hen Galan, she explains, survives the centuries because of its shared tradition among families. They all know what day it is and what the day comprises. The songs sung outside each house are engrained – they are not in need of books or scores.

'Some years back, every farmer's wife was always at home. When we were children, you knew you would always find someone at home as we travelled around, but now so many farmer's wives have to work off the farms.'

The once heavily-manned small farms have given way to larger ones with more machinery and few staff. For haymaking, 24 workers would have once been fed around their kitchen table. Small farms of 65 acres would have been viable and kept a family but the economics of upland hill farms no longer make the sums add up. These days, wives and husbands leave their land to work elsewhere. Hedd, their son, who farms the neighbouring property, has a mobile ewe-scanning business to report the coming year's lambs.

'Russian television came to the Gwaun Valley once,' says Mrs Davies, preparing tea and cakes. 'Pembrokeshire isn't the only community that observes the old calendar – some communities in Russia do too. We are not freaks or traditionalists clinging on to a sepia past. Hen Galan is simply

The once heavily-manned small farms have given way to larger ones with more machinery and few staff.

the observing of a ritual that is a living part of our community, the same as birthdays or Christmas would be marked.'

Llyr is one of the Davies's grandsons. He is joining his grandparents for tea between the last jobs on the farm and before the falling light and perishing cold end the day early. He is the fourth generation to farm here after his father, grandfather and great-grandfather. This isn't so much a choice, but a calling; even given an alternative, this is what he would want. The mountains and the animals have always been in his blood – why would he want to work in an office? How could you aspire to earn a living inside when the outside is so breathtakingly beautiful, although today, also frozen? And so, the same families that have always farmed here go on, even though the work changes.

There are children singing outside the farm door now. The same pupils that started their day early this morning at their school have made it to the top of the Gwaun Valley and the roof of the Preseli Hills. They complete one verse before the door is opened and they rush in. They know the drill by now and take their places around the long kitchen table for another round of cake, sweets and pop. Later, they will leave with more sweets and a coin each. One of the little girls thinks she has been given seventy coins, all stored safely in her knapsack, although the sweets won't last there long.

In a country where few of us grow up and go to school with our neighbours, this looks like an idyllic childhood. It seems to make for deeply happy children who are grounded in a clear love and affection for their families and their way of life. Despite two dozen children being under the same roof, there is no fighting or shouting. Instead, the older children instinctively look after the younger ones, who are now becoming weary.

Looking out for each other has been a necessity in the Preseli Hills. Long before the health service, social security and the welfare state, there was, and still is, a deep-knitted community here. When the soil is thin and the seasons harsh, all you have is each other. Here the gathering of the sheep off the mountains, the hay-making and the dipping would have been too much for individual families, so families worked together, and still do. Despite the distance between homes, the bond between people is close. The old ways survive, because they work.

The evening is falling fast around Penlanwynt Farm. The quickening darkness ushers in an even deeper cold. Tonight, the old New Year will be celebrated in Bessie's by those who live in the bottom of the valley and those who live at the top will gather in Gellifawr. Many will perform their party piece and sing the old Welsh hymns, Calon Lân and the traditional songs, and later, when the beer is flowing, Tom Jones and Max Boyce ballads too.

Tomorrow will be the start of the New Year, but tonight a feast among friends in kind, warm surroundings is enough to break the bleakest of winters and the cruelest month.

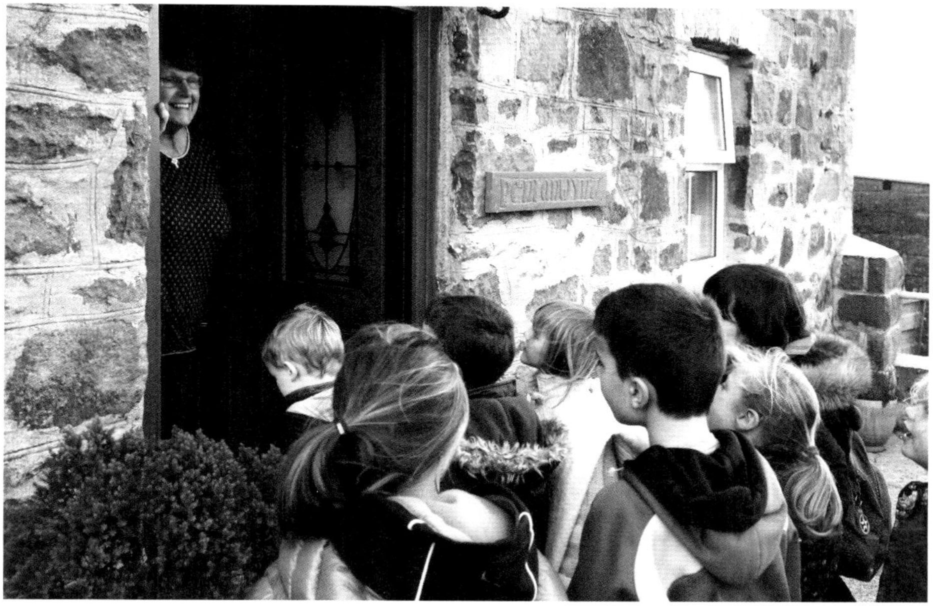

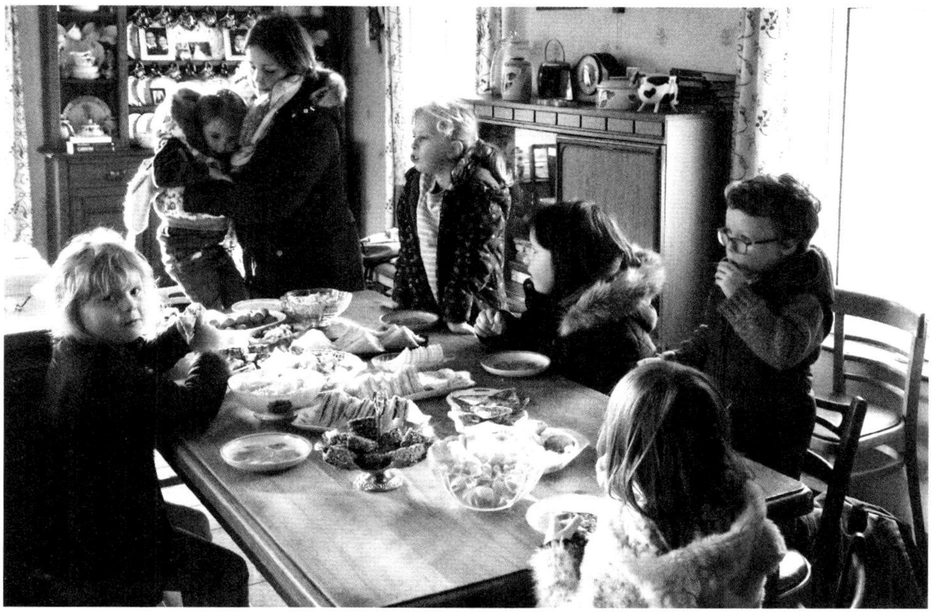

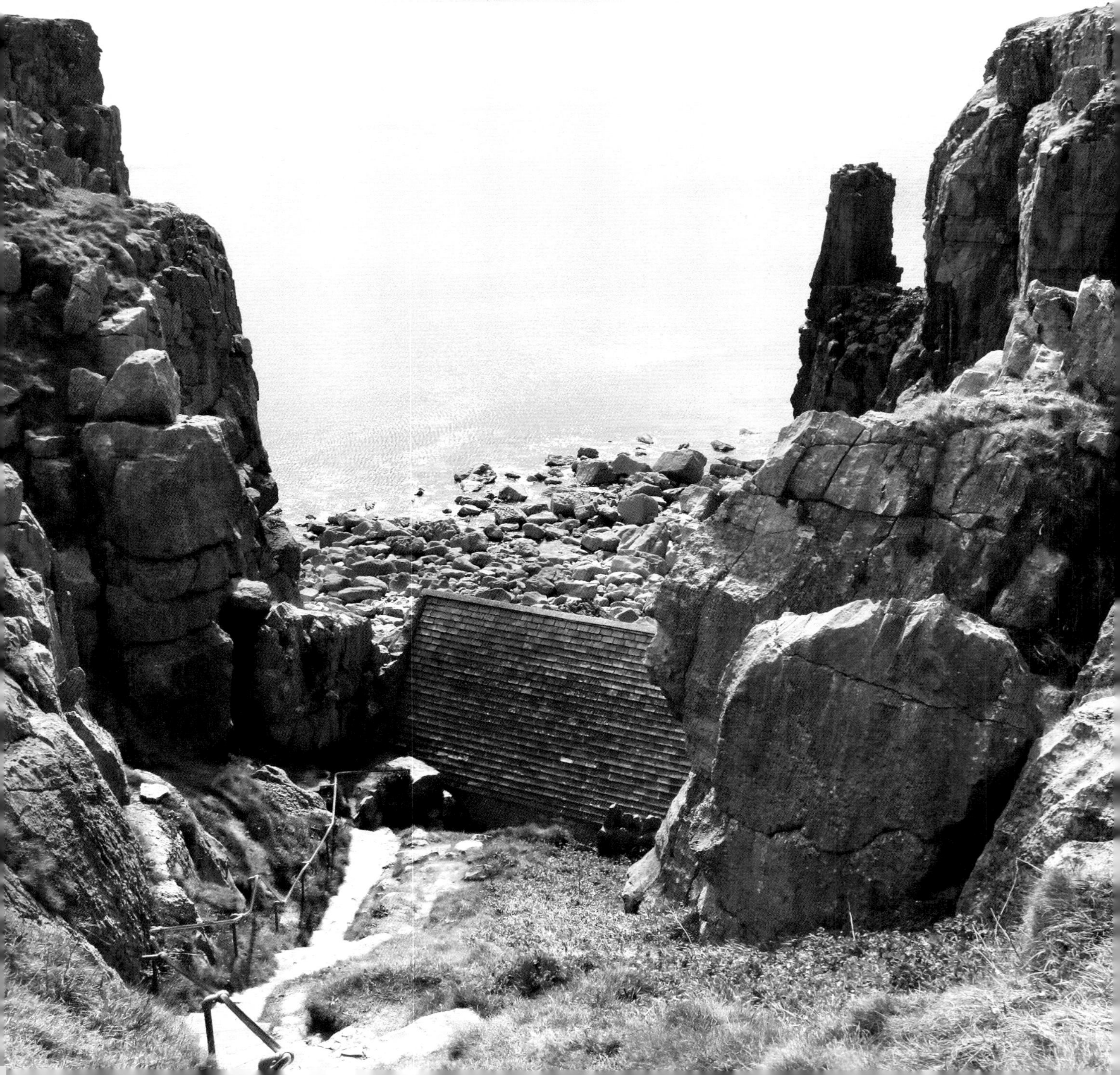

Castlemartin

St Govan's Chapel and the gathering of the flock

It is spring on the south Pembrokeshire coast. Its arrival is accompanied by storms and sunshine. The desolation of winter gently becomes the season of new beginnings.

At St Govan's, a coach-load of white-headed tourists is slowly making its way back on board after an hour's peek at the 13th-century chapel beneath the cliffs. The risky booking of a week in Wales so early in the season has rewarded them with kind weather. Thirty intrepid travellers are folding their Nordic walking poles and stowing their rucksacks after the adventure of a bright morning walking on the edge of the ocean.

From here, in clear skies, you can see the coast of Devon, Lundy, and the Gower Peninsula. Half a dozen white-sailed yachts pass slowly behind Caldey Island, and nearby a coastal tanker sitting low in the water waits for a radio message before making its way into Milford Haven to off-load its cargo.

This is a rare treat; often the road to St Govan's is closed to family cars and buses to make way for army battle tank training exercises. The Castlemartin Peninsula is home to a Ministry of Defence firing range and admission to these treasured acres is not always assured.

Although the military range dates from the 1930s, this coastline has been fought over for thousands of years. St Govan, who, depending on who you believe, was perhaps an Irish monk or Gawain, one of King Arthur's Knights of the Round Table, is said to have fled here escaping from pirates.

The pirates have long gone, but the coastline and villages are pock-marked with each generation's torment – hillforts and castles, Napoleonic fortifications and defences from two world wars.

A long flight of stone steps cuts through the cliff to the medieval chapel below. The present building perhaps dates from the 13th century. A steady stream of camera-laden pilgrims gingerly descend from the breeze of the cliff top to the shelter in its shadow.

The chapel is no larger than a static caravan, hewn from slate and stone. But on entering its walls, the cold wind lulls and, even in its unforgiving monastic severity, tucked into the cliffs it offers a spiritual calmness punctuated only by the sound of rolling waves.

So who was St Govan? Half myth and half legend? If we know little about his life, historians state with certainty that he died in the year 586. He was a hermit who lived in a fissure on the side of the cliff. What we now call St Govan's Chapel was built much later.

Two rock climbers weighed down with ropes and shackles clatter over the fallen boulders strewn between the chapel and the tide. From sea level they will spend their morning groping up the sheer cliff face to their heaven, accompanied by the startled sound of a bird song magnificat.

A few fields from the sanctity of this holy site, a small army is gathering; not a military platoon, but a band of shepherds. Today will see a farming ritual that brings together north and south Pembrokeshire. For a county that is divided by the Milford Haven waterway, Pembrokeshire can often seem like two distinct and separate communities – and this was even more pronounced before the building of the bridge across the River Cleddau.

But today, north and south are united in purpose. Spring marks the gathering of the flocks of sheep from the gentle lowlands of the Castlemartin ranges and their return to the Preseli Hills for summer grazing. The army's activities will soon replace them.

The main entrance to the range is flanked by two tanks. There is no ambiguity about what this place is for. South Pembrokeshire's military range is a school for war. The Royal Armoured Corps took over the land more than 80 years ago. Conflict is a growth industry and the ranges developed further during the Cold War. Its attraction is clear from the map.

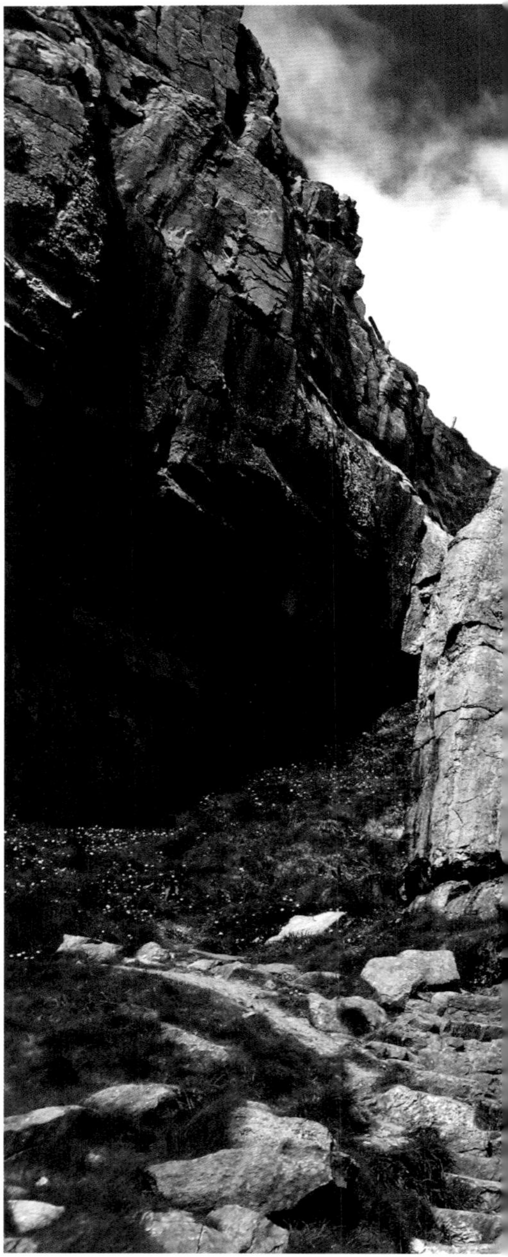

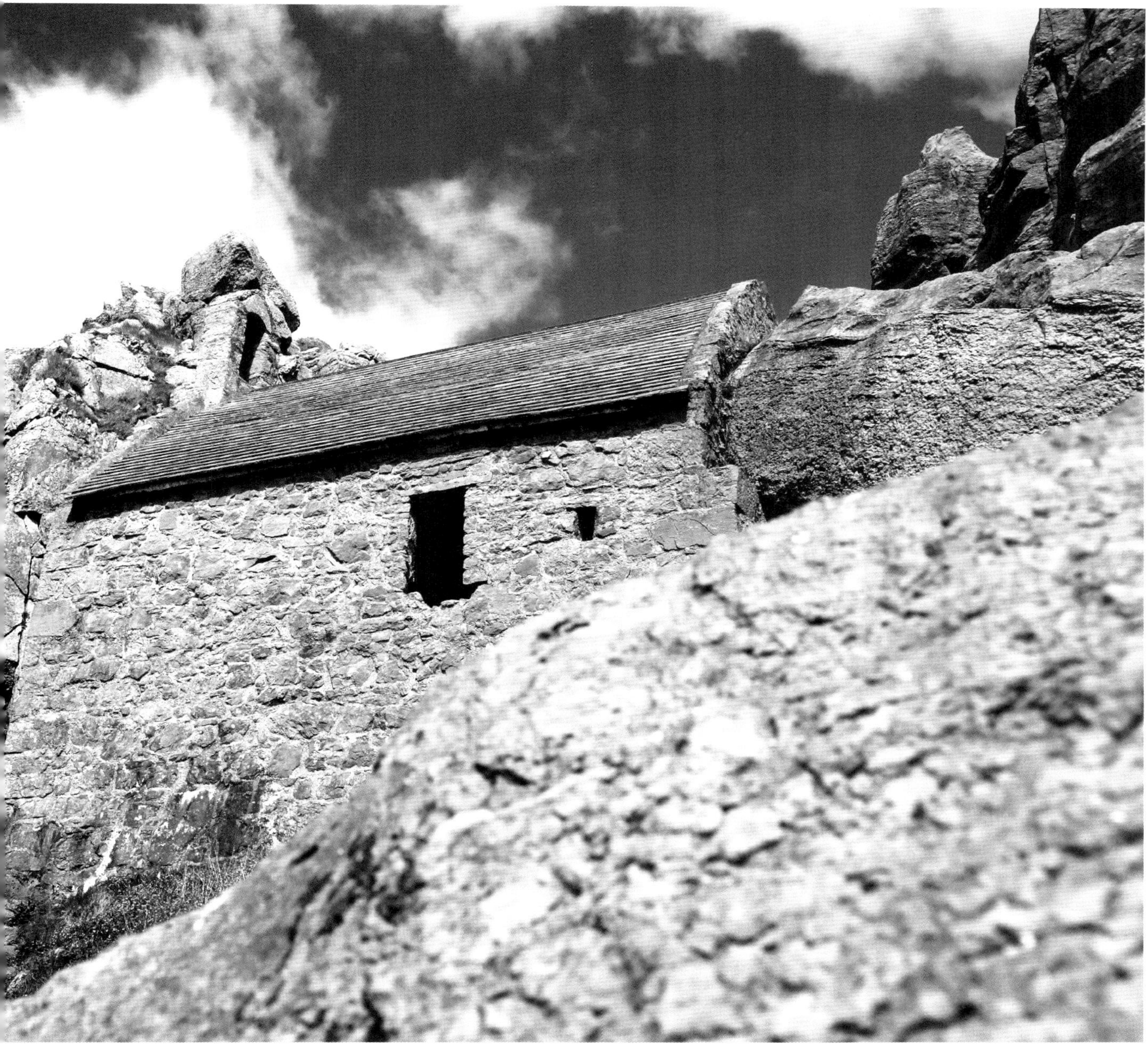

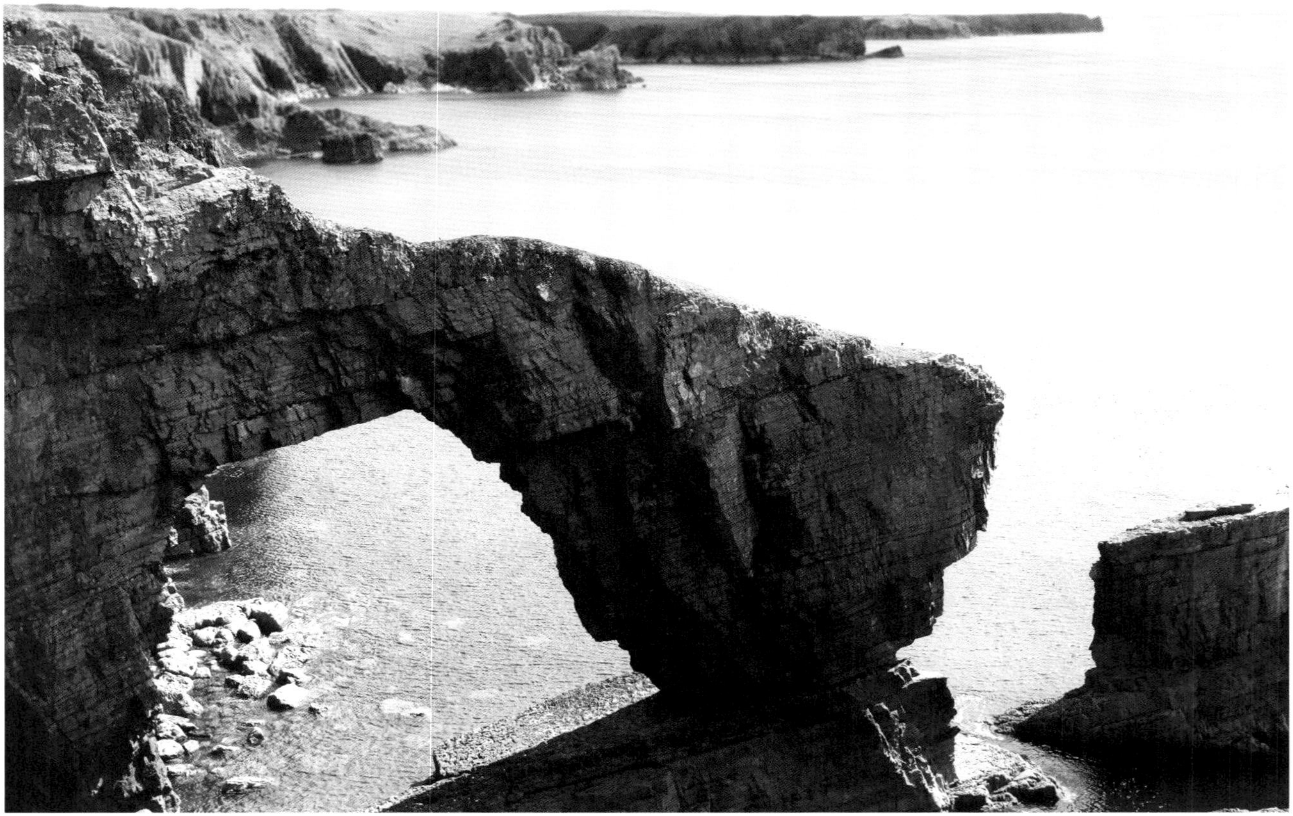

52 Green Bridge of Wales

Peninsulas appealing to religious communities for their seclusion and proximity to the sea also make the land easy to isolate and keep the wandering public away.

Generations of soldiers have passed through these gates and trained on the flat lands of Castlemartin for conflicts in foreign fields. The unpredictability of farming with its changeable seasons and markets makes way in Castlemartin to the world's most reliable and constant business – warfare.

Today the General is Cerwyn Davies; his officers number a dozen other shepherds, as many sheep dogs and half a dozen quad bikes and Land Rovers. The sheep are gathered from wide-open ranges and herded into pens before being taken by lorry to the Preseli Hills from where they came. If you're a ewe, today is the beginning of an unwelcome summer holiday at the hands of some brusque tour couriers.

The movement of livestock from high land to low is known as transhumance. Over the coming days an exercise of near military scale will unfold. Transhumance is not unique to Pembrokeshire or even Wales, but was once widespread throughout the farming world. The Preseli Hills are brutal in winter and the lower pastures of Castlemartin, closer to the sea, are kinder.

Pembrokeshire's transhumance, at least in modern times, can be traced back to the severe winter of 1947. At Glynsaithman Farm, near Maenclochog, less than 10% of the flock survived the snow, and all this following a bad harvest in 1946. W.H. Jones was the field officer who would be instrumental in bringing together Preseli sheep farmers facing ruin and a military range than would revert to bracken if not grazed. South Pembrokeshire came to north Pembrokeshire's rescue.

Cerwyn's father took the farm's first flock from the Preseli Hills to Castlemartin in 1950. There were 12,000 sheep that year.

Pembrokeshire in the 1950s was a different country. Austerity extended far beyond the Second World War and Britain's food cupboard was bare. The wartime drive to encourage Britain to become more self-sufficient in food saw rapid mechanisation coupled with rural depopulation as returning servicemen sought better-paid work in the towns.

Glynsaithman Farm was a holding of 250 acres and took half a dozen men to run it. The farm's Welsh Mountain sheep were the product of hundreds of years of breeding to withstand the cruel north Pembrokeshire winters. The breeding ewes would be bought at auction in Aberystwyth and then moved by train to Preseli. This was, as it is now, sheep farming with little human intervention. Put the sheep on the mountain and let them get on with it.

Castlemartin is coastal and spring can come six weeks earlier here than on higher ground. Its open spaces, a peninsula warmed by the sea and excellent soil are all the perfect ingredients for livestock or crops.

The movement of livestock from high land to low is known as transhumance.

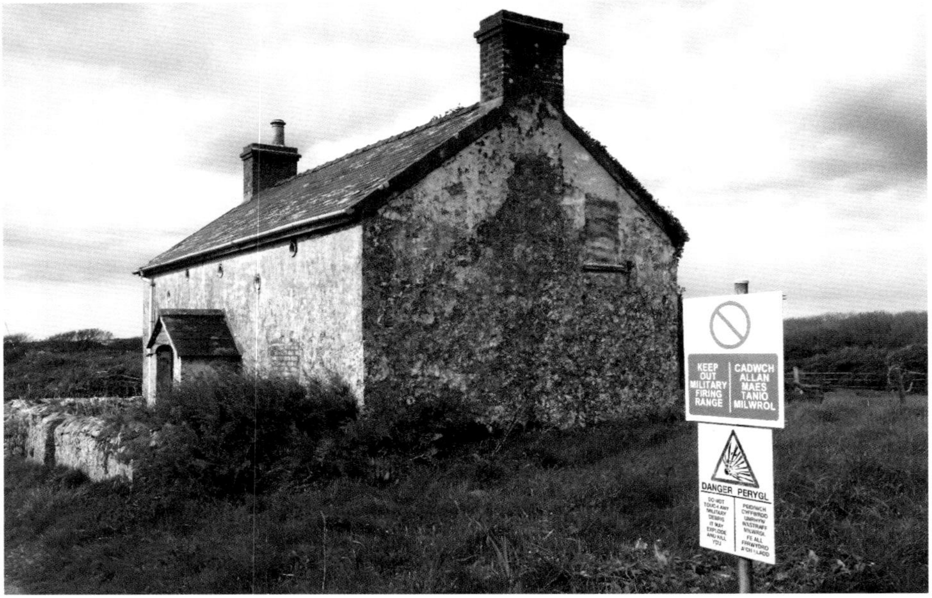
KEEP OUT MILITARY FIRING RANGE
CADWCH ALLAN MAES TANIO MILWROL
DANGER
PERYGL

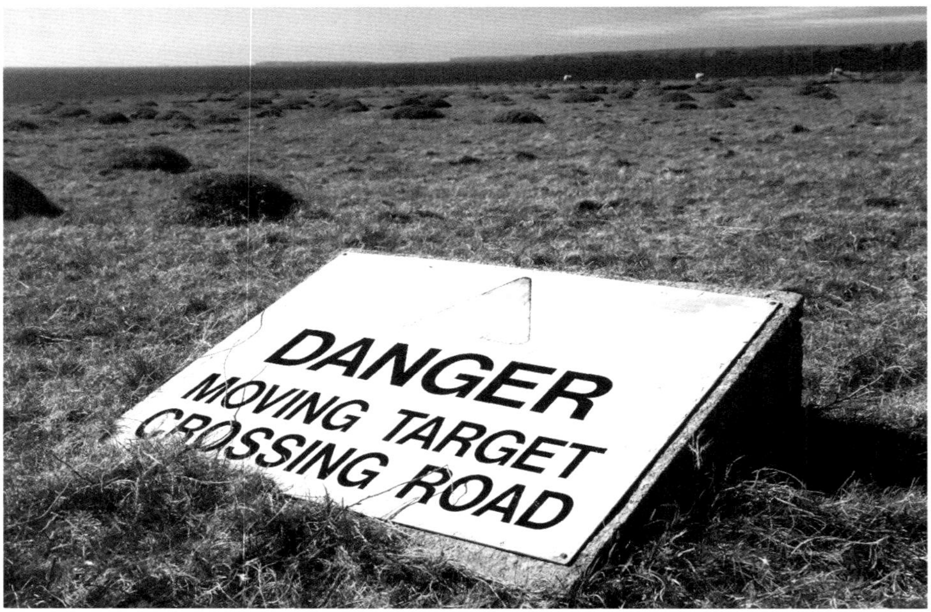
DANGER
MOVING TARGET
CROSSING ROAD

Cerwyn, overseeing today's operation, remembers the gathering when he was a boy. From the age of seven he would sit down to communal lunchtimes – the attraction was the quality of the food, not the task of sorting the sheep. In those days the gathering of the flocks might take a fortnight; now thousands of sheep are rounded up in days.

While quad bikes and 4x4 vehicles have transformed the speed of the operation, many of the shepherds involved today still walk with their dogs. Different dogs are required for different jobs. Some excel at the long sweep round-up – others better for closer work when a lamb makes a dash for freedom. The younger dogs watch and learn from their peers and some elderly ones are here just for the ride. It's difficult to know who is most enjoying a day by the sea in bright sunshine, the sheepdogs or their shepherds.

There are 13 graziers here and at least 13 flocks of sheep. All the sheep are mixed together. When they are gathered they'll be sorted into their separate flocks before being loaded into lorries for the journey north. Each animal is marked with its farm colours sprayed onto its fleece but also electronically ear tagged. They look like punks from the animal world.

In the heyday of sheep farming, wool was a significant part of the animal's value. Now it just covers the cost of the shearer. Much of the wool from these sheep will find its way into the carpet trade and the meat will be sold to the halal market. The best breeding ewes will be kept back for next year's stock.

Cerwyn only farms sheep – 1400 breeding ewes. Each lamb will cost between £40 and £55. None of this enterprise is big business – it couldn't be more distant from the grain barons of East Anglia and their easy, flat agriculture. This is farming gripping on tightly for survival. Many of the shepherds are able to continue working on the land either because of inheritance, second jobs or a partner's income. Cerwyn's wife is a teacher.

Our gathering today is dominated by older men, but there are a number of women here too. The average age of a Welsh farmer is 60. Not many want the long hours and the seven-day weeks. But there are reasons for optimism – some of the next generation of Pembrokeshire farmers are here, seduced by a life in glorious countryside rather than an office.

The graziers collect their military passes from the range sentry point and then drive onto the vast open expanse of land, where green fields meet blue ocean and Pembrokeshire falls into the sea. I was born and brought up in Pembrokeshire but I have never before visited the forbidden land of Castlemartin Training Area.

When the historian George Owen of Henllys came here to write his *The Description of Pembrokeshire* in 1603, he found:

'The chiefest corn land in Pembrokeshire is the hundred of Castlemartin as that which yields the best and finest grain...the best wheat...and bread fairer than any other.'

Centuries later, the naturalist R.M. Lockley described Castlemartin in 1957:

'The best soil, richest agriculturally, overlies the red sandstone and carboniferous limestone of the south, and this southern part also has the mildest and driest climate.'

Lockley railed against, as he saw it, the waste of outstanding farmland:

'The fertile limestone fields are despoiled as a result of this misuse of valuable agricultural land. The nearby farmhouses lie in ruins, shell-riddled or leveled to the ground, and ugly anti-tank bunkers have been thrown up to mar the once smiling plain.'

If Lockley's generation struggled with Castlemartin's requisition as a British military firing range, the next decade would see a decision that would vex many in Pembrokeshire who had served in the Second World War or been bombed by the Luftwaffe flying over Pembrokeshire. In 1961, 16 years after the war ended, German Panzer tanks headed for Castlemartin. After the war, our enemies had become allies and the Germans were back in Pembrokeshire, but this time to train. Protesters lined the streets, but an equal number came out to cheer them and the economic boost Cold War combat training would bring.

The truth was that the young Germans stationed in Pembrokeshire were not Nazis and hadn't been involved in the war, but for communities who had borne the full force of German aggression, it was at first difficult to accept.

Pembroke Dock was bombed during the conflict. In my street, even decades later, we played in the grassed-over bomb crater on the Barrack Hill and walked past houses still showing the structural cracks of air raids. We had new faces in my primary school who, in our ignorance, we generously called Nazis – but soon realised they were children just like us.

My father was interviewed on the local television, vigorously demonstrating his opposition to the German invasion. Years later, when the Germans left, a documentary crew sought him out and he was delighted to eat his words. By and by, the visitors and the Welsh mixed and there were a number of marriages. After its shaky start, the German tank range would remain in Pembrokeshire for 35 years, local road signs even becoming trilingual – Welsh, English, and German – to accommodate our guests.

Some 84,000 German troops passed through Castlemartin, firing 270,000 rounds, and there were some 140 'Panzer bride' weddings between German soldiers and Pembrokeshire women.

Only too aware of their controversial presence, the Germans had gone out of their way to become good neighbours. Their base provided work for local people and they invested their time to win hearts and minds. Friendships don't need physical memorials, but if you wander into St Mary's Church in the hamlet of Warren you'll see how German soldiers helped restore the medieval building. If you climbed the roof you would almost be able to see the Milford Haven waterway, where Pembroke Dock's oil tanks burned for weeks following the Luftwaffe's raids.

In 1996, the German soldiers returned to a cheaper range closer to home. The fall of the Berlin Wall changed the politics but also the economies of Europe. Their departure was almost unanimously

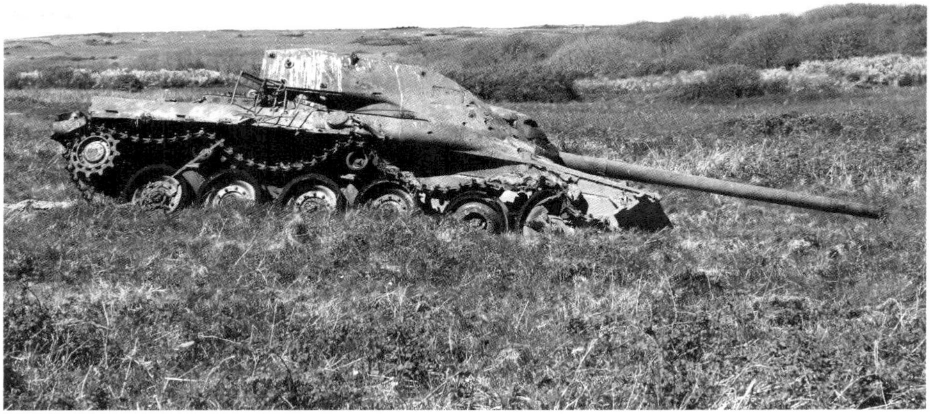

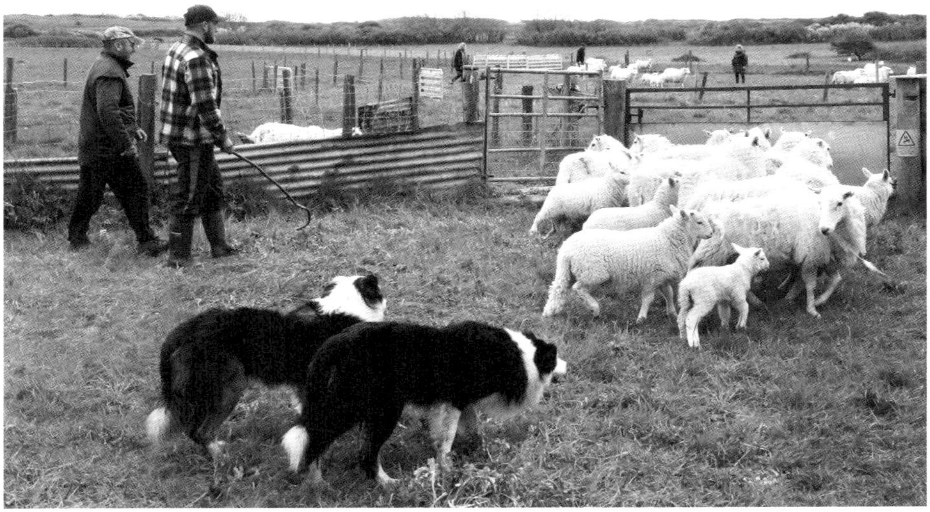

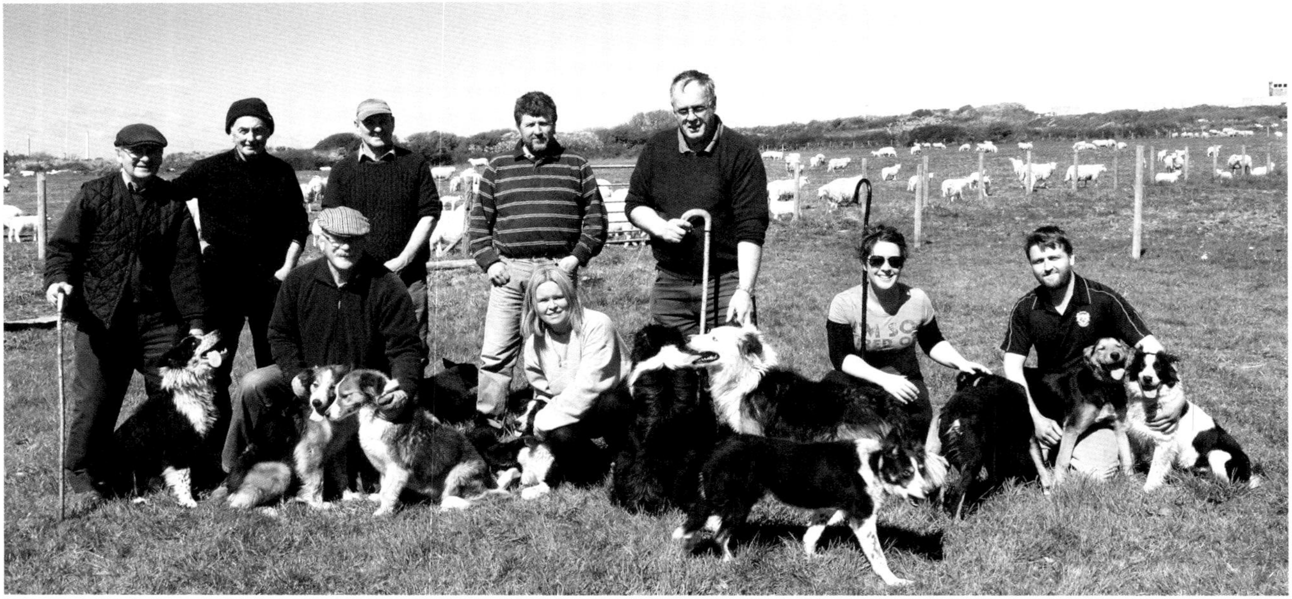

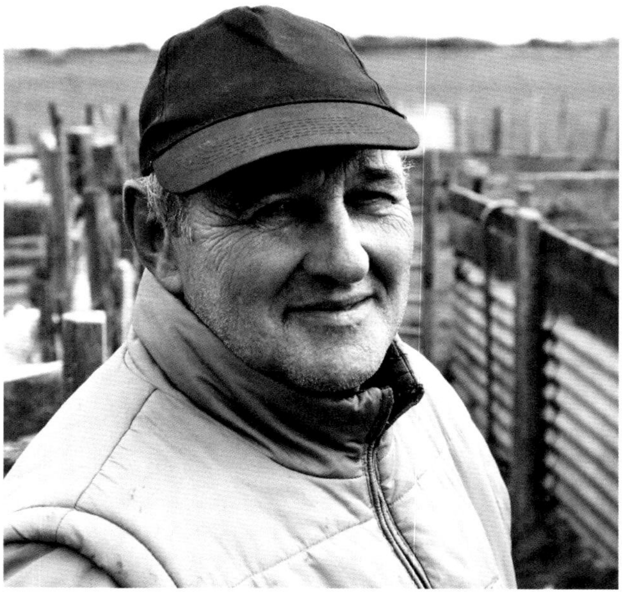

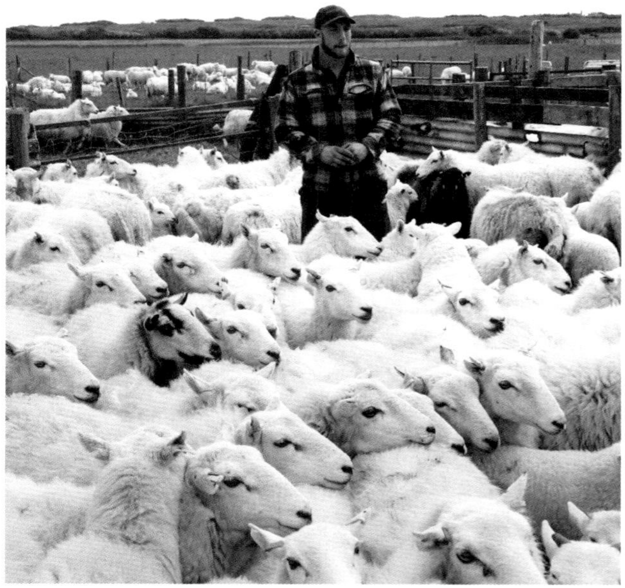

mourned. Foes had become friends. Their absence would not be just financially missed; they had become part of the community.

Today's Castlemartin is a largely British affair. Its name and surroundings are familiar to many of us who are local, but it has been for generations a rather private and secretive land. The Castlemartin Range is an unreal landscape. In the middle of the National Park, utilitarian military buildings, look-out towers, control rooms, shelters and barracks, punctuate the treeless land, devoid too of hedgerows. The architecture is brutal Cold War concrete. Narrow roads race across wide fields, all of them flat pastures, bar the regular craters. Two ancient rusting tanks rot, motionless and neutered, their firing days long past, their last days now spent as cannon fodder for trainee tank commanders.

With the same precision of any officer mustering his troops and outflanking his opponent, what now follows is something akin to ballet on an epic scale. Agreeing that the final goal is the fenced area where the stock will be sorted before being driven away, Cerwyn orders half the graziers to peel off in vehicles or quad bikes to carry out a loud, wide sweep of the edge of the range. The tooting of horns and barking of dogs funnel the first thousand sheep from their scattered grazing to run towards their intended destination. The orders have been given, the commands shouted and the operation begins.

The story of this farming community is one of unending resilience. The odds of survival might seem stacked against Pembrokeshire's shepherds, but on a perfect blue-sky day beside a quiet ocean, their choice of vocation is easier to understand.

Whatever the challenges of international markets, the changing seasons and the thuggery of supermarkets, Pembrokeshire lamb, nurtured on the grass of the mountains and the coast, will always find buyers. The meat prized for its succulence will always taste better than something reared in a shed that has never seen daylight; its production is sustained by passion and habit rather than hard-headed profit.

There is a sweet irony that the shepherds of the Preseli Hills have invaded the south of the county to graze on Castlemartin. In 1946 the UK Government considered siting a further firing range in the Preseli Hills. The proposal was deeply controversial and vigorously opposed by a formidable band of priests and poets, teachers and farmers, but post-war Britain understood that military threats hadn't evaporated with the conquest of Germany. Triumphant communism presented a new threat to a struggling, war-ravaged country.

Legend has it that Prime Minister Clem Attlee took a holiday in Newport, Pembrokeshire. The Prime Minister was a keen walker and enjoyed the gentle challenges of Preseli. It was here that he is said to have met the bailiff John Llewellyn, who took him by the arm and persuaded him that it would be a terrible idea to agree to build a military range in north Pembrokeshire. And so it never happened.

Now, all these years later, the Preseli shepherds who take their flocks to help graze the fields when the tanks are not exercising might well have found themselves turfed out of their farms in the

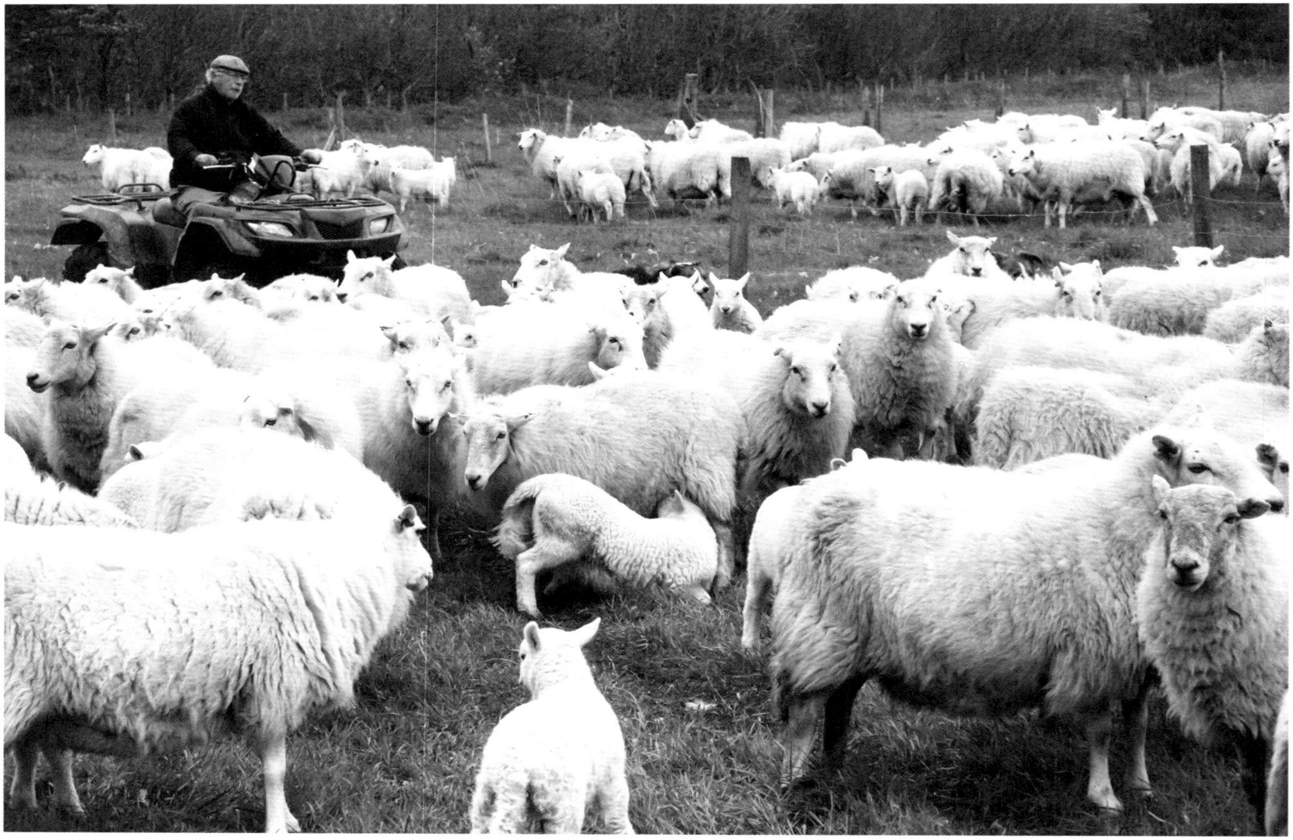

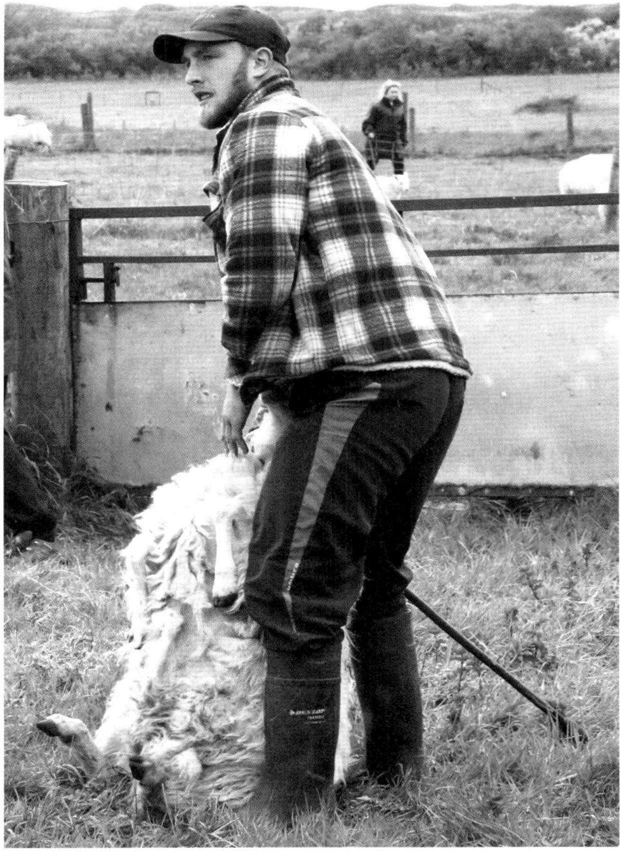

mountains to make way for the military, had history fallen differently. And so the sheep and the soldiers take their turn in sharing the land and the seasons.

Our day ends near Linney Head. In a scene unchanged from medieval times, a handful of shepherds and their dogs herd the last thousand sheep on the cliffs above Freshwater West. On a stormy afternoon this task would have been a soaking penance, but we are now in our t-shirts and our faces burnt from a day in the sun. When I was a little boy we played on the wet sands below. At the end of the shore where the sand ran out, signs on the cliffs warned NO ENTRY and MILITARY FIRING RANGE. I often stood in my shorts with my bucket and spade and wondered what lay beyond the barbed wire in the strange land with German road signs and military vehicles. What lies beyond is perhaps the most beautiful stretch of the Pembrokeshire coastline. In an age of satellite images that show you all of the earth, where you think you know every corner of the world, today I've discovered somewhere new and something quite magical – a foreign land in the heart of home, another country, a quiet battlefield on a sunny day.

In a scene unchanged from medieval times, a handful of shepherds and their dogs herd the last thousand sheep on the cliffs above Freshwater West.

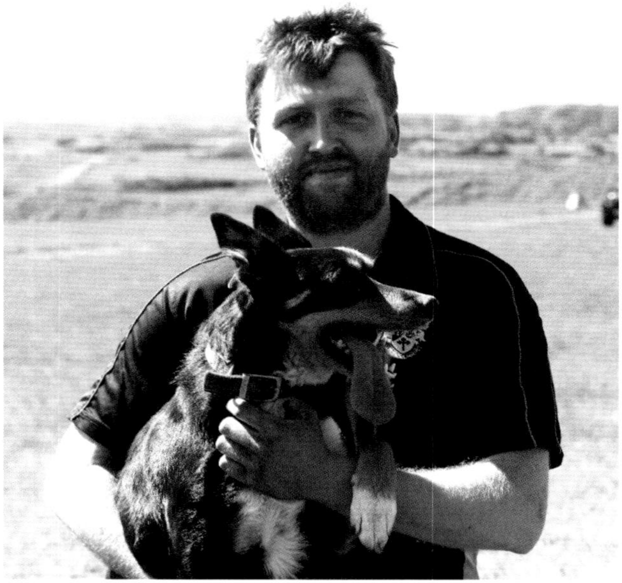

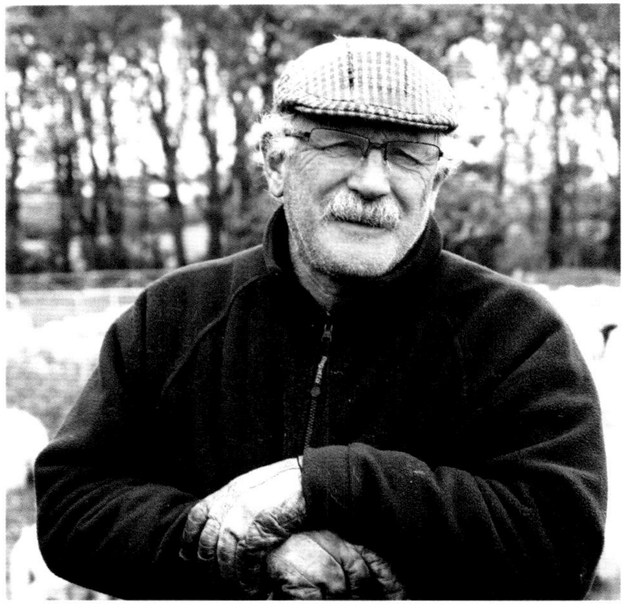

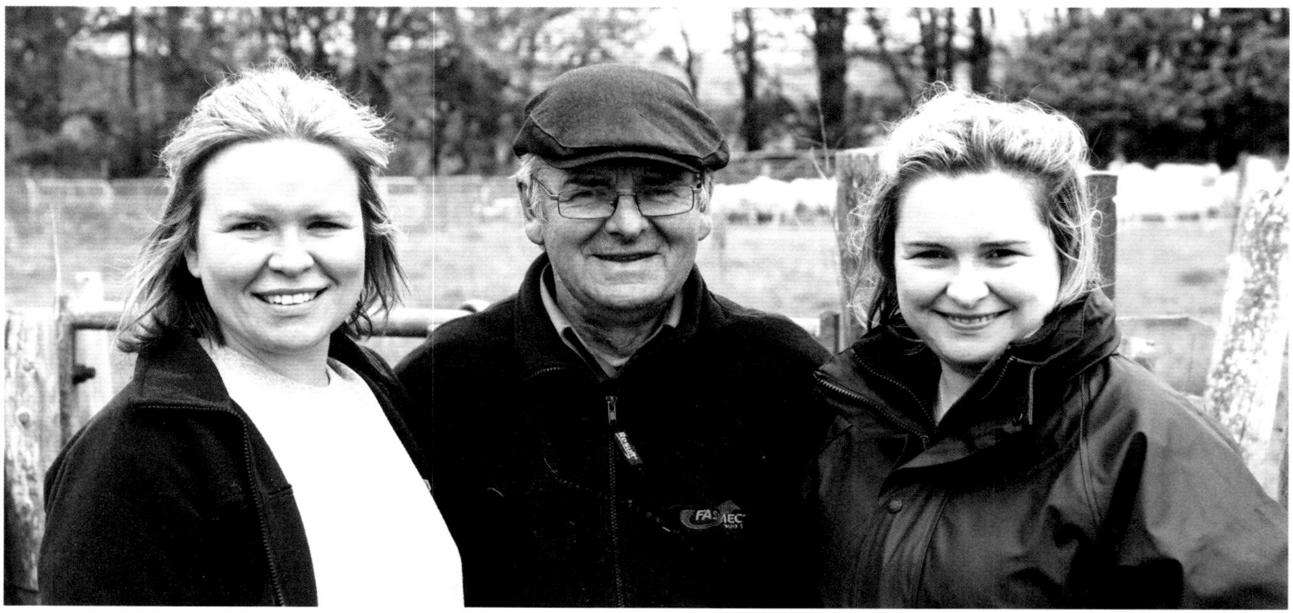

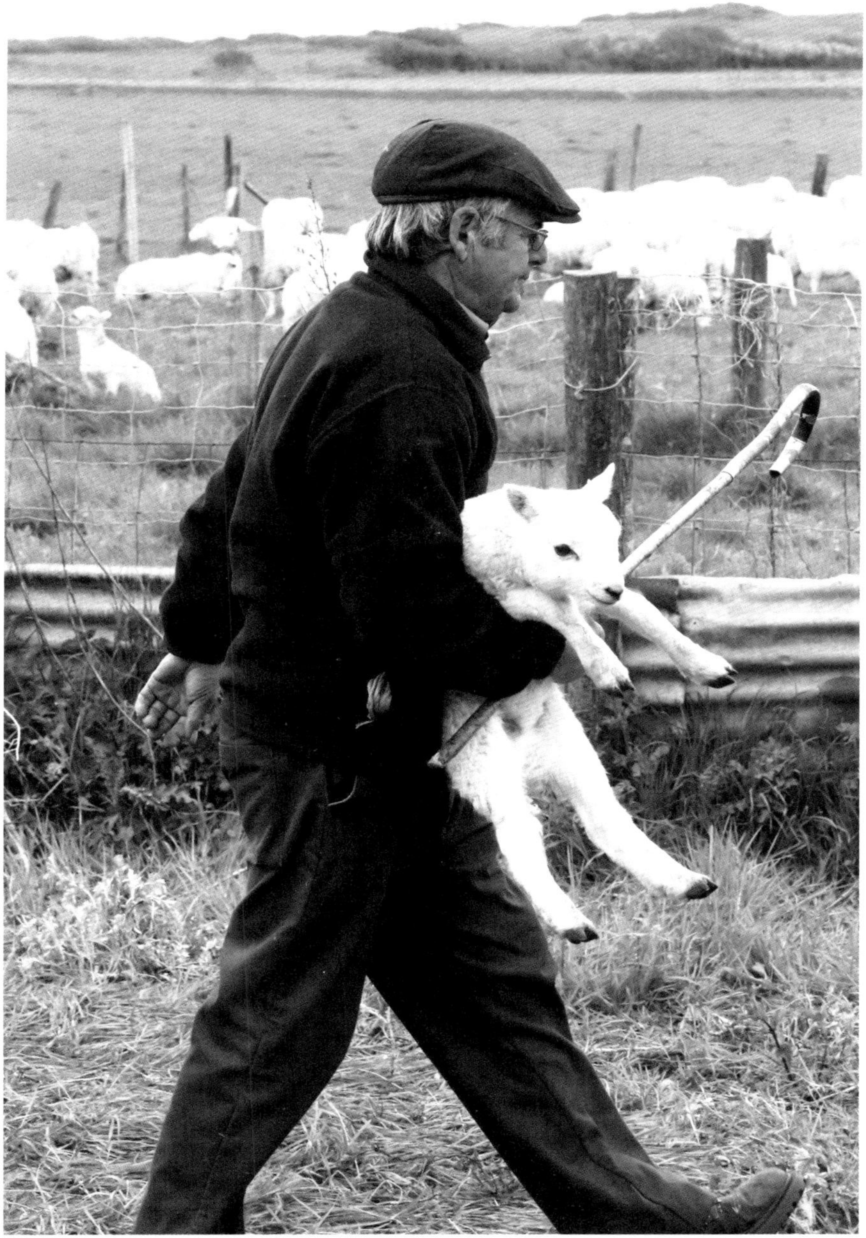

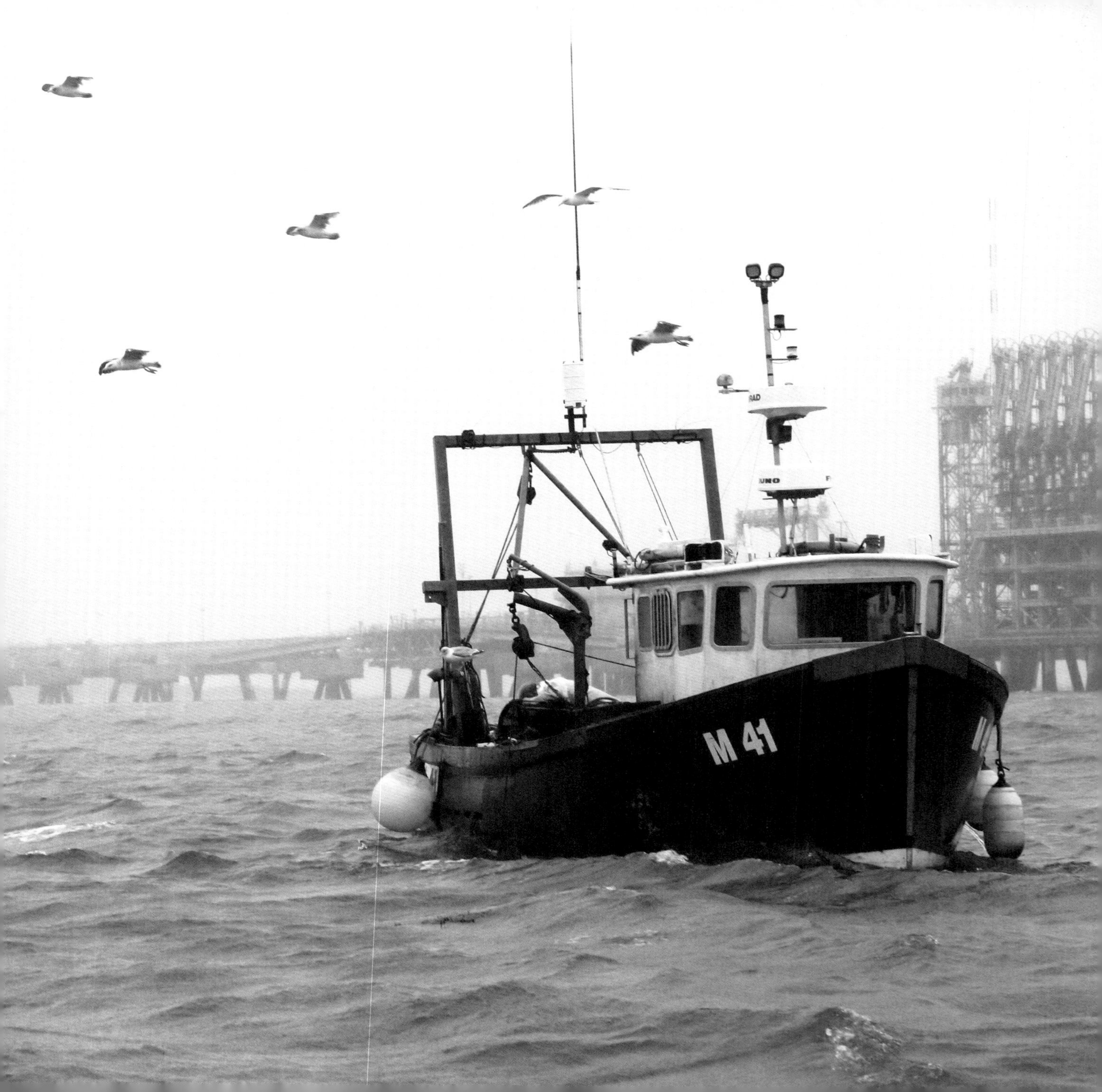
M 41

Sailing the Haven

A voyage to the heart of the county

It's 6.30 on a September morning and still too early for the dawn chorus. It's dark on the shortening days of autumn. This morning, high tide is at 7.00 on the Milford Haven waterway and timing and tides, as every boatman knows, are crucial for a voyage on the River Cleddau. Mistime and you'll pointlessly struggle against the unseen power of water; choose well and it'll be your silent force beneath the waves.

Clad in fleeces, waterproofs and lifejackets, we're sailing from Neyland Marina on a day-long voyage up and down the Milford Haven waterway. First we'll travel up the Cleddau as far as Landshipping and then double back on ourselves to Lawrenny, then head out towards Angle and Dale, before Milford Haven spills into the Irish Sea, sailing deep into Pembrokeshire's heart before the tide turns and the water flows out of the river. The Cleddau will empty at its highest reaches to leave shallow streams in glistening mud.

Before the age of road and rail, the sailing boat was how travellers arrived and departed Pembrokeshire. The haven was the highway to the world. Today, we'll sail past what were once the front doors to Pembrokeshire's towns and villages. 21st-century drivers arrive in our communities by the tradesmen's entrances, but today we'll see the view from the water. Downriver, the waterway is still how the oil, gas and petrochemical industries transport their precious cargo in their supertankers, but the upper reaches of the Cleddau are another world, lost in time.

Our morning destination has lost its ancient industries. Up river, you'll spy a few ageing jetties, moss-covered quays and straight-cut inlets on the yachtsman's chart of the Milford Haven waterway, but these days upriver is mostly a paradise for pleasure. The commercial boats, the trade ships and the coal barges have slipped into history.

Our boat is a catamaran sailing yacht called *Sea Legs*. Our crew consists of Andrew, known as Sam because he was a fireman, and Bob, a former submariner. We're hoping not to have to draw on Bob's extensive experience below the water's surface. After the initial frantic activity of untying ropes and all hands on deck to aid our slow reversal from the pontoon, we settle into the quiet contemplation of watching the still dark world slumber.

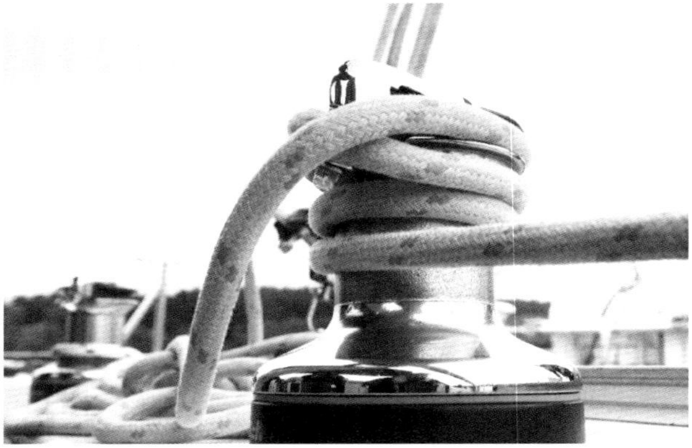

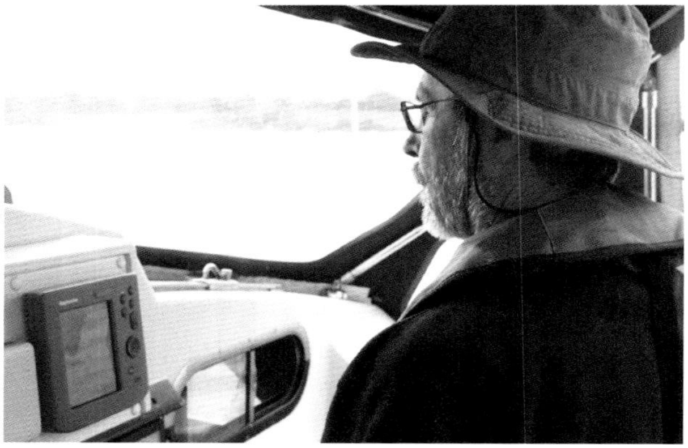

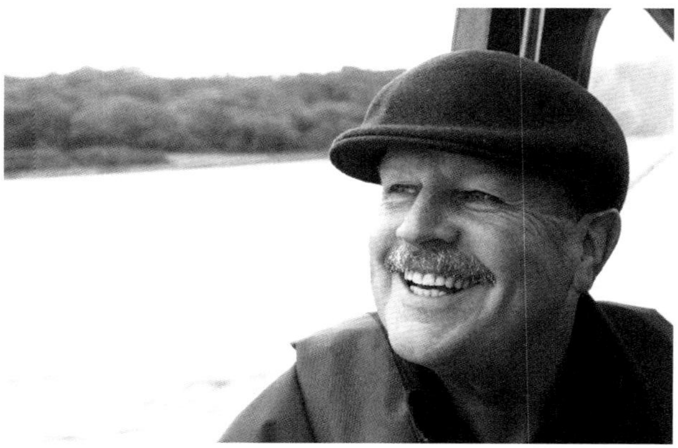

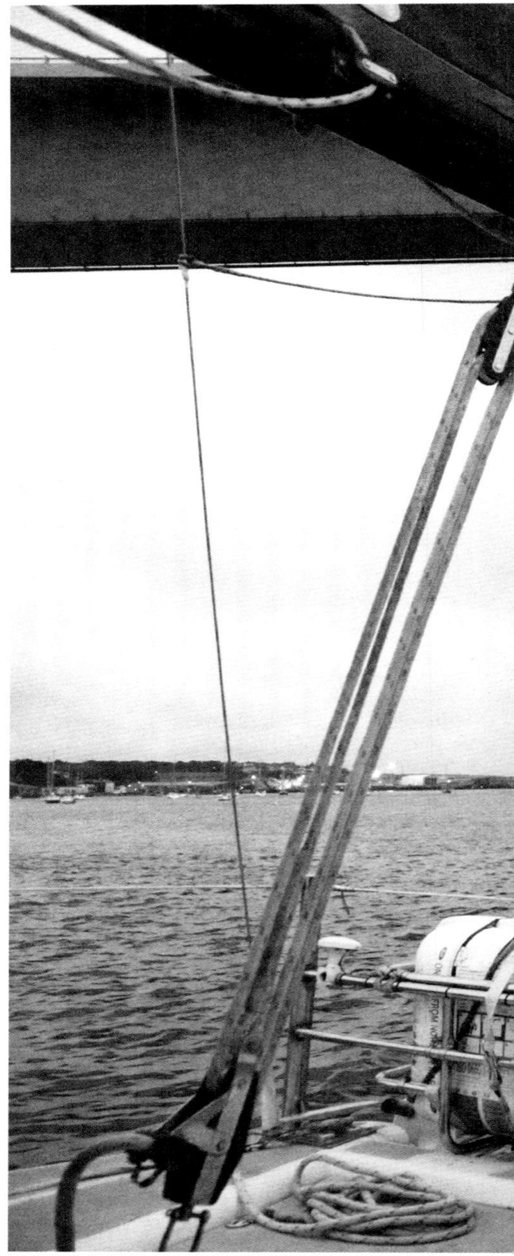

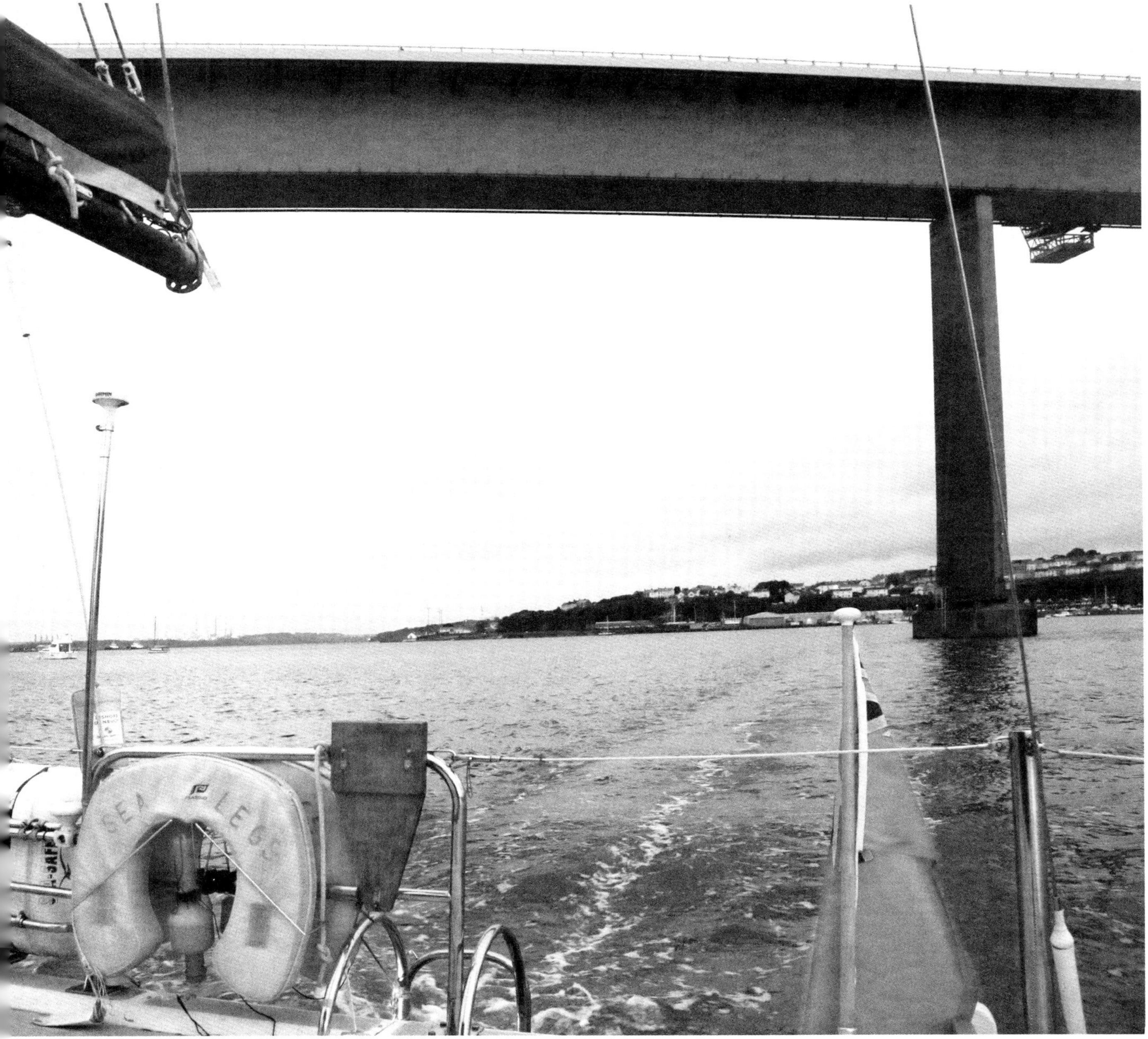

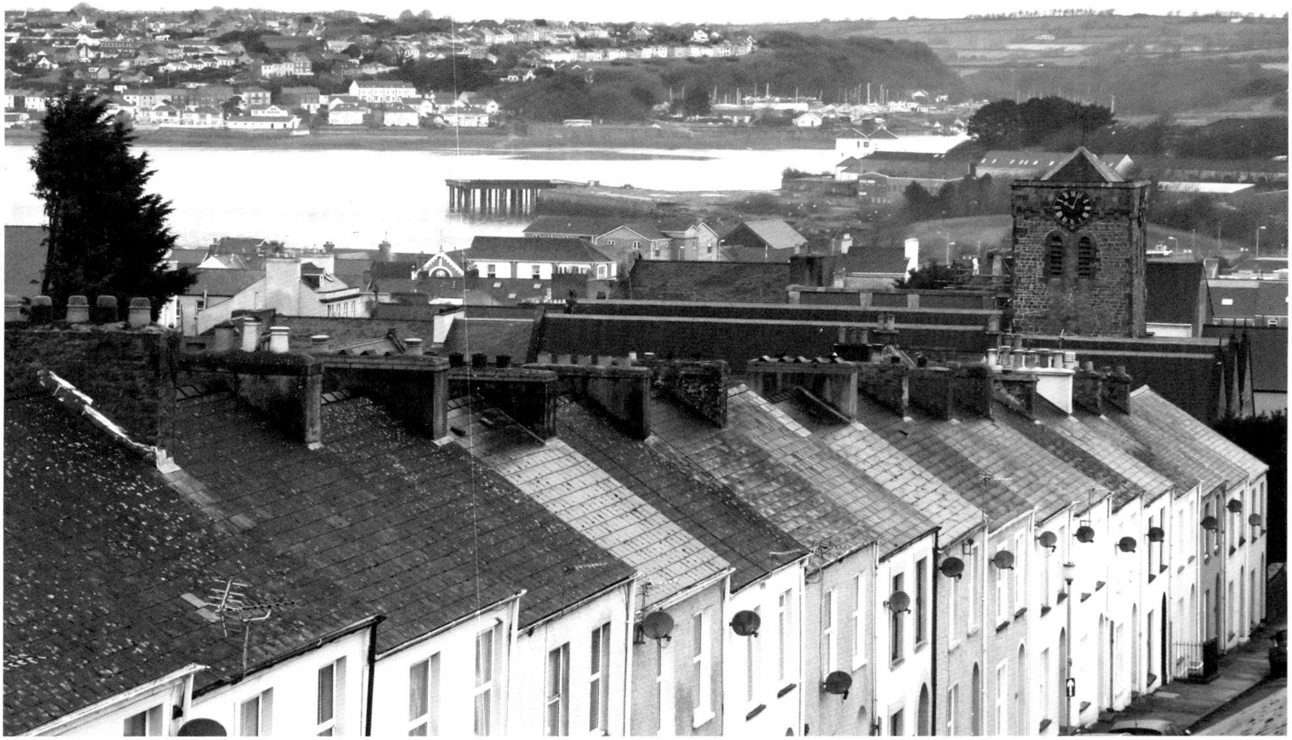

Neyland has reinvented itself as a marina town, though the yachts and motorboats are for the most part empty this morning. The working vessels, a few fishing boats, the police launch and firing range vessel occupy the deepest berths close to the mouth of the marina. The pleasure boats are tied on the pontoons beyond the boatyard, waiting for a weekend's play. Boats are primarily white and plastic. Wood is too much like hard work, although there are some old yachts here too – throwbacks and relics from the grand old days of sail and winters spent varnishing their planks.

Above the new waterside houses, Neyland's older colourful terraced cottages stand high above the inlet and look down upon where the port and rail yard once worked hard for a living. Neyland is waking slowly now, the windows blinking on their lights in the disappearing darkness of a deep-blue dawn.

In the 1850s, Neyland became the western terminus of Brunel's Great Western Railway with a transatlantic terminal remaining a busy rail and sea town until the mid-1960s. I have fond childhood memories of sitting in my parents' Mini in a queue of traffic, waiting for the *Cleddau King* to ferry us from Neyland to Pembroke Dock. The ferry service stopped when the Cleddau Bridge was opened, after it first collapsed during construction in 1970. We came after school to see the aftermath of the accident, the half-built bridge, broken like a Meccano toy. In the 1980s, they built this marina.

Today, we slip the ropes and motor quietly and slowly out of the still waters of the mouth of Neyland Marina, into the channel and under the Cleddau Bridge.

There are few motorists this early, rush hour begins late in Pembrokeshire, but there is a lone walker high above us, striding across its span.

We pass Trinity Wharf in the village of Burton, staring across the water to the woods where the decaying hulk of HMS *Warrior* was once moored. The dinghies and sailing boats on their moorings all face the same direction, but, like synchronised swimmers, they'll soon swing around in the tide. Cosheston Pill lies off to our right along with the water sports centre where children go to learn how to sail.

They've ploughed the low-lying fields in front of Burton Mountain, where the brown-lined earth reaches down to the shore. The acres behind are dotted with round, black, plastic bales of hay, awaiting tractor and trailer to take them to the farm.

We sail at walking speed past Mill Bay. Lawrenny lies off the right fork in the river, to which we'll return later in our voyage. In the trees on the opposite bank, the Union Flag is fluttering in the breeze above the stout stone tower of Benton Castle.

After the growing sprawl of Neyland and Pembroke Dock, the upper reaches of the River Cleddau are dominated by thick forest, its canopy still in full green, stooping low to touch high water mark. We have escaped the towns into an ancient landscape, seemingly unchanged in generations. But the chart of the river on the navigating table tells another story: a once-busy thoroughfare of commercial activity – the quarries, jetties and mines the map remembers are all lost in the woods. Garron Quarry and later Llangwm Ferry Quarries were once sharp shapes cut into the rock, now smoothed over by time and oak trees.

Ahead of us now, beyond the green water's edge, alive with islets of seaweed floating in the slack tide, is Coedcanlas House. It's set back from the shore and a few fields from the river. Coedcanlas was once a house and garden of distinguished social standing. The earliest reference to the manor house dates from 1363, and it is claimed to have been the gathering point for troops going to fight at Bosworth in support of Henry VII. From the boat I can't quite make out the stone-mullioned windows or what's left of the formal garden, but they are there, carved into a landmark from more troubled times.

The formal garden's remains lie in the field to the south of the house. Many of its distinguished visitors might have arrived by sea and walked from the shore past the gardens to the hospitality of their hosts.

In the early 20th century the house was owned by the Thomas family, grandparents of the jockey and novelist Dick Francis. Dick was born here and learned to ride in Pembrokeshire.

Past Llangwm now, settled by the Flemish in the 12th century and once home to miners and oyster fishermen. The Cleddau splits east and west before us and we make our way to Landshipping, passing Picton Point and the vast Picton Estate. It's time for a mug of morning tea; making tea on a moving boat is not for the uninitiated. Andrew and Bob take it in turns and sensibly keep their inexperienced new crew members out of the galley. Steaming cups are passed through the hatch to the parched passengers at the stern. Regardless of the breath-taking scenery, your author and photographer drop camera and notebook for a cuppa.

The half-restored, twin bow-fronted walls of Landshipping House, built in 1750 and owned by the Owens of Orielton, are just beyond the shore. Owens were the Landshipping Coal Agents, with the design of the house inspired by Slebech Hall and Picton Castle, both just up the river. The house at Llanshipping fell into disrepair and by 1890 it was a ruin. Even from the water it's easy to imagine its status – its huge windows offering sweeping views of the river and parkland beyond. A document from 1857 described Landshipping House as having bedrooms, hall, parlour, dining room, drawing room, nursery, library, servants' offices, stabling, coach house, saddle room and granary, walled garden, orchards and a wood.

The house was originally owned by Sir John Owen, later passing to his son, Hugh. Hugh lived there until 1856 with five servants. He was a landowner of considerable means and Lieutenant Colonel of the Pembroke Militia. This square mile of Pembrokeshire was the centre of power, patronage and wealth.

Alun Lewis has made it his life's work to restore the house to its former glory. It will take him a lifetime, but there can be no finer legacy to leave this community than to breathe new life into a landmark that would have been lost were it not for his extraordinary passion.

Past Sam's Wood and Black Tar Point – these moorings are home to the proper sailors who take to the water every day, rather than once in a blue moon. These boats are older and scruffier but are used more often than their white and clean weekending cousins sitting in the marina at Neyland, where we began our voyage.

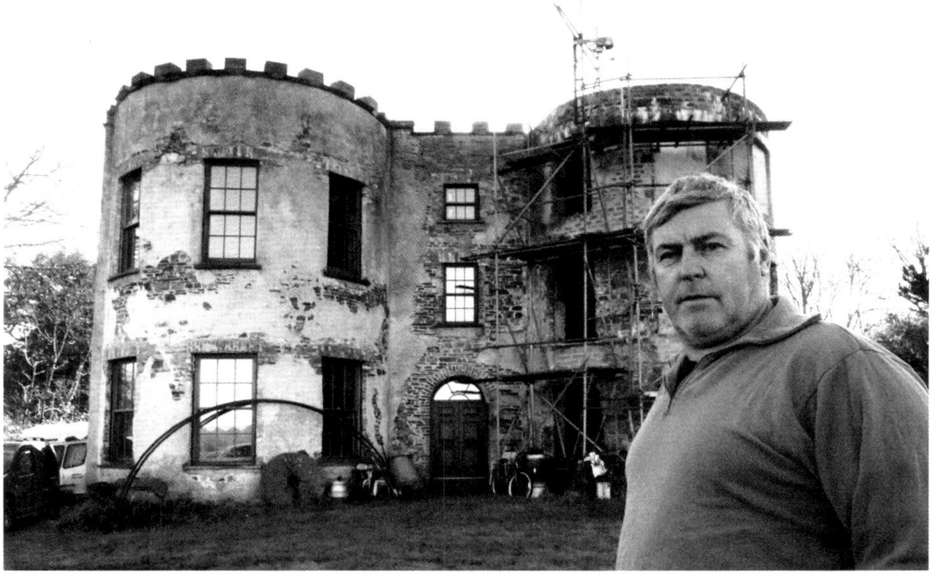

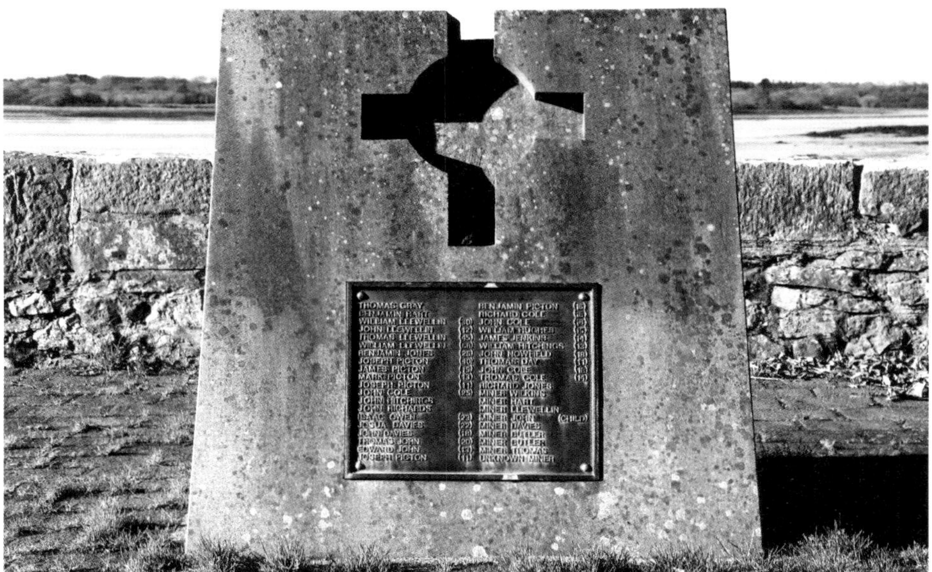

Alun Lewis and Memorial to Garden Pit Mine disaster

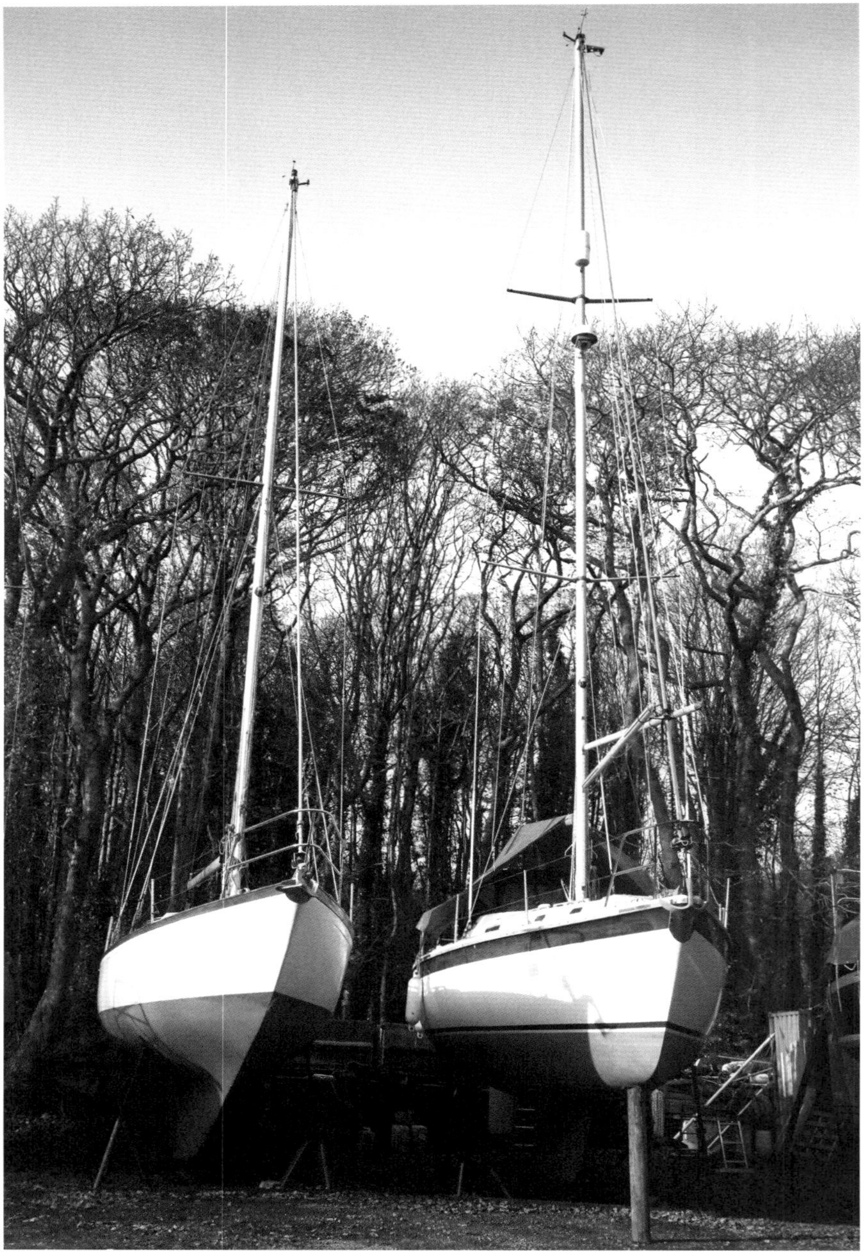

Sailing past the bucolic surroundings of woods and fields, it's easy to forget the upper reaches of the River Cleddau were home to thriving industries, including mining. There had been mining in this area since the Middle Ages, but it had been a rather gentle endeavour. In 1800, Sir Hugh Owen installed the first steam engine in the Pembrokeshire coalfield and the industry expanded, soon mining over 10,000 tons of coal each year. Few communities in Wales have dug coal and escaped the industry's tragedies and the Pembrokeshire coalfield was not exempt. In 1844, 58 men, women and boys were working in Garden Pit Mine at Landshipping. The pit workings extended under the river and 40 miners drowned when water burst through the roof of the mine.

The cause of the disaster was said to be the pressure of the water; there were no mining inspectors to check on safety. The names of the dead are engraved on the memorial and many were related. The same names reoccur: Llewellin, Picton, Davies, Cole, Hart and John. Joseph Picton died with three of his sons, leaving his widow and five more children. Several of the names on the memorial plaque say simply 'Miner'. These were probably women, even though legislation preventing their employment underground had been passed in Parliament. Other names listed give ages as young as 9 or 11. One is listed simply as 'Child'.

At Picton Point, the River Cleddau divides: the western Cleddau turns away to Hook and Haverfordwest and the eastern Cleddau flows towards Slebech, Minwear Wood and Blackpool Mill. A cormorant flies over our catamaran and we turn around. This is as far as we will sail up river.

The depth of water, the turning tide and weather forecast make us retrace our route for a mile.

There is time for a second brew as we sail past Knapp Farm and towards Beggars Reach. The mouth of the Lawrenny river remains hidden until we are almost upon it. The moorings and the boatyard dominate the yacht station. Lawrenny was originally developed around fishing, boat building and as a collection jetty for limestone quarried further up the Cleddau. There'll still be a few sunny weekends to sail the waiting yachts here, before they're craned in to sit on the concrete for winter. Behind the boatyard, the log cabins enjoy the best view in the village, looking across the water; their lawns have been mown for the last time this year.

Lawrenny has a number of claims to fame. The village gave Wales its first and only Grand National winner, Kirkland, at Aintree in 1905, and its war record was distinguished. Lawrenny was a base for Walrus seaplanes and a training centre operated by the Fleet Air Arm. Its calm, long and sheltered stretch of water was the perfect spot to take off and land.

In the distance, Carew River and Cresswell River beckon. Cresswell Quay and its intoxicating beauty lies at the end of one arm of the inlet and Carew's castle and its tidal mill on the other. The water stretching out before our bow is deceptive; its seeming depths conceal mud banks inches below the surface. Our detour to Lawrenny is short and restricted by the dropping tide and depth of water. This channel isn't deep enough for a yacht with a keel. We risk getting stuck on the mud if we go much

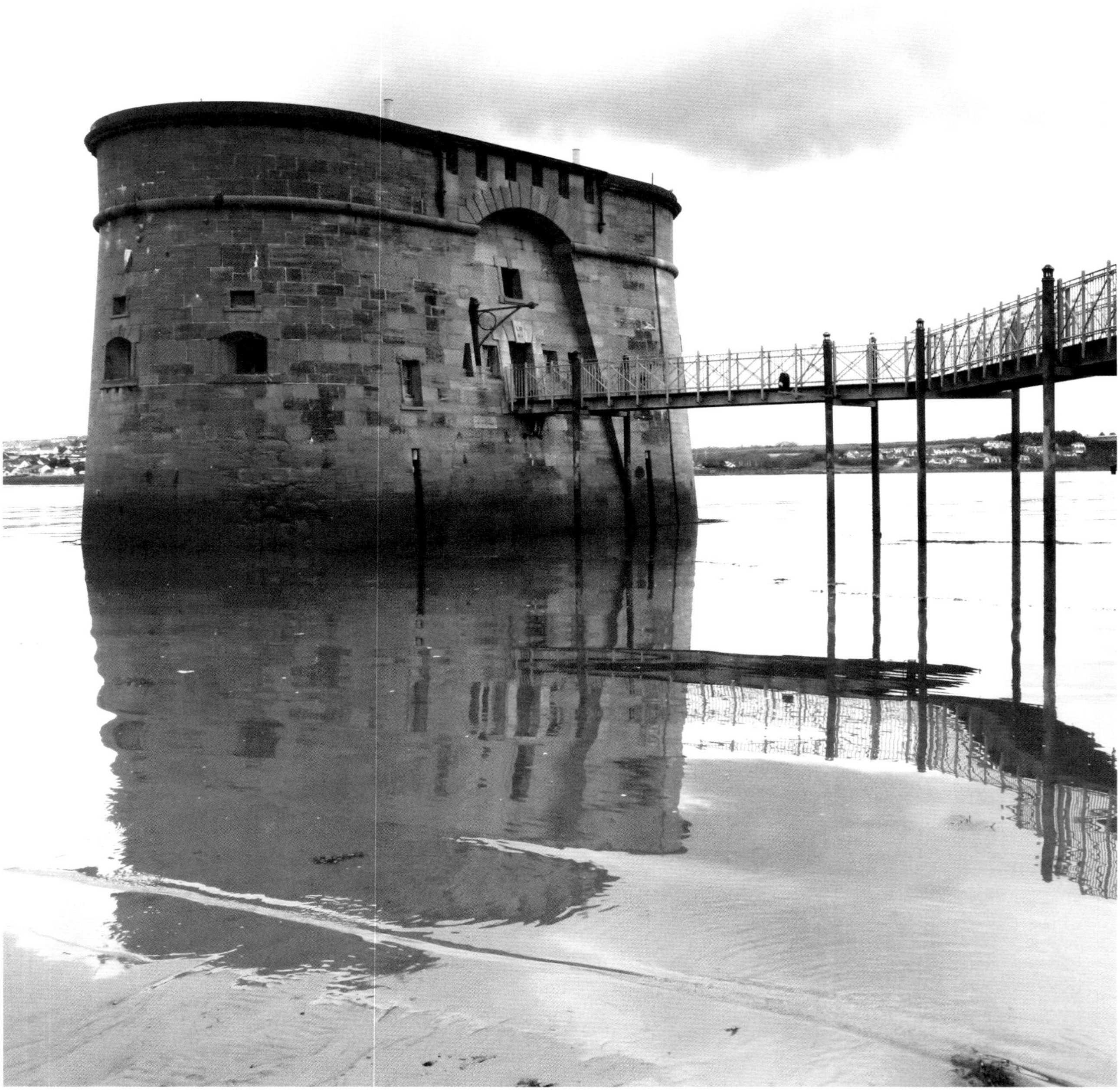

further beyond Black Mixen Pool, so we turn back for deeper waters and Jenkins Point. We resolve to return at high tide and in a rowing boat next time.

This stretch of the Cleddau was the playground of my childhood. My brothers and I spent summers exploring the estuary in a ten-foot boat. Its engine was so unreliable we were all proficient rowers. So many happy days were spent on this stretch of water between Hobbs Point and Lawrenny, with the constant accompaniment of a picnic and the whiff of two-stroke petrol. This is where I fell in love with Pembrokeshire; here on the upper reaches of the Cleddau in a small boat on summer days, taking forever to go not very far to nowhere in particular. They were simple pleasures: a boat trip, a knapsack full of food and the company of friends and family. Here we watched the forests go by, the cormorants fish and the sun scorch our skin.

In a bend of the river before Burton, Pembrokeshire's two stories lie before us and behind us, ancient and modern. Like the fluttering pages of a hymn book, the old songs slip into the distance to the ancient woods crowding the banks of the river. Stretched out in front of us, the new themes of Pembrokeshire – the story of oil, gas and wind turbines and the, as yet, untapped energy of waves.

Underneath the Cleddau Bridge again, past Neyland, our starting point, and onwards to Pembroke Dock. Front Street's small, square cottages hide behind the Martello Guntower that is still keeping watch. Only from the sea can you really appreciate the once mighty naval dockyard; its enormous slipways and dry docks built in dressed stone, as good today as when they first opened. Behind the slipways, newer giant steel sheds dwarf the older, more distinguished Admiralty buildings.

One of the nearby hangars was secretly used in the original Star Wars trilogy. The dockyard, that had been a central part of Britain's defence in virtually every war in two centuries, was called on to build the Millennium Falcon. The second Star Wars movie, *The Empire Strikes Back*, was already in production when the filmmakers needed a life-sized, moving prop of the Falcon. The town's skilled workforce and enormous aircraft hangars, home to the Sunderland flying boats during World War Two, clinched the deal.

Pembroke Dock once more played a small part in the battle between the forces of good and evil.

This clever little town of shipwrights, carpenters and engineers built 263 Royal Navy vessels and five royal yachts over the 112-year lifetime of the Royal Dockyard. My paternal grandfather, an engineer, worked on prototype submarines. I never knew the man in our fading photographs in his pork-pie hat and neat dickie bow, but he and his friends were helping to push the boundaries of combat at sea. This river, its rise and fall, its high tide and low tide, its war and its peace, its happiness and its sorrow, is the story of our family for generations and generations. I think of my grandfather walking to the

This stretch of the Cleddau was the playground of my childhood.

dockyard with his bag of tools and of Dad's stories of growing up here, swimming across the river in the age before the oil tankers.

These days, it's the huge Irish ferry which keeps the spirit of Pembroke Dock's maritime story alive. The Ferry Terminal is empty now, waiting for the lunchtime *Isle of Inishmore*. In total, 62,000 vehicles and 325,000 passengers make the crossing through Pembroke Dock every year. Twice a day from Rosslare, the ship belts across the Irish Sea then slows to gently pirouette in the tight confines of Milford Haven's waterway to dock alongside the jetty at Pembroke Dock.

We move past half a dozen tugs moored together, all of them waiting for a job like taxi cabs on a Friday night. These vessels are the ship handlers. They push and pull enormous, clumsy and slow super-tankers into position. They are the safety nets ready to intervene if any ship loses power and they are also the firefighters, should the worst happen.

The LNG tankers and their cargo necessitated the world's most powerful fleet of tugs, constructed to handle the world's biggest carriers. This is a community that watched the tragedy of the *Sea Empress* oil disaster in 1996 unfold a few miles away. They say the lessons have been learnt. If you are an incoming tanker, there is now a well-rehearsed compulsory routine. A tug follows the tanker from the mouth of the channel and a rope is attached to the larger ship. If anything should go wrong, there is less chance of an accident if the ship is tied to a following tug. The tugs are the sheep dogs of the sea – following out wide, keeping their distance, until a friendly nip is required at close quarters.

We gather speed and skirt outside Carr Rocks. At high water, we're safe from the rocks rupturing our hull, but many unknowing boatmen have come to a juddering halt, catching their keels on the stones.

From the 790s until the Norman Invasion in 1066, the Milford Haven waterway was used by Vikings looking for shelter from the Irish Sea. In 854, the Viking Chieftain Hubba spent winter here with his ships, lending his name to Hubberston. This waterway tells the story of Britain, of its invasions, the rise and fall of religions and the ebb and flow of its immigrants and industries. Each chapter is etched into its shores.

The four low chimneys of the new Pembroke Power Station slip past us on our voyage towards the sea. This is a gas-fired station which replaced the oil-fired unit in 1997. Oil replaced the coal industry here, and now gas is slowly replacing oil. This is the largest gas-fired power station in Europe, generating enough power to supply 3,500,000 homes. It looks across the water at the next chapter of energy – a handful of huge wind turbines on land once occupied by Gulf Oil Refinery. Behind the spinning turbines, the half-submerged tanks containing liquified natural gas shipped from Qatar try to hunker down in their fields, like elephants hiding behind a tree.

The big new houses at Pennar Point occupy a windy perch looking down the haven towards Pembroke's Valero refinery. Locals will remember this plant being called Texaco or Regent. Some will remember the explosion here, which blew out the windows in Milford across the water. Valero is one of the largest, most complex refineries in Western Europe,

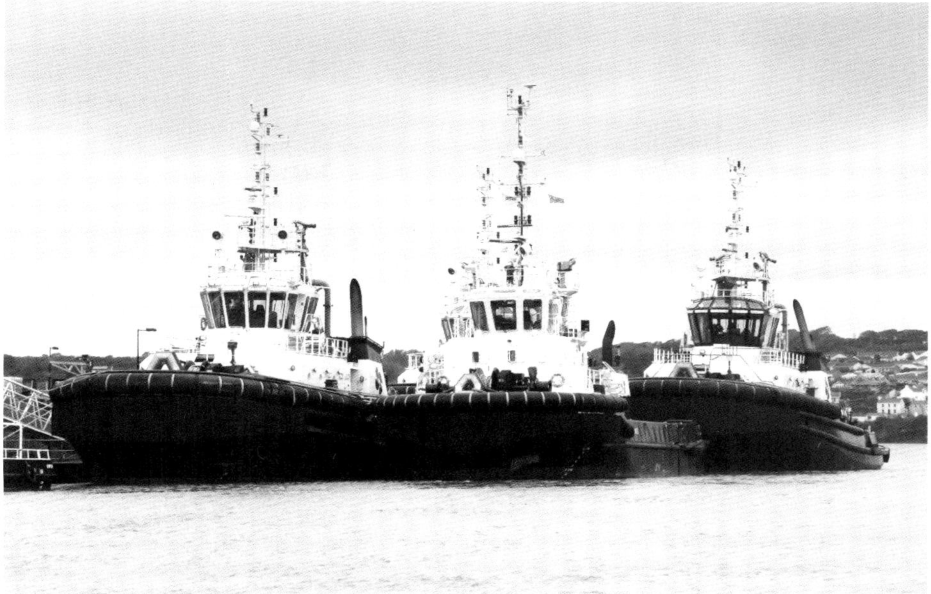

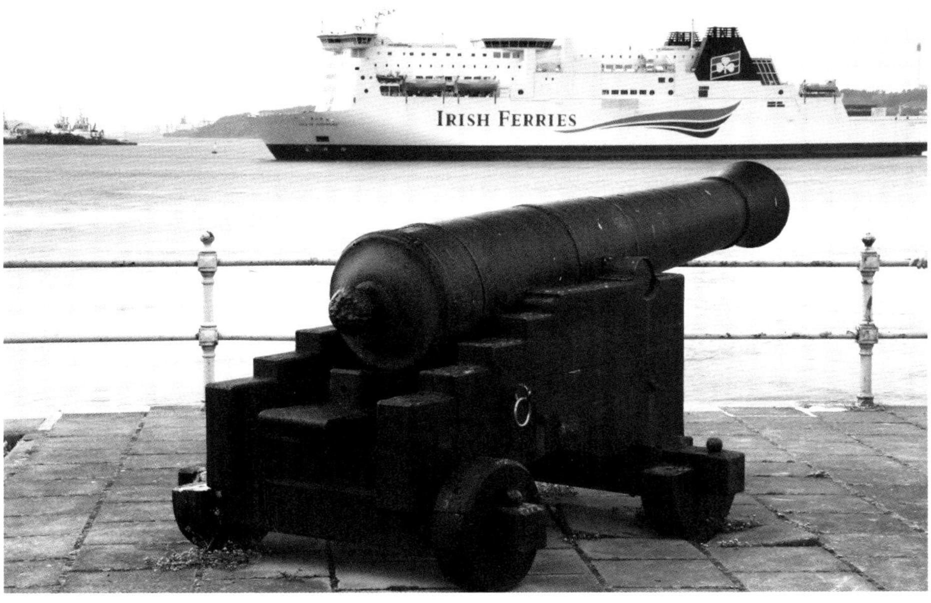
IRISH FERRIES

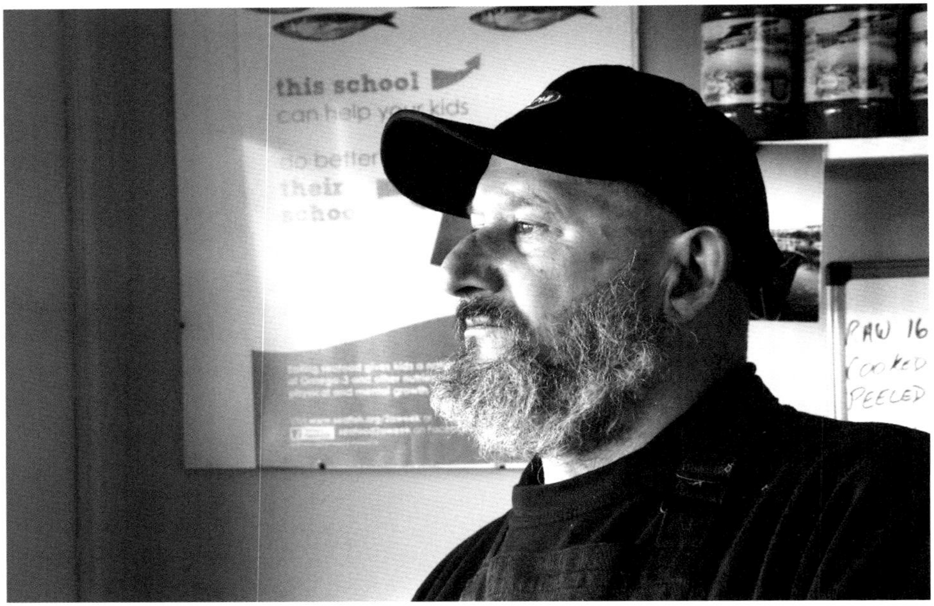

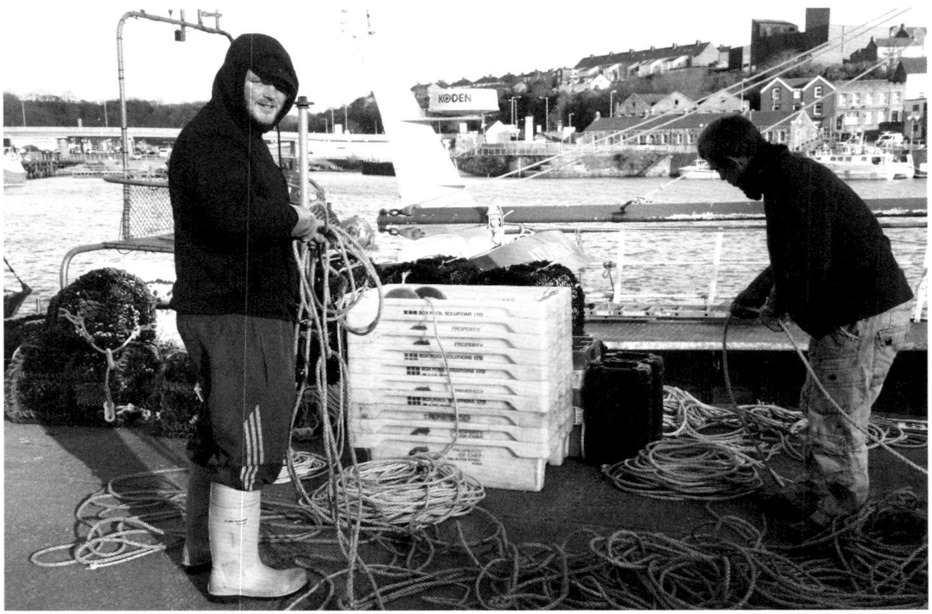

 Steve Mackay and trawlermen

making gasoline, diesel, kerosene and liquefied petroleum gas.

Long before the energy industry, it was fishing and fighting that helped to establish these towns along the haven. Milford was founded in 1793 by Sir William Hamilton, perhaps better remembered for his younger second wife, Emma Hamilton, Horatio Nelson's mistress. Nelson visited the Haven, along with the Hamiltons, describing it as the next best natural harbour to Trincomalee and 'the finest port in Christendom'.

Sir William's nephew, the Hon. Charles Francis Greville, invited seven Quaker families from Nantucket and Martha's Vineyard to settle in Milford and develop a whaling fleet. The business of fighting, or war, began in 1800, when he persuaded the Navy Board to develop a dockyard for building warships. Seven royal vessels were launched here, including HMS *Surprise* and HMS *Milford*.

In 1814 the Royal Dockyard was transferred to Pembroke Dock and Milford's fortunes grew around fishing. By 1906, Milford had become the sixth largest fishing port in the UK. The *Pembrokeshire Herald* reported in 1912 that 'the fish trade is Milford's sole industry...the population of the town has doubled.'

Milford Haven, like Pembroke Dock, has experienced a roller coaster of boom and slump.

Milford Haven, like Pembroke Dock, has experienced a roller coaster of boom and slump. At the height of the fishing boom, it was said that 'every day was a pay day'. My father remembered running across the decks of fishing boats from one side of Milford to the other, there were so many trawlers. In 1921 674 people were working in the fishing industry, but you'll be pushed to find more than a handful of fishing boats today. Steve Mackay moved to Milford from Great Yarmouth at the age of six and was an apprentice fish-filleter in the old fish market. He did his time on trawlers and now you'll find him in the fish shop on shore. You sense he might be one of the last of the line.

The oil industry helped to boost the town but the slumps have been severe. During the 1980s and 1990s, the unemployment rate at times topped 30%. These communities have known hard times. Energy and tourism are now the big earners. Cruise ship visits have increased, with hundreds of liner passengers calling every year to explore the county's castles and cathedral, but it's the energy industry which is the dominant player – this waterway transports 25% of Britain's motor fuel. Sailing up the Haven today, watching the ships go by, this stretch of water is never still. It's a successful, international shipping destination. Milford Haven's waterway supports over 5,000 jobs in Wales and 30% of jobs in the local economy are in oil refining, gas processing and power generation. After our love affair with petrol and diesel is over, Milford Haven will reinvent itself again, as it has always done. Wind, solar and tide will generate a new home-grown industry after the oil and gas ships stop coming.

The tanker *BW Thames*, resplendent in green and red, is tied to the jetty, sitting high in the water, waiting for a cargo. We sail past the old mine depot as we make our way past Milford. The Admiralty bought Thomas Ward's ship breaking yard in the 1930s. By the outbreak of war the Mine Depot consisted of six armament sheds, tunnels built into the neighbouring valley and a reservoir, in case of explosion. At the height of the Second World War, a thousand people worked here. Today it's ghostly and quiet.

On the south bank of the Haven the crude oil tanker *Nansen Spirit*, all 66,563 tonnes of her, sits at the jetty. Built in 2010 and home port Nassau, her crew on deck walk briskly about their tasks to shorten her stay. These seamen will travel the world, but few will spend much time in port.

We're mid-channel and there's a gentle whiff of crude oil. Our yacht that seemed so substantial when we boarded at Neyland now feels inconspicuous beside looming supertankers. We are surrounded by thriving international big business.

The *Axelotl* is berthed at Valero's jetty. It has journeyed here from Amsterdam. Just over its bridge, perched on the mainland, Popton Fort comes into view. The fort was built in 1864 as part of the defence of Milford Haven on the orders of Lord Palmerston, along with Fort Hubberstone on the opposite side of the Haven. They are dwarfed by the might of the ships that slip beneath their sights. Like old soldiers sitting on the bench, their wars are done.

In the middle of the channel, off Angle's Lifeboat Station, the fishing boat *M41* slowly hauls up her pots on the winch. Lobsters and crabs fly upwards, caught in the cages from dark, deep blue and into the light. The little ones and the females will be thrown back, but the adult males will make a tasty lunch.

The relaxed nonchalance of sailing in the upper reaches of the Cleddau is now long gone and swapped for constant head-turning vigilance as we look out for faster and infinitely larger ships. We've exchanged the maritime equivalent of the empty back roads for the speeding motorway of the sea.

Thun Gothenburg steams into sight, riding high in the water. She's travelling empty into Milford to collect chemical products before making her way to Liverpool.

These ships are sailed by a handful of crew and lots of new technology, but regardless of the technical advances there is still something mesmerising about watching a ship voyage to its destination. It's entrancingly timeless.

We are making 10 knots. The sails are full and aside from the waves slapping the hull there is near silence on deck. We'll turn around before we reach open sea; our passage down Milford Haven is almost done.

The lunchtime Irish ferry is closing in on us, thundering in from the distant horizon, an indistinct white dot becoming larger by the minute. Milford Haven's newest arrivals are about to drop anchor – the latest visitors in a long line extending back through the centuries.

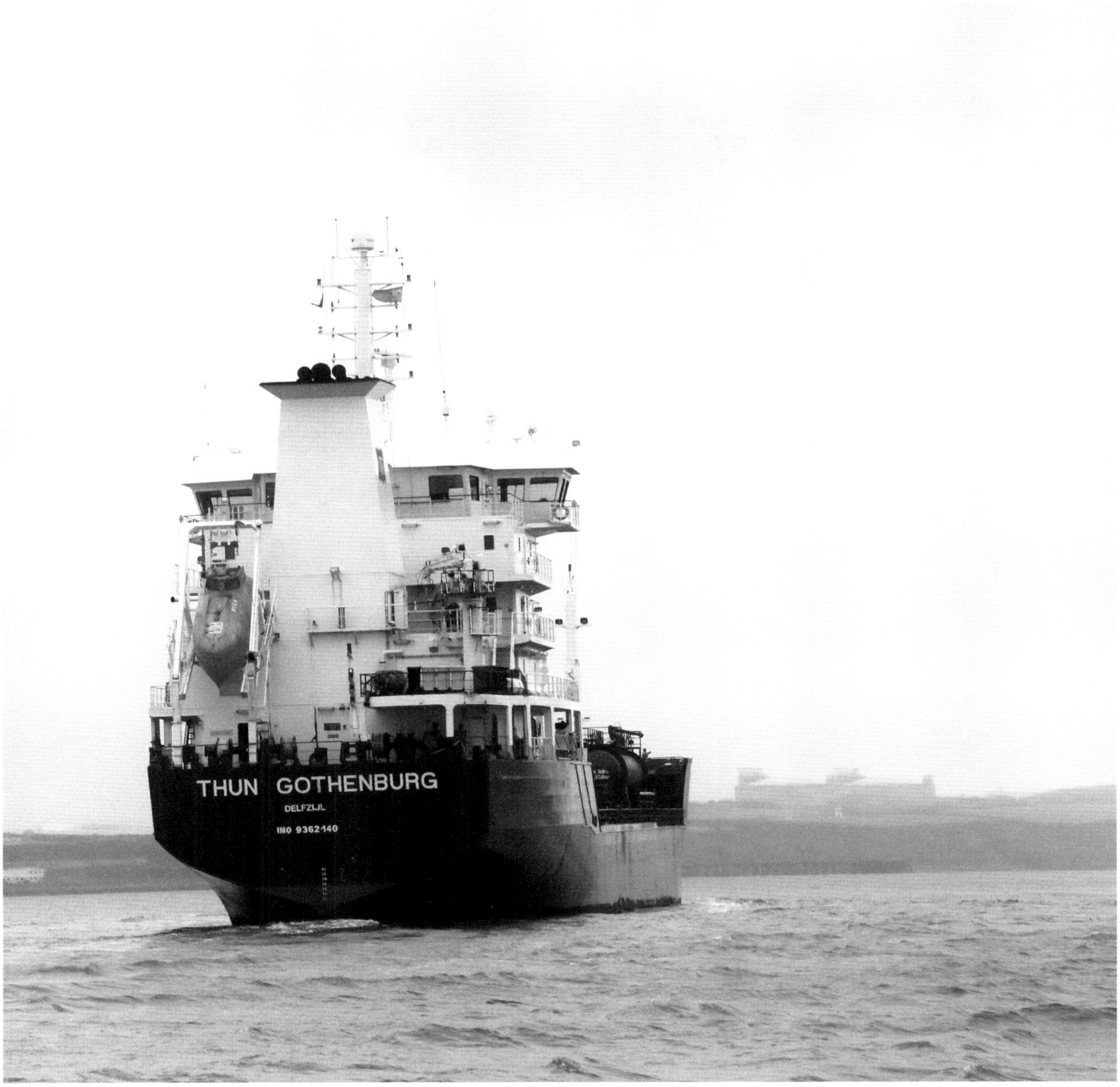
THUN GOTHENBURG
DELFZIJL
IMO 9362140

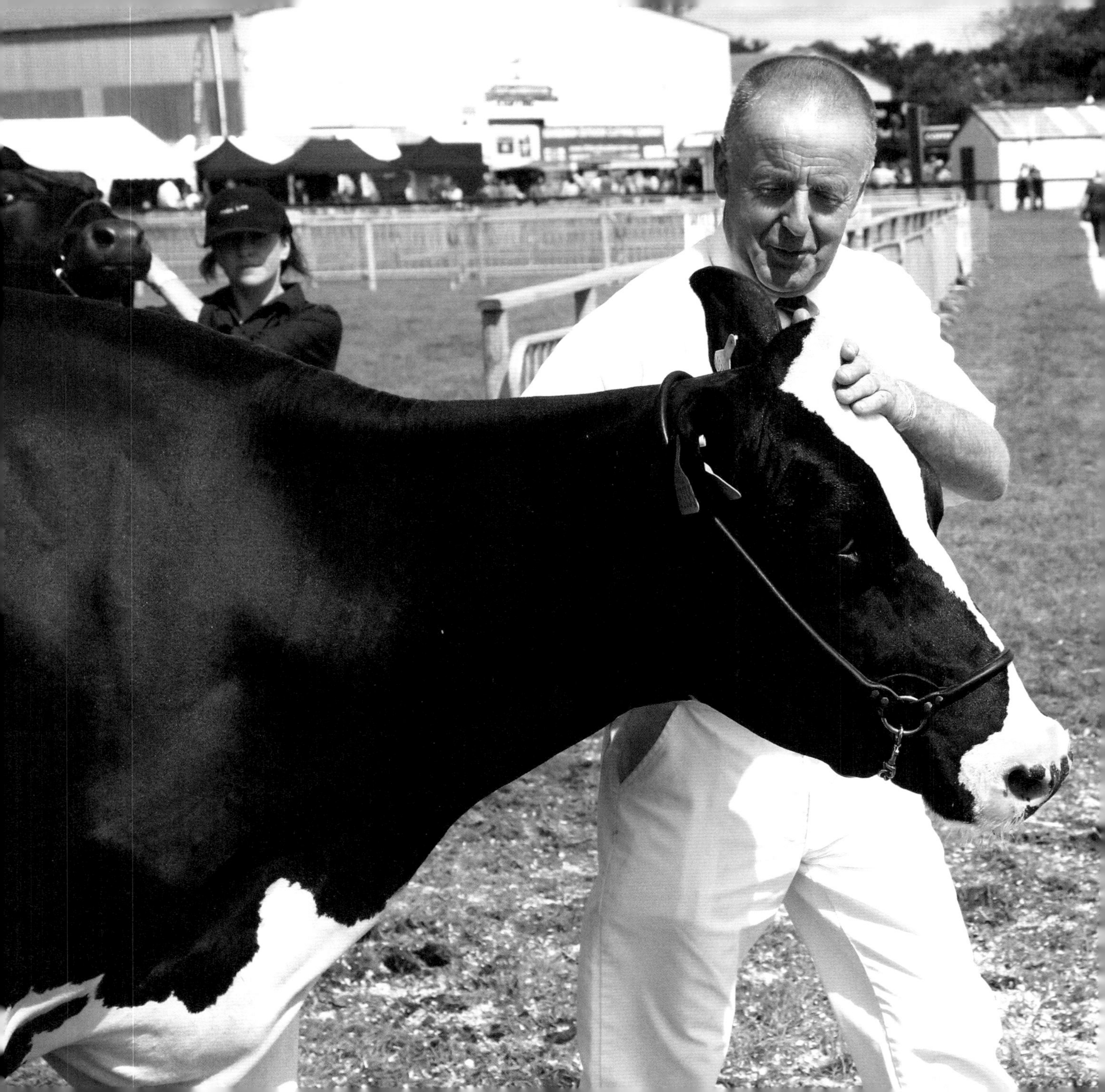

County Show

Pembrokeshire's beauty contest

The truth is that August is probably the wrong time of year to hold an outdoor agricultural show. The leaden days leading up to mid-August have been unkind and the warmth of summer has slipped away. It is forbidding autumnal grey skies that greet visitors to Withybush Aerodrome on the outskirts of Haverfordwest. It has rained for days; the car parks are sodden, the main ring waterlogged and high winds are forecast for this evening. But for the farmers who are the stars of the show, this is the perfect time of year. The hay is cut, the baling done, and the sheep are grazing in the summer pastures. August is downtime, if there is such a thing in farming circles. August is the time to look back and plan ahead. Here, tractors and implements will be traded; cars will be bought and sold and meetings with the moneymen, the bankers and the insurers, will take place over a cup of tea in their trade stands.

This agricultural show is a three-day event, one of the largest in the UK. The show will promote the most talented young people: the breeders, the handlers, the riders, the cooks. It will demonstrate new technology, offer a myriad of competitions for every rural skill and allow the opportunity to wallow in the nostalgia of vintage machinery. But this is not just a celebration of the past; it is a shop window for the future of food production too. A much-vaunted robotic milking parlour is already gathering a small crowd for its demonstration – presumably comprising of many dairy farmers desperate for a lie in of a morning. This week will offer the chance to meet with friends and family and catch up on many busy months.

Days start early at the Pembrokeshire County Show. Judging of the Welsh ponies Section A begins promptly at 8.30 – it is the curtain raiser on a programme that will fill the day until sunset and events will change every half hour. Shire horses, the Grand Parade of Horses and Cattle and the Parade of the Foxhounds by South Pembrokeshire Hunt each have their billing, until finally the motorcross team close the day with their loud stunts. The show jumping and horse arenas are set to host the UK championship's qualifier rounds and the Junior Show Jumping Championship and Shetland Grand National respectively.

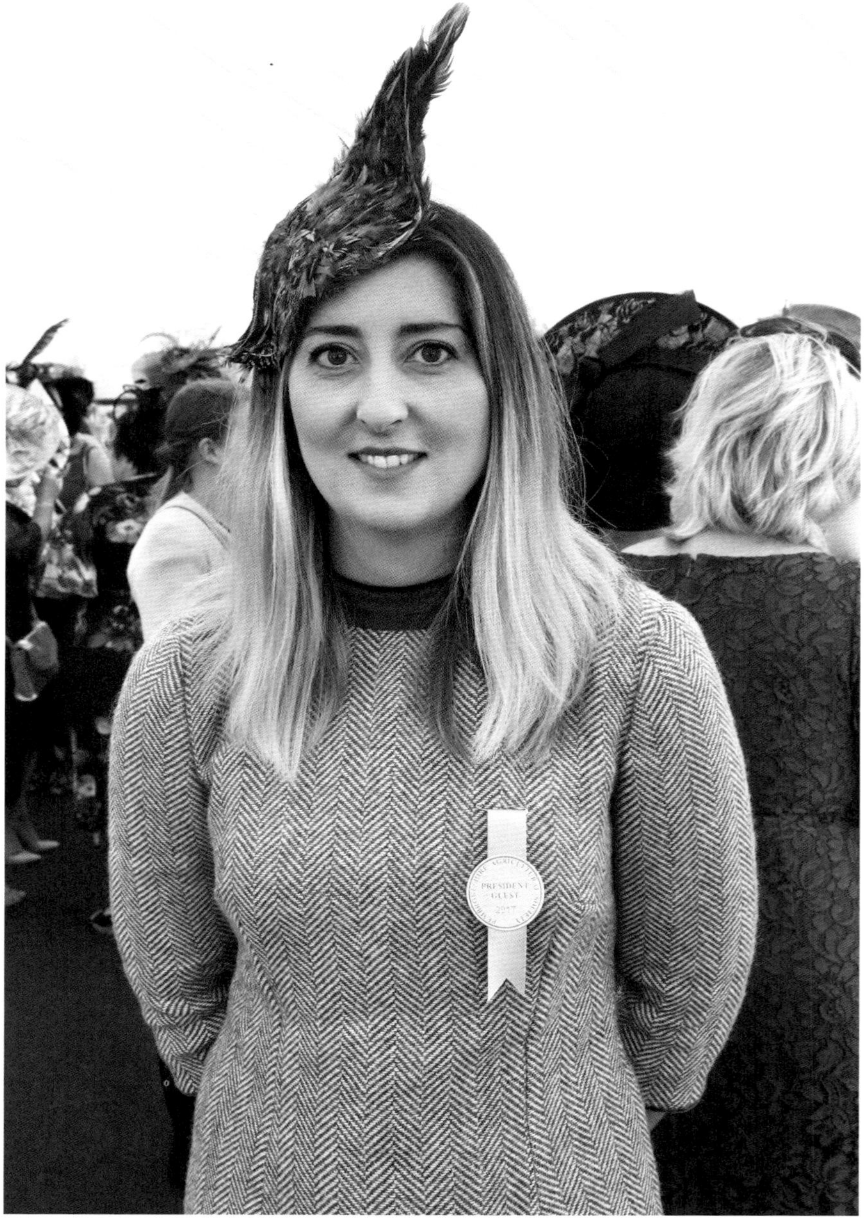
PRESIDENT
GUEST

In the livestock arena, Ayrshire, Jersey, dairy shorthorn and brown Swiss lead their owners to the dairy cattle classes.

The Show awards the county's best animals – but it is also the countryside's equivalent of the Academy Awards for rural skills. The crops competition will be judged at 10 o'clock, followed by prize giving for craft, horticulture and cookery. The poultry exhibition is housed in a large hangar and draws larger than usual interest when the rain becomes determined. The axemen's display, the gundogs, the falconers and ferret handlers are all surrounded by the curious and the converts alike.

The gathering breeze and spitting rain won't deter the wide-hatted and new-frocked guests tottering in high heels, swapped moments ago from wellington boots. It is Ladies' Day in the President's Marquee and champagne is to be served to a female-only gathering. It is here that the real networking of Pembrokeshire's farming community will take place. Up and coming business women who have made it through the cruel gestation of start-up businesses will be celebrated in front of the county's VIPs. The chairwoman of the National Park is here, MPs, Assembly Members, county councillors, other female entrepreneurs and the Bishop of St Davids, plus 200 other guests. This morning, these ventures will receive influential attention and order books will be filled.

Clare Johns is a young farmer who is to be showcased today. She nervously tells the hundreds of women of her endeavours. She grew up in a council house on the other side of the county. She and her husband are working with Pembroke School farm. Their aim is to infuse a passion for animals and food that perhaps couldn't be ignited in classroom teaching. If that ambition wasn't admirable enough, she is turning her sheep's wool into tweed for the high-end fashion industry. For so long sheep farmers have struggled to make any money from their wool, now the television programmes are beating a path to Clare's door. Soon her new shop on the high street in Narberth will open and the rapt crowd listening will certainly support her.

Clare established her own luxury fashion label a couple of years ago. She sells high-end handmade clothes. Some of her pieces will set you back £500. Nothing unusual about this, in what is a crowded global marketplace, but what is different about Clare's business is her insistence on keeping the entire process from shearing to sewing in Pembrokeshire. So many of the UK's fashion labels have off-shored their manufacturing to cheaper, low-wage economies, but not Clare. Her unique, luxurious clothes are made from the wool of her own animals and transformed into garments almost within the same postcode.

At the gathering for Ladies' Day in the President's Marquee, some women are perhaps wearing expensive designer haute couture made on the

Clare established her own luxury fashion label a couple of years ago.

other side of the world, in questionable conditions and then shipped halfway round the globe. They listen intently to Clare's plea for a more sustainable fashion industry, where local people make local clothes supporting the local community. It's a mark of how removed we are from the countryside that we marvel at making clothes from the animals on our own doorstep. There are more sheep in Wales than people, but few of us would stop to think of buying clothes made from Welsh wool, although many try to buy locally-produced food. A growing interest in sustainability and a quiet revulsion at sweat-shop conditions in the global fashion industry has turned the tide, all of which is good news for Clare.

At Ladies' Day, Clare's story is an accurate snapshot of farming in Pembrokeshire. This steely sisterhood ensures that generation after generation, the disparate, isolated business of farming maintains wider support. The good news stories will be shared and those who need support will find it. This group of Pembrokeshire VIP women spend the morning networking, while their men talk outside and watch the world go by. It is the womenfolk who will quietly but determinedly look after the county's interests. Today is their day at the County Show and, for too brief a moment, they will be acknowledged and rewarded.

Farming and fishing once employed thousands of people in Pembrokeshire as the dominant industry. Now it is the public sector, the NHS, schools, the council and oil and gas that are the big employers. Agriculture keeps only a fraction of the population. Mechanisation on farms has reduced the workforce and liberated many from the drudge of low-paid jobs, and agricultural contractors now complete in days tasks that would have once taken weeks. Yet despite the exodus from the land, Pembrokeshire's office workers and urban dwellers still come in their thousands to enjoy this festival of rural life. Perhaps they come to rekindle some fading family memory. They will come to look at animals with their children, enjoy the show ring displays, shop at the stalls and wonder at our distance from the land and the food it produces. Maybe they also yearn for a different way of life. This is an escape for a day from office careers and urban employment, escape from neighbours and life in suburbia, an escape to an imagined Eden not so far away.

Whatever the dreams, the reality of rural life is somewhat harsher.

Pembrokeshire's rich farmland, its lowlands and fields, were fought over by invaders for a thousand years. In recent times, the farming community's battles have been closer to home. Foot and mouth disease, BSE, Bovine TB, milk quotas and the falls in the price of food have driven many from the industry, or at least driven husbands or wives off the farm to find other income. Those who remain in farming are the survivors who have chosen the good life over the easy life.

This is a meeting today of two Pembrokeshires. The County Show claims to promote agriculture to the farming community but also to the wider general public. Town meets country here, but they are two distinct peoples. The people of the countryside have a boundless energy demanded of living off the land.

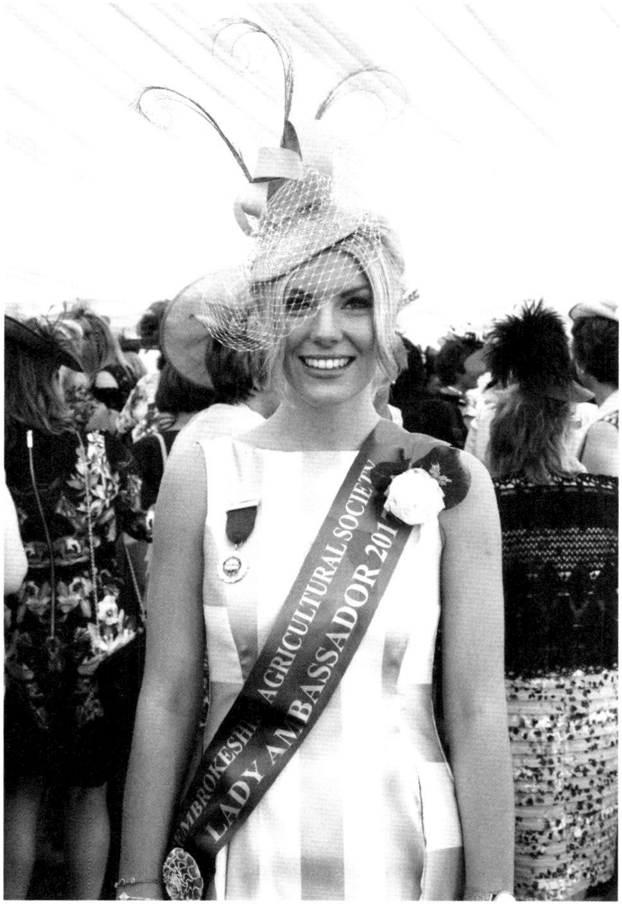
AGRICULTURAL SOCIETY
LADY AMBASSADOR

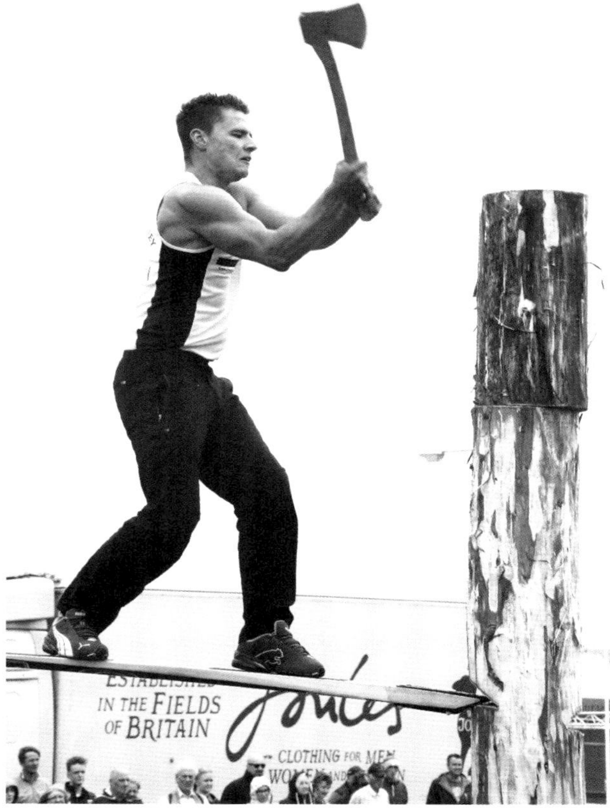
IN THE FIELDS
OF BRITAIN
Joules
CLOTHING FOR MEN

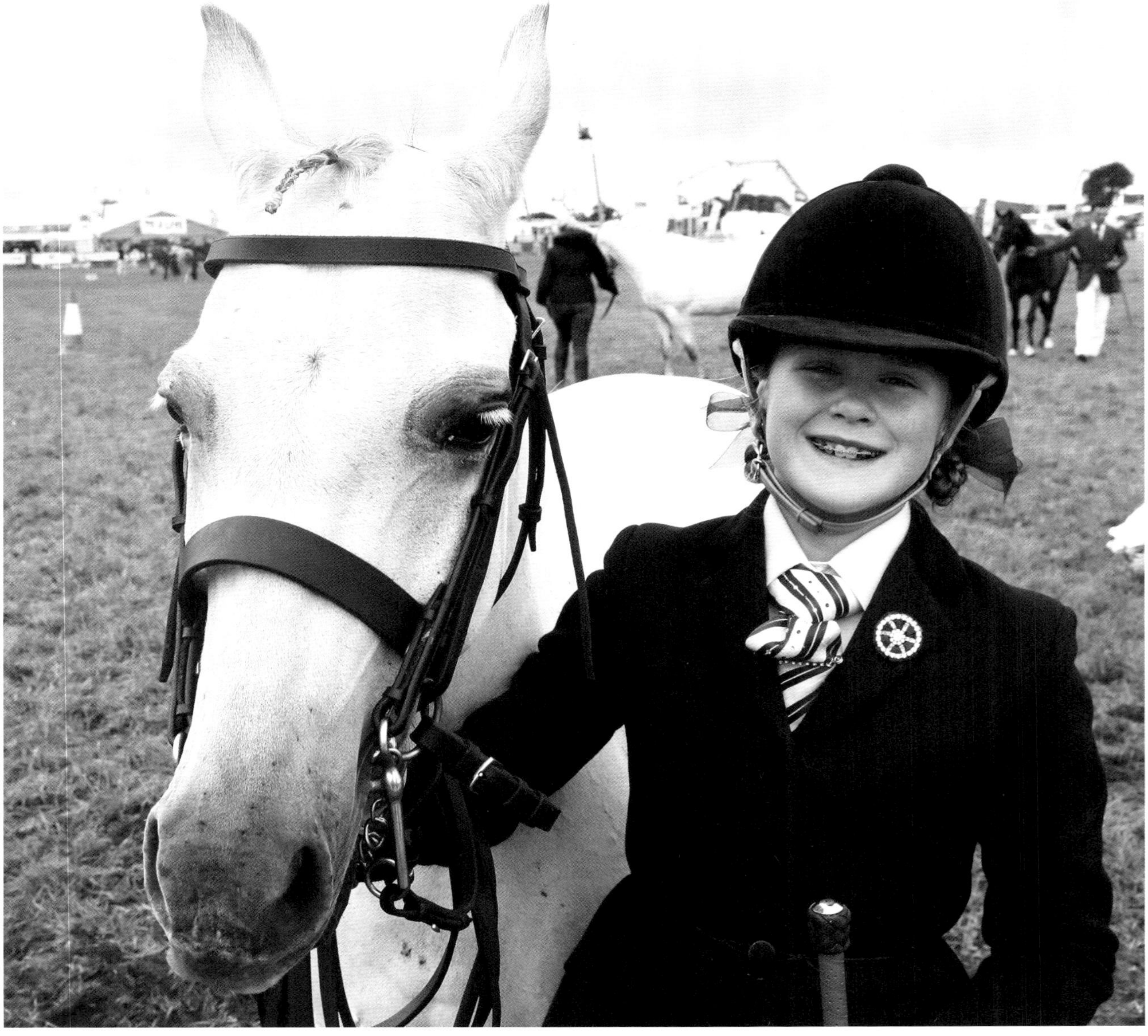

In all-weathers they are capable of herculean physical strength – they are wiry and whippet-fit. There's no time for hours hunched over computer games in days ordered by milking, calving, lambing and combining. The Pembrokeshire farmer is worthy of a prize for still being here, against all the odds.

The primary purpose of the County Show is to award excellence – the best in breed, the finest skills and outstanding produce. Bowler-hatted, besuited judges, mostly men, stand emotionless as they ask teenage riders to first walk their Welsh ponies, then run and then stand. The judge watches how the animal and human both pick up their legs. He then motions them to mount up and walk in a circle, before lining up for final judging. The tweed-jacketed, cream-jodhpur wearing riders await the verdict in reverse order – third, second, first.

Choosing local judges wouldn't be a wise move in such a small community, so they come from far and wide. Roger Hunt comes from Penn, near High Wycombe. He's been around Welsh ponies for 70 years and is to judge the Section A and Section B entrants. He says he's looking for an animal that can walk well; its hind foot should rest in the same position as the front; it should trot and be capable of a regular canter and a gallop should be demonstrated. In his last judging class an almost perfect presentation was let down by a pony that wouldn't gallop.

Mr Hunt is a kindly man but there is little informality or small talk. There is no engagement before or afterwards with the entrants. The riders may be young, but they are expected to meet exacting standards. He looks for correct confirmation that the animal is well-proportioned. The perfect Welsh pony should possess short legs with good bones. The Welsh Cob is designed to carry weight and the weight capacity of the animal is derived from its cannon bone, to which the judge pays particular attention. These ponies were bred to work hard and be cheap to keep. Our national breed didn't have an easy time; often there was not an abundance of food, so the ability to live off rough forage and the willingness to do all the work required on the farm and then pull a trap on Sunday to go to church was what made them indispensible.

There is more than one competition for Welsh Cobs here. The Welsh Cob is primarily distinguished by height and also by variations in type: the smallest is the Welsh Mountain Pony (Section A); the slightly taller but refined Welsh Pony of riding type (Section B) – popular as a children's show mount; the small but stocky Welsh Pony of Cob Type (Section C) – popular for riding and competitive driving; and the tallest, the Welsh Cob (Section D) – that can be ridden by adults.

The Cobs have been replaced on farms by the tractor and the car but there is an enduring love for the animals. They are an old and noble breed and a Welsh-type Cob was known as early as the Middle Ages. Throughout their long history they've had many uses, including as a cavalry horse or pit pony, as well as a working animal on farms. The original Welsh mountain pony is thought to have evolved from the prehistoric Celtic pony and their ancestors existed in the British Isles prior to the arrival of the Roman Empire. Mentions of them can be found in medieval

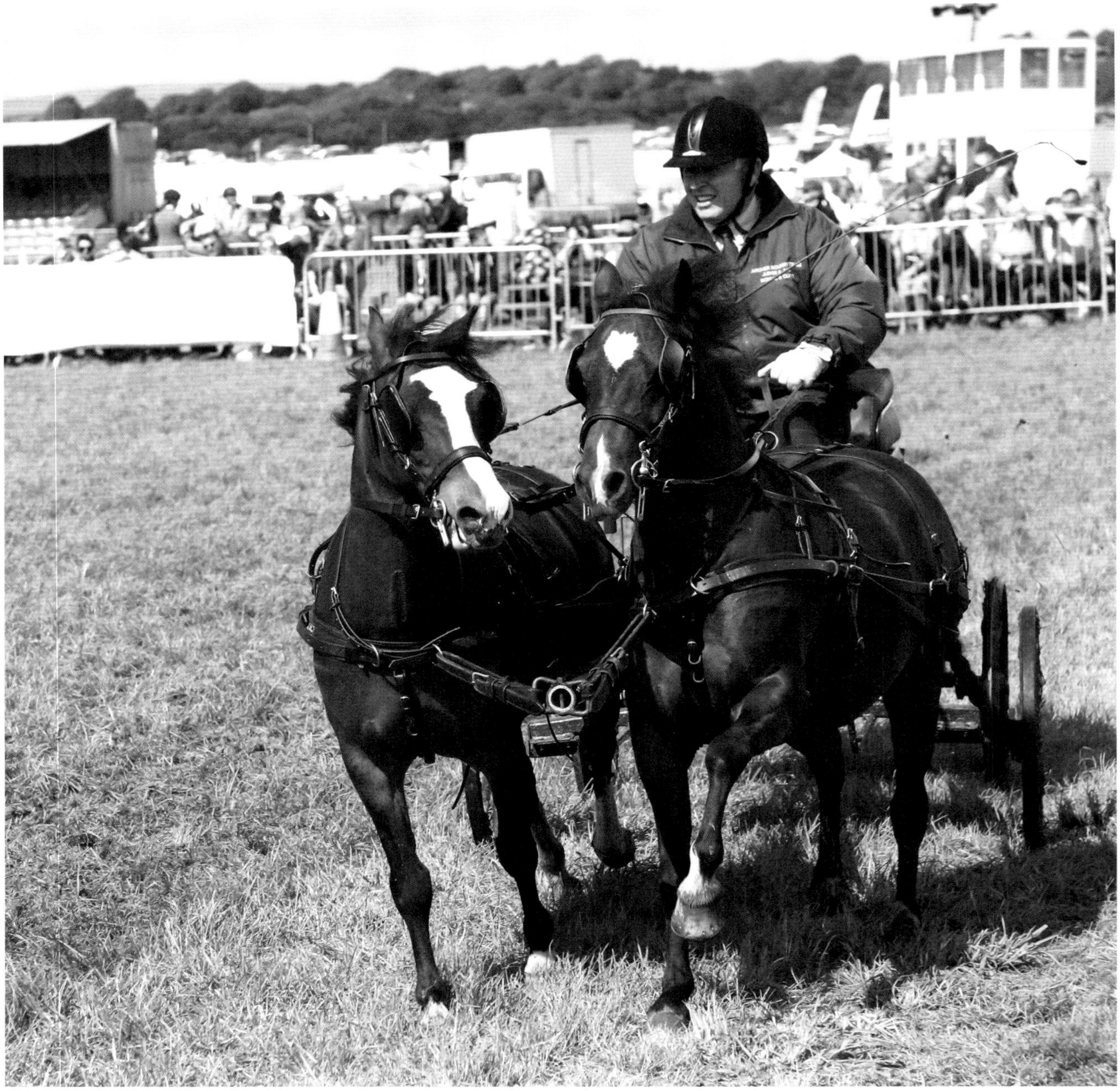

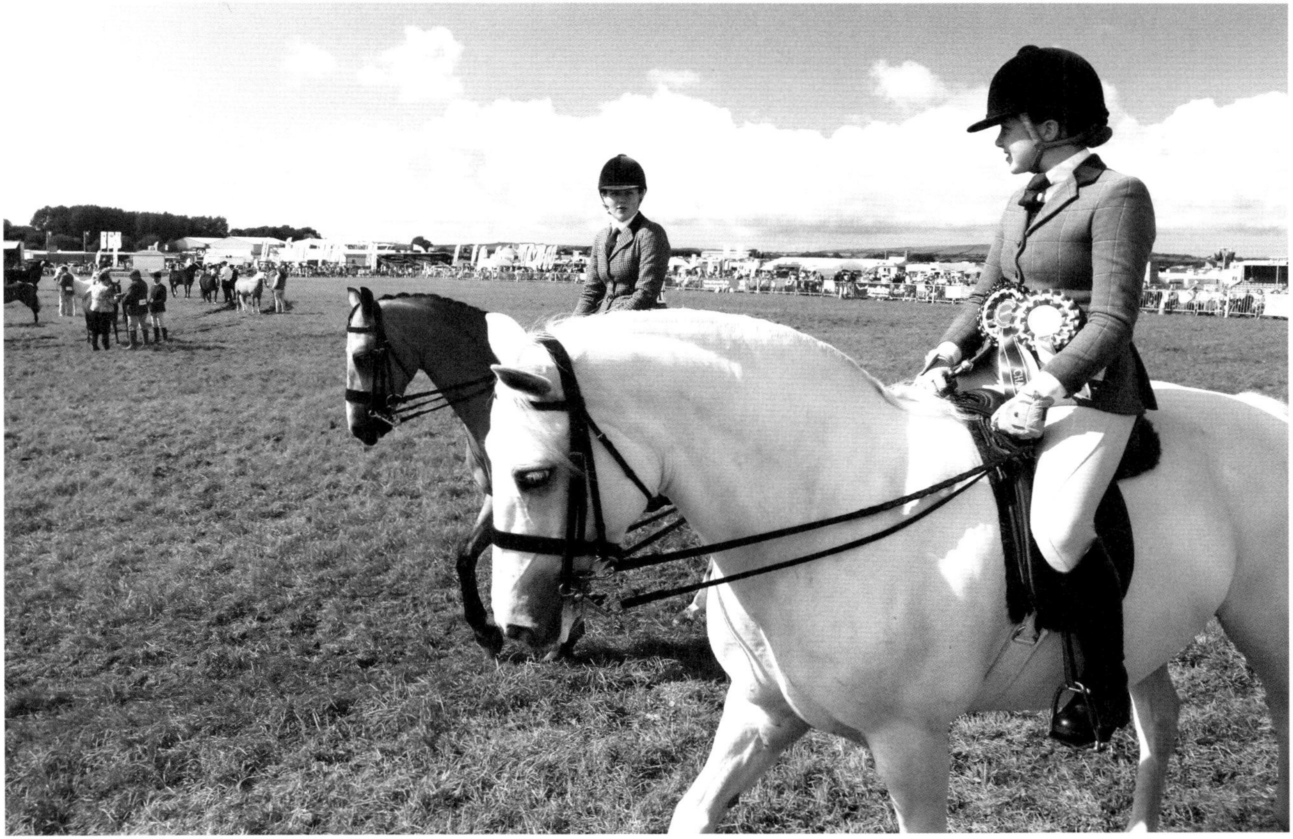

Welsh literature. In 1485 the Welsh Militia, riding local animals presumed to be related to the modern Welsh Cob, assisted Henry Tudor in gaining the English throne.

The characteristics of the breed as we know them today are thought to have been established by the late 15th century, after the crusaders returned to England with Arab stallions from the Middle East. But the existence of the Welsh Cob after this period is remarkable, given Henry VIII's desire to 'improve breeds of horses' and in doing so wipe out the little Cobs. In the 16th century, Henry wanted to improve war horses. He ordered the destruction of all stallions under 15 hands and all mares under 13 hands in the Breed of Horses Act 1535. This royal decree was partially repealed by Queen Elizabeth I in 1566 on the basis that the poor lands could not support the weight of the larger horses because of 'their rottenness', and fortunately for the future of Britain's mountain and moorland pony breeds, many animals, including the Welsh breeds, escaped slaughter.

Judge Hunt stands before the final line up of Cobs and riders. He has made his decision and in reverse order the rosettes are arranged. Julian Williams from Bwlch, near Brecon, wins the red rosette. The other competitors came from far afield to compete here.

The prizes are awarded. This is one of hundreds of competitions taking place and the crowds gather around the ring and offer a ripple of gentle applause. Roger Hunt has been breeding these ponies for 50 years. He sold his childhood pushbike and bought a Cob for 20 pounds in 1953. Even now you can pick up a cheap foal for not much more than that, but it's a lot cheaper to buy a horse than to keep it.

The judges' tent contains a human encyclopedia of a lifetime of knowledge on every animal in the country. The voices and accents are not local but a tapestry of excellence: Mr Zoet has travelled from Holland to judge the Welsh ponies; Mr Boustead is from Lancashire to judge the Shetlands, and all the way from Wakefield, Mr Evans will decide who wins the fruit, salad and vegetables competition.

Stephen Hipps is sitting in the Judges' tent enjoying a cup of tea between duties. He's a Yorkshireman and made the long journey here to judge Ryeland sheep. He sets out his criteria to win silverware:

'The breed has definitive characteristics which I will want to see. Is the animal true to type? A straight back? Good confirmation? Is the mouth right? I see a lot of poor mouths. It's a wool sheep, so I'll want to see the quality of the wool, its colour, crimp and its strength. Does the animal stand properly, walk straight and is it well turned out, well-presented?'

As with the other animals, a winning Ryeland spells more money for breeding or sale. Winning means the flock and shepherd are recognised by their peers and will attract buyers. The Ryeland breed has an ancient story. In the 1300s, the wealth of the country was built on wool. Sheep shaped our landscape and built our churches. The Ryeland came from Herefordshire and was reared by the monks of Leominster. They are a smallholder's sheep, a non-commercial breed. A survivor. The monks of Leominster grazed them on the rye pastures, giving them their name.

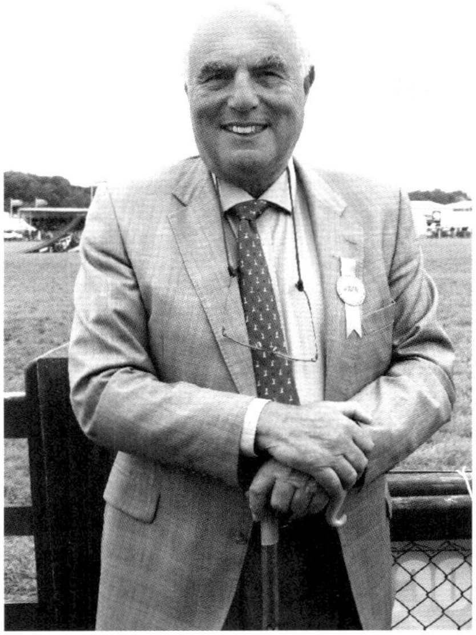

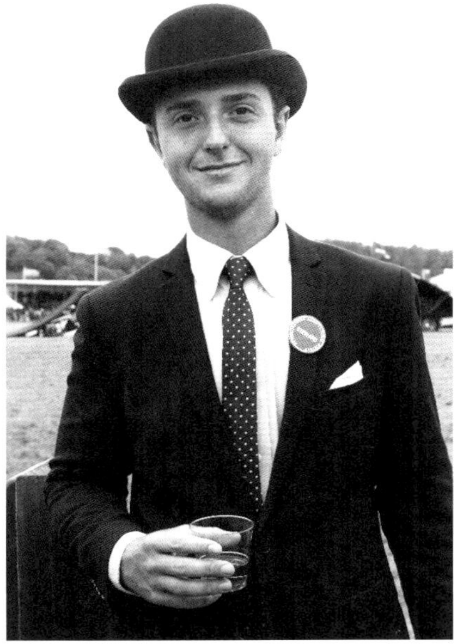

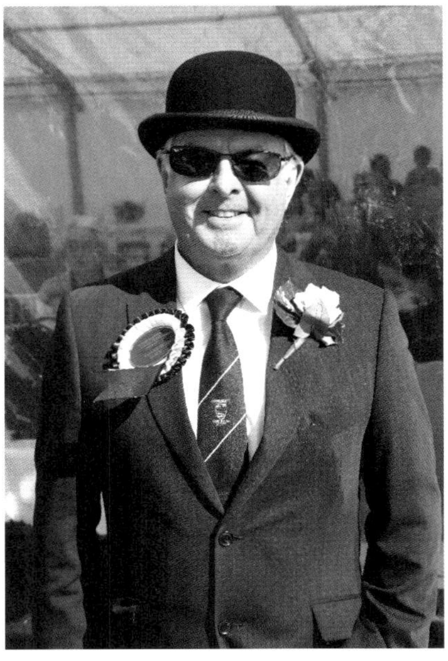

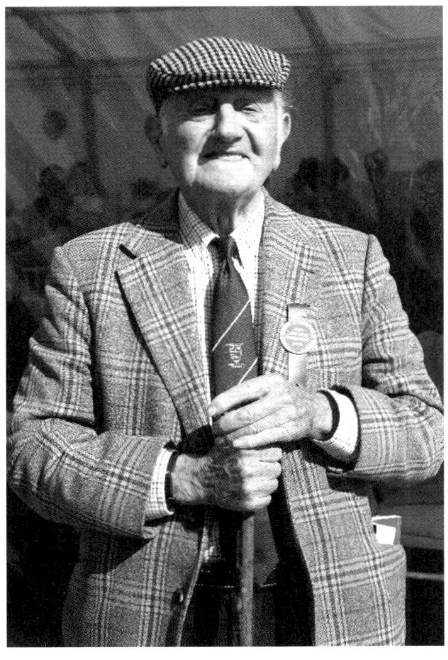

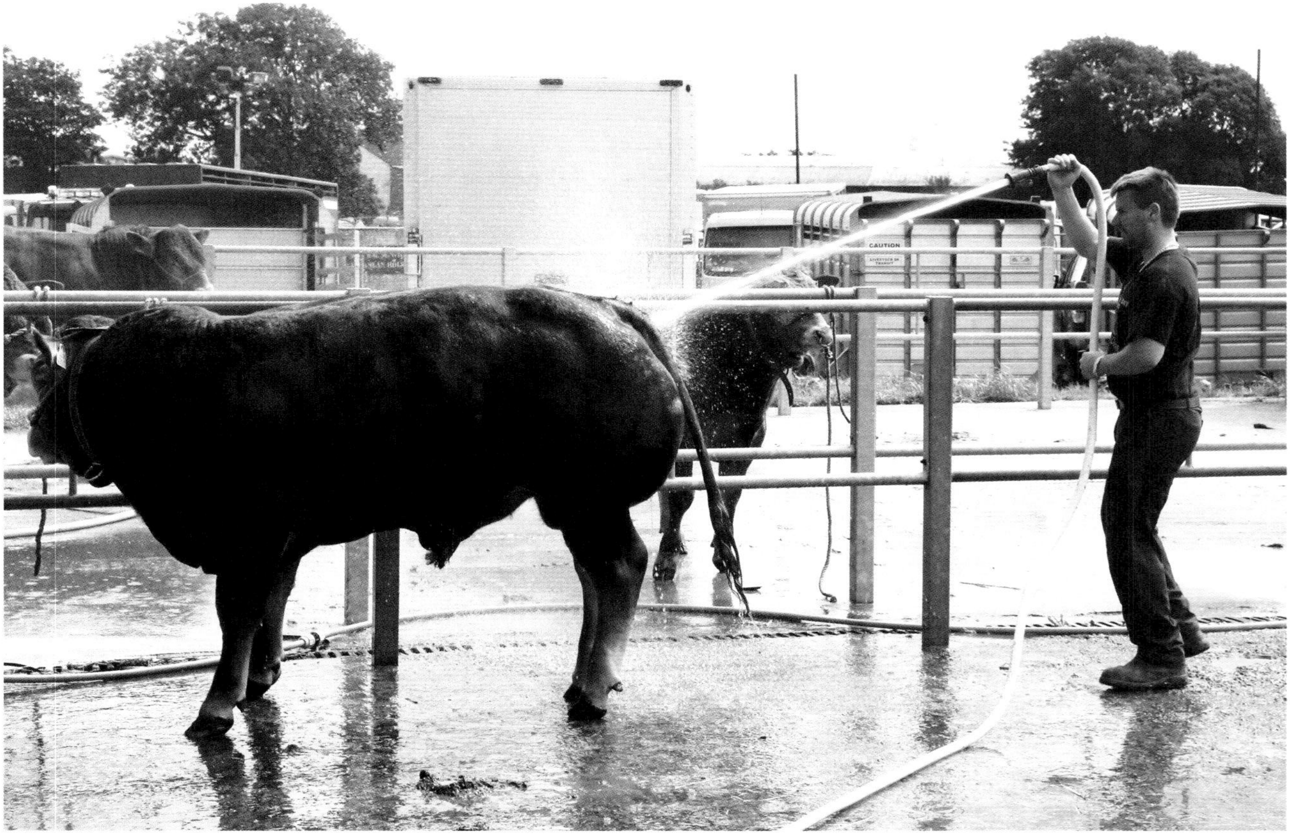
CAUTION

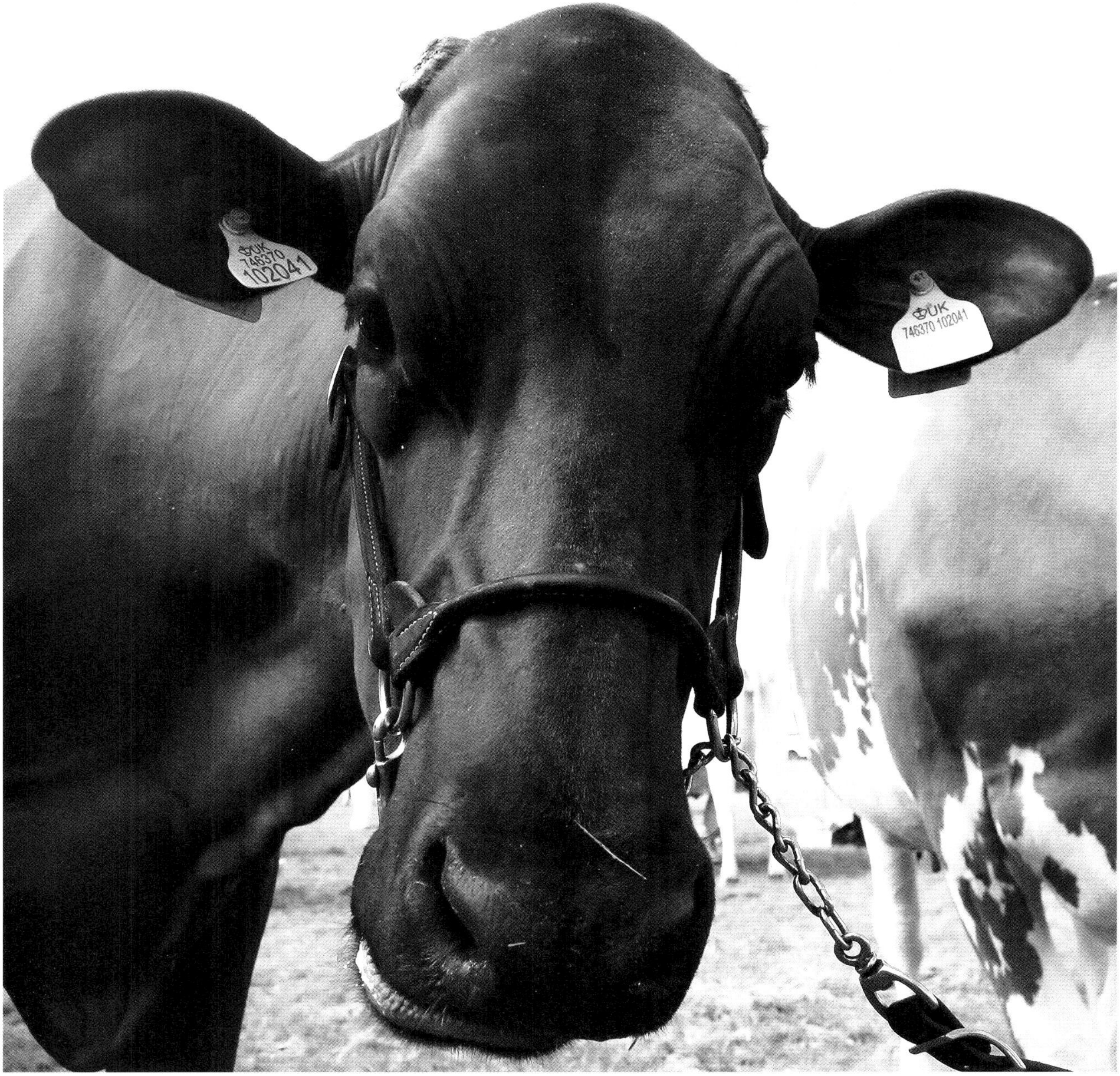
UK
746370
102041
UK
746370 102041

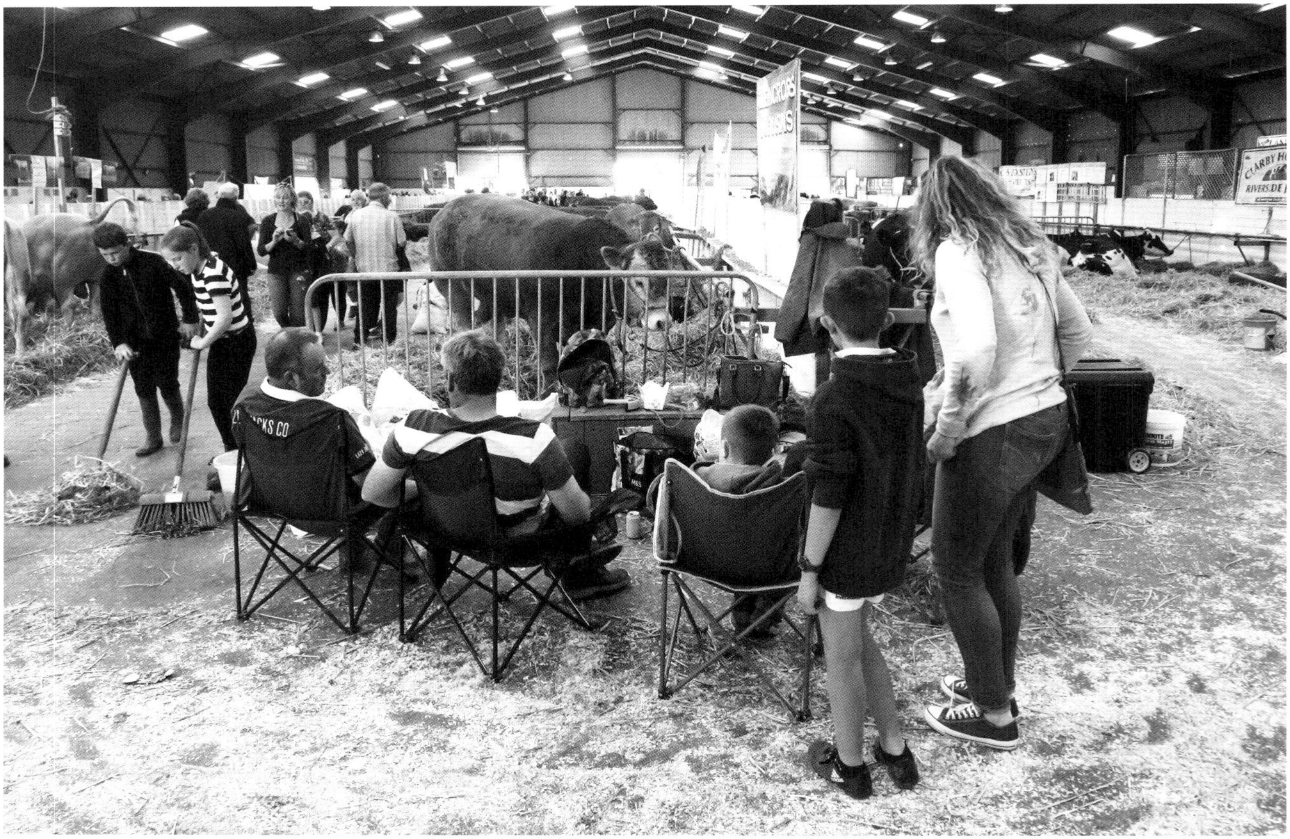

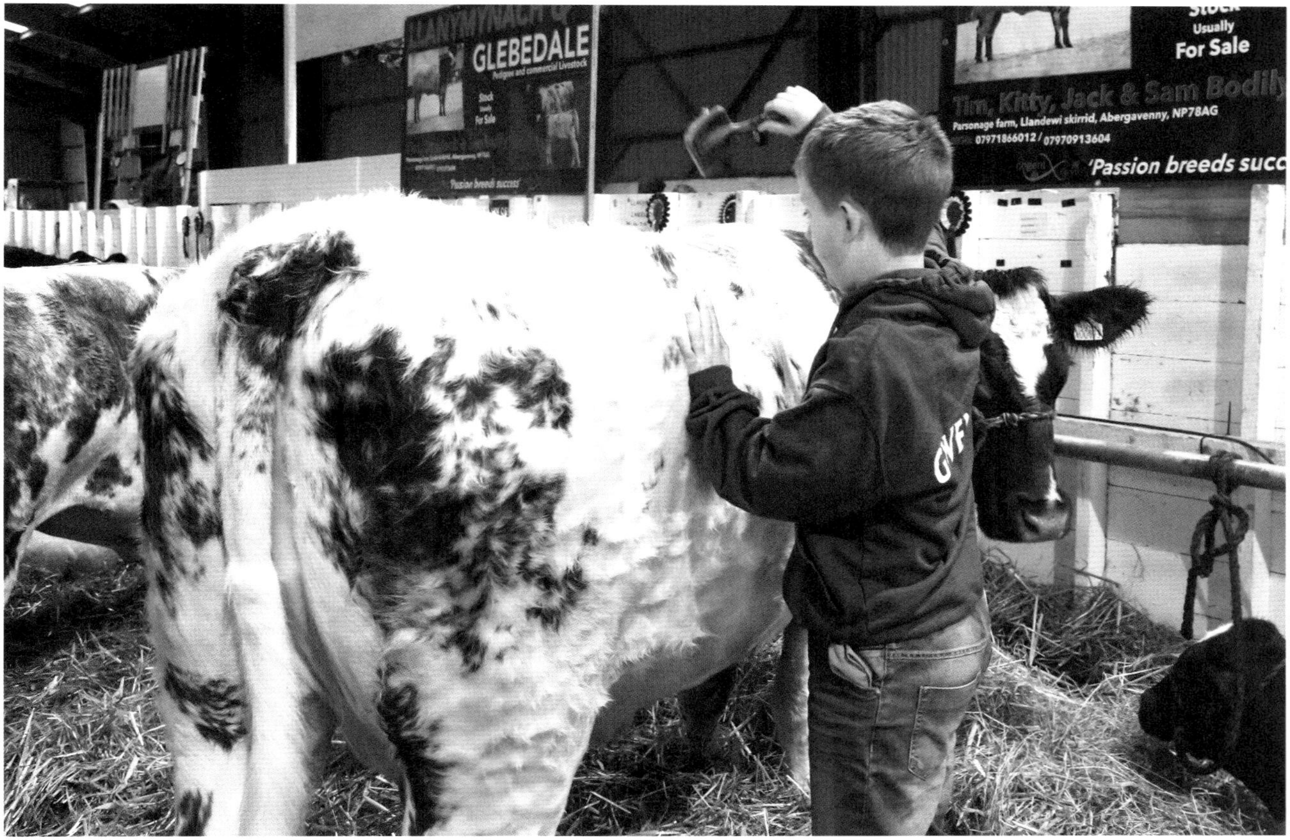
GLEBEDALE
Pedigree and commercial Livestock
Stock
Usually
For Sale
Tim, Kitty, Jack & Sam Bodily
Parsonage farm, Llandewi skirrid, Abergavenny, NP78AG
07971866012 / 07970913604
'Passion breeds succ

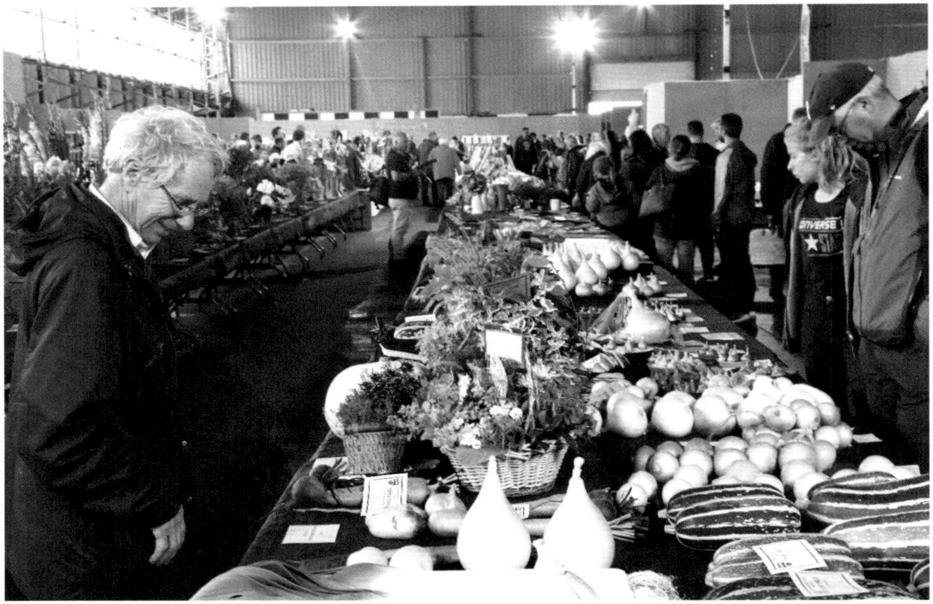

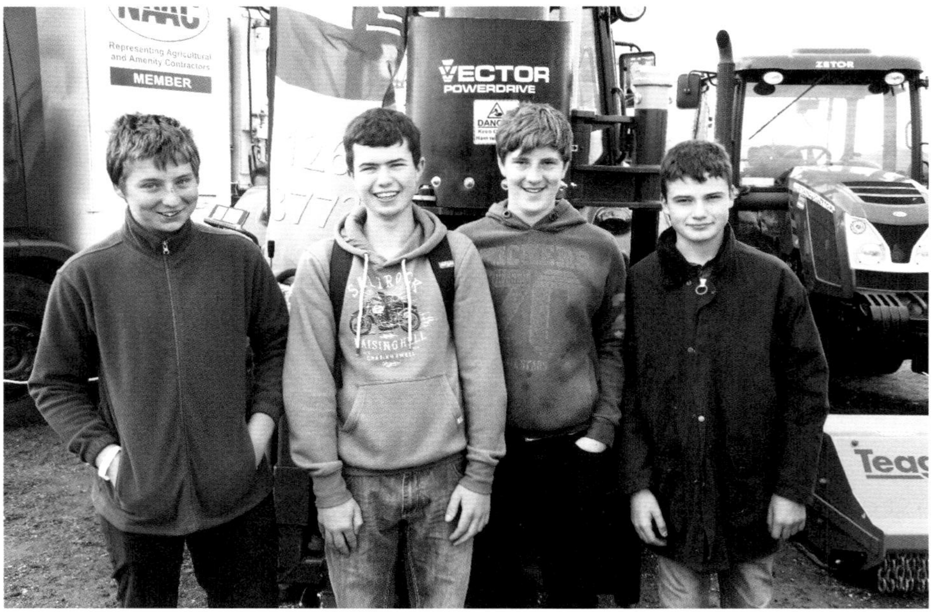
Representing Agricultural and Amenity Contractors
MEMBER
VECTOR
POWERDRIVE
ZETOR

This breed is raised primarily for meat. Ryelands are docile animals, unlike their wilder Welsh mountain cousins.

Ryelands were considered to have the finest wool of all British breeds of the time. Queen Elizabeth I was given 'Lemster' wool stockings and it is claimed she liked them so much that she insisted thereafter on 'Lemster' Ryeland wool. But the Queen's underwear needn't detain us here; there are more rosettes to be distributed. The winning Ryeland, a Ram of two years and over, is owned by the Morgan family of Court Farm, Eglwyswrw. Other Ryeland entrants have driven from Gower and Presteigne.

Not all the competitions are for livestock. In the Craft and Horticulture section of a vast barn-like building, tables as long as rugby pitches groan under the weight of plates of food, jars of produce and bottles of drink. None of it is for sale or to be eaten, it is here simply to be judged. Rosettes for first, second and third litter the perfection of blood-red tomatoes, deep green runner beans, a bouquet of rhubarb, enormous onions, marble-like new potatoes, apples like cricket balls and heavy beetroot, all sitting like the muse for a still-life painting.

On another trestle table, visitors respectfully file past Kathleen Griffith's champion Dundee cake and her winning Madeira cake. In what is starting to look like a Chinese election result, Kathleen's nearby Cherry cake has also secured victory. Red rosettes too for Victoria sponge (jam filling), chocolate sponge (not decorated, cream filling), Welsh cakes, gingerbread, Swiss rolls and shortbread; all taste success, never to be eaten. Kathleen has had her cake and eaten it. A few words of appreciation are exchanged but mostly admiration is quiet, as though walking around a museum. In all, there are 4000 exhibits and all of them amateur. These displays are the work of endless days of gardening, growing, gathering, making and baking. They exude love.

White loaf, brown loaf, current loaf, date and walnut loaf – all under cling film, works of art. The judges came early and gave out their prizes. Strawberry jam, marmalade, chutney (any variety), pickled onions, pickled beetroot (sliced), pickled red cabbage and honey have all been tasted, tasted again and marked. The prize will be no more than a few pounds and a mention in the *Western Telegraph*, but there are few greater rewards than winning at the Pembrokeshire County Show.

Megan Richards' rhubarb wine 2012 wins first prize in the white wine class. Her blackberry wine and sweet and plum wine are highly commended. It is turning out to be a vintage year for Megan. Her 2015 Sloe Gin picks up first prize too. It'll be doubles all round at Megan's tonight.

This is all the work of the amateur enthusiast. All that is here is done for passion and yes, perhaps a little pride too. There is a world full of growers and

These displays are the work of endless days of gardening, growing, gathering, making and baking. They exude love.

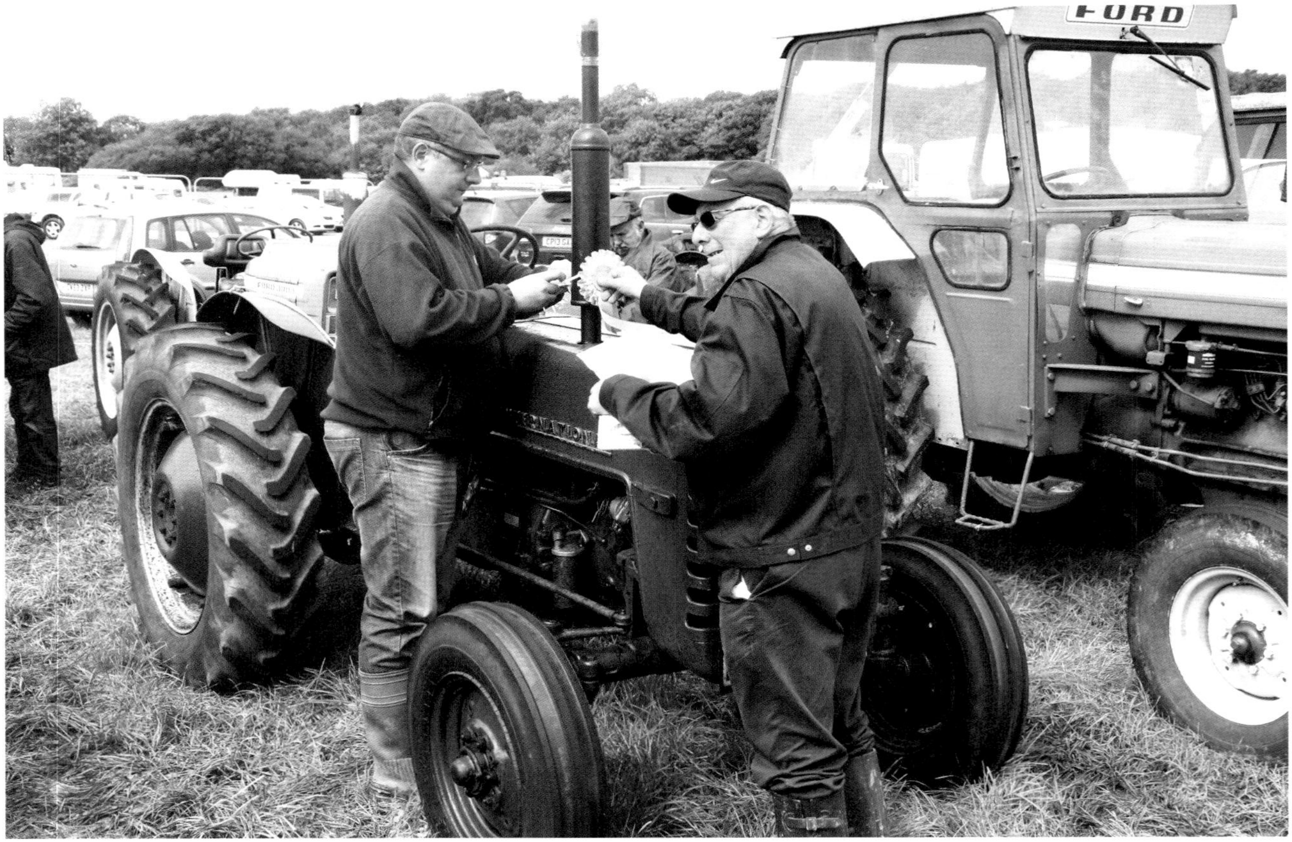
FORD

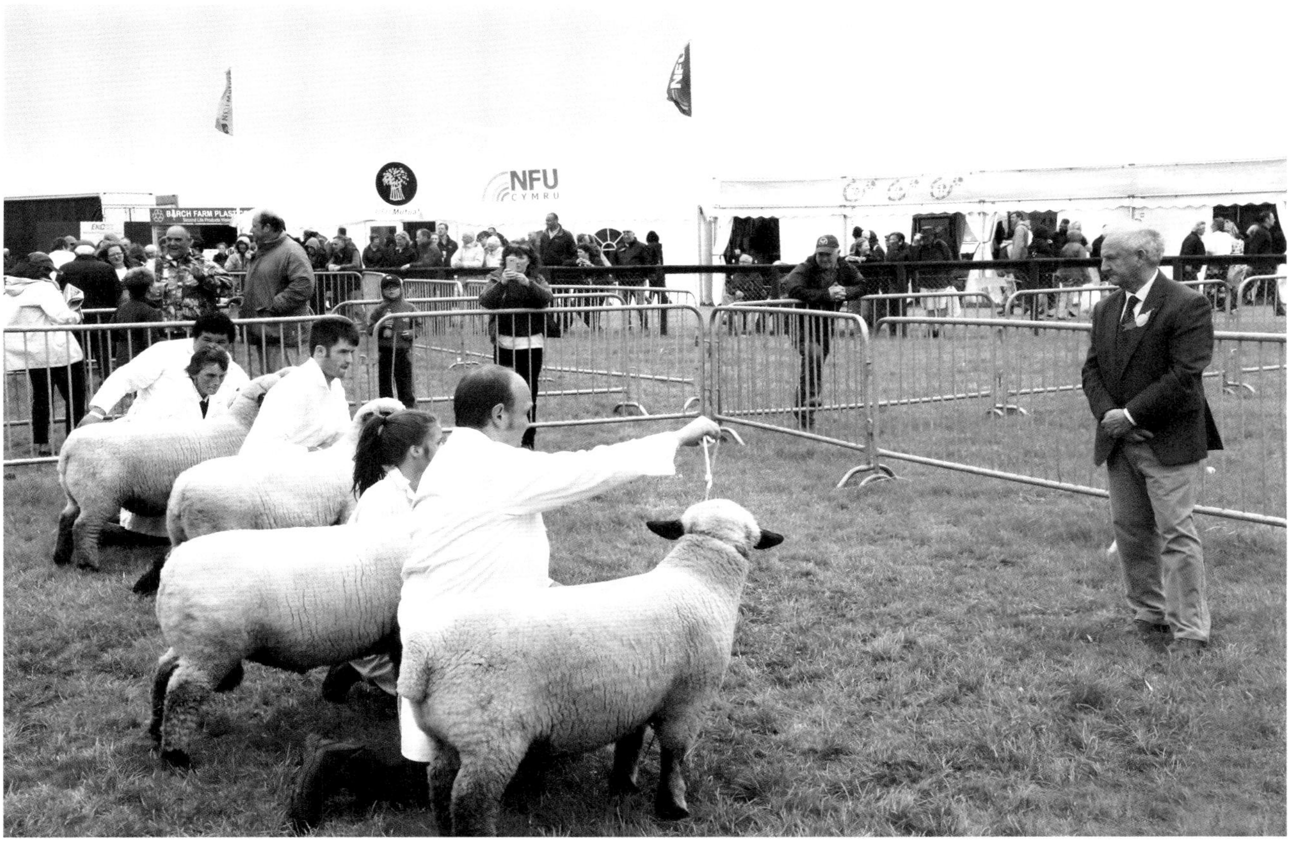
NFU
CYMRU

makers who spurn the easy and the quick. Similar items to everything displayed here can be bought cheaply and quickly in the supermarket down the road, but how much better to have grown it, picked it, brewed it, stewed it, strained it or baked it.

The newspapers left neatly folded on the tables in the judges' tent report the headlines outside the showground this week: America divided on the latest controversy to befall President Trump; Britain's politicians squabbling over Brexit and North Korea's nuclear ambitions. In the madness of the outside world, the discipline, orderliness, familiarity and repetition of the County Show stands in marked contrast to the seemingly intractable problems beyond. Here, as they have done for two centuries, judges will perform their duties in their immaculate dress, the country crowd will wear their best clothes each day and competitions will take place with the punctual regularity of the ticking clockwork in the tower of St Mary's Church in Haverfordwest. Somehow, life is richer for the earnest attention given to the Supreme Pig Championship, the search for the best fruitcake and the winner of the best goat competition. True sanity is to be found here, a sense of things that really matter.

Nevertheless, this is a world beginning to disappear. Few who come here to marvel at the animals and watch half-remembered skills from childhood will buy their food from anywhere but a supermarket day-to-day, delivered after a click on a computer. But many who smile at the sheep championships or wander past the goat pens may lament how we have become so removed from the people who make our food. Today will offer a little in the way of reconnection.

Perhaps the Pembrokeshire County Show's greatest gift to its visitors is a gentle reminder of the richness of time. A reminder to count the changing seasons in a country where they have all but vanished. Many of us now live and work indoors. The show is a reminder of years invested in the land in all weathers – in raising cattle and crops. It is the culmination of months spent training animals for exhibiting and a celebration of the long-term in a world obsessed with the instant. An increasingly urban population drowning in communication technology seems to feel the need to renew a life more earthy and rewarding. So they come here in their thousands, year after year.

At four o'clock, the rain sets in and the afternoon's gentle truce of threatening grey cloud turns into gale force wind and heavy rain. The meandering crowds sauntering past stalls now sprint towards shelter, a well-earned cake and afternoon tea. Outside, beyond the flapping marquees, like a grudge rugby fixture, the judging in the main ring continues defiantly, though the spectators thin. The judges and stewards forge on and pull down their bowler hats to keep the rain from their eyes.

The show is a reminder of years invested in the land in all weathers– in raising cattle and crops.

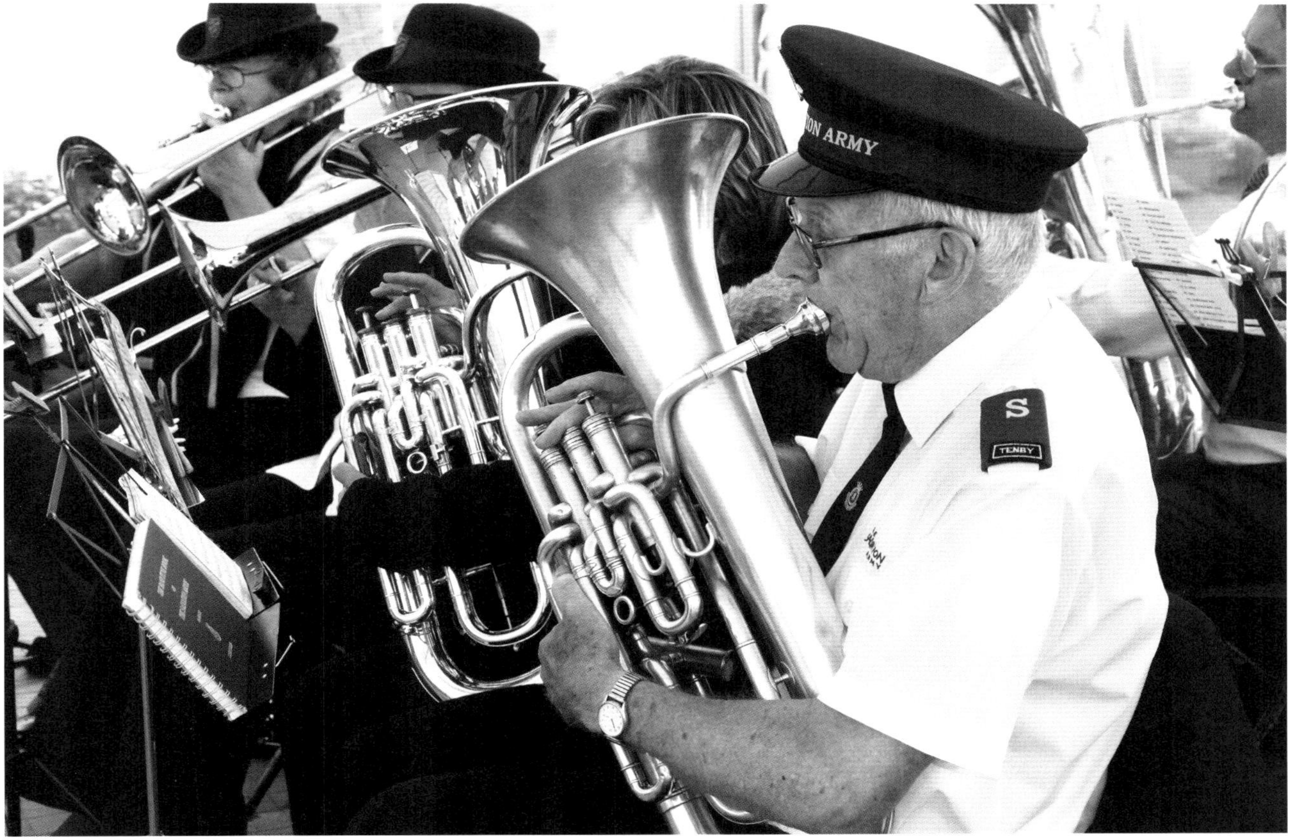
ION ARMY
S
TENBY

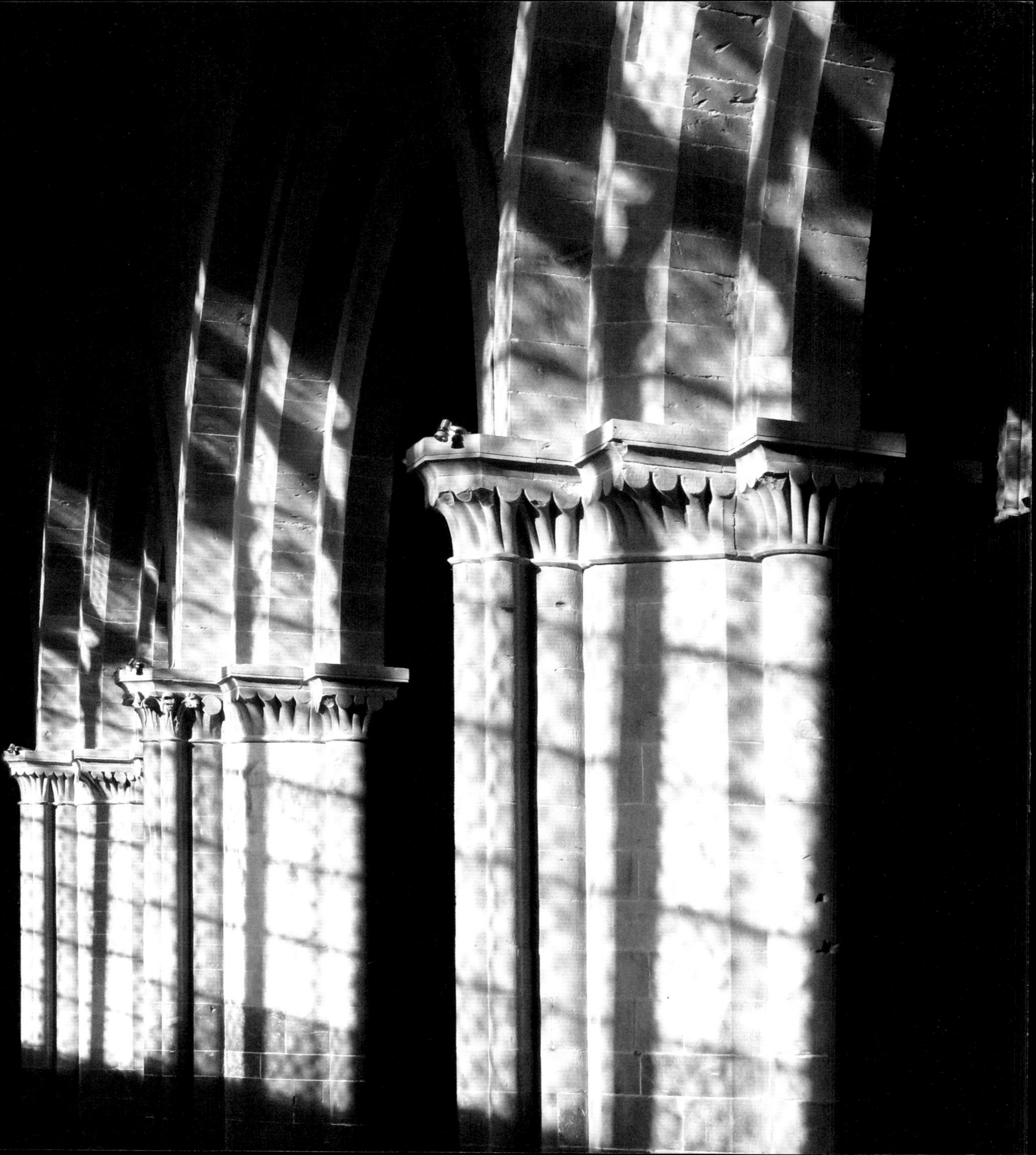

St Davids
Christmas in the Cathedral

It doesn't much look like Christmas from the new slipway of the lifeboat station at St Justinians. The Irish Sea, grey, cold and uninviting, swims around Ramsey Island, just off the coast. The water lies calm this morning, like an alligator half-asleep. This stretch of sea can turn within a flick of the eye. This will be a Welsh Christmas, rather than a white one: wet, foggy, windy and mild.

This is the headland of the ancient saints, St David, St Justinian and St Non. Saints and pilgrims drawn to the islands and peninsulas of Wales found their calling on the edge of the ocean, once the superhighway of the Celtic world. Above the lifeboat station, the ruins of the Chapel of St Justinian are roofless and eyeless. Like the Chapel of St Non, this was a place of pilgrimage for medieval travellers to St Davids. Pilgrims who arrived on the Pembrokeshire coast by sea had a few miles more to journey over land before arriving at the Cathedral. This place marks the beginning and the end of journeys. After St Justinians, the land falls into the sea. This is the end of Wales, the rocks that mark the beginning of Pembrokeshire.

St Non is said to have been raped and that her child was St David. On the day of Non's labour, David is claimed to have been born in a great storm, yet the place where Non gave birth was bathed in light. This is a land writhing in storms and sunshine. Here the earth is pock marked by holiness and violence. This is where the lightning races across an ocean and touches landfall. This is where mortals grow up fearing the sea.

Many contemporary visitors to treeless, windswept St Justinians come here to walk the Pembrokeshire Coast Path or to enjoy one of the boat trips to explore Ramsey Island's spectacular cliffs and birdlife. Others come to see one of Britain's most important grey seal colonies, though October's storm Ophelia killed a generation of pups. But for one group of regular visitors the road to St Justinians is sometimes a more tense affair. The men and women who make up the RNLI crew drive from nearby homes along this narrow single-track road, never knowing what their pager summons will require of them. There is little reliable mobile phone coverage here.

St Davids Lifeboat has been involved in saving more than 330 lives over its long history and the community has lost a number of its menfolk at sea in this service. Those who live on this peninsula never forget that this life-long watery companion knows no loyalty or affection, despite the years of intimacy.

The Welsh name for Ramsey Island is Ynys Dewi – David's Island, and it is said to have been the home of St David's confessor, St Justinian. Viewed from the top of the cliff above the lifeboat station, Ramsey lies tantalisingly close to the mainland.

Its cliffs echo with the prayers of a century of lifeboat crews launching into the storm. For the crew, the whale-like hulk of Ramsey Island is the last familiar landscape they see before setting course for the unpredictable and the unknown, responding to the ancient call for help at sea from strangers whose lives depend on kindness and bravery. The treacherous stretch between the island and the mainland is known as The Bitches, with good reason. This is a coastline littered with lighthouses, lifeboat stations and wrecks. From the golden age of sail to today's laden super-tankers, the business of moving people and goods by sea has never gone out of fashion – and neither have its inherent dangers.

The Welsh name for Ramsey Island is Ynys Dewi – David's Island.

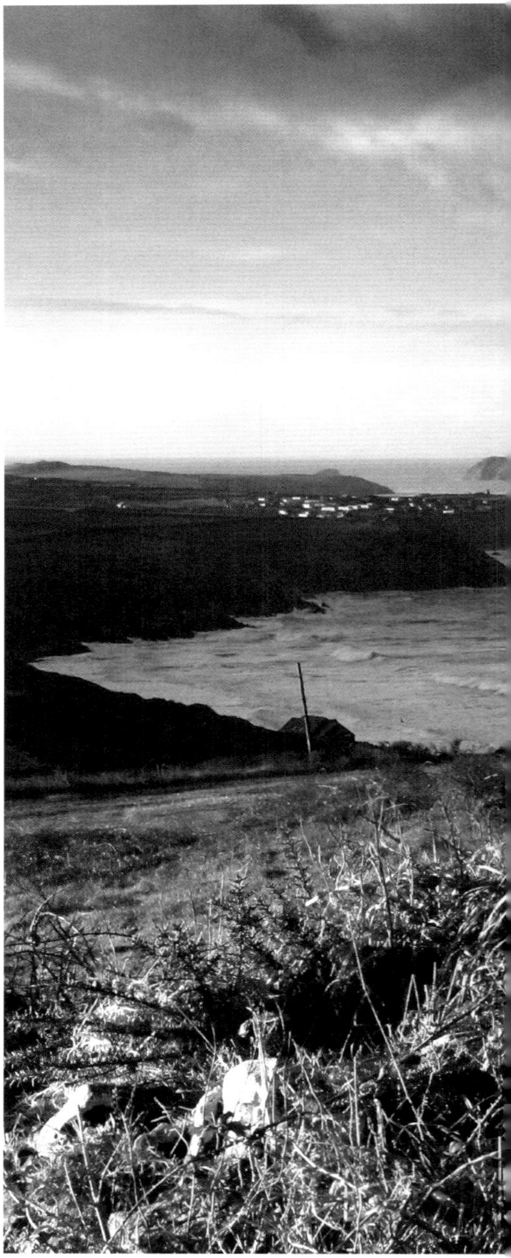

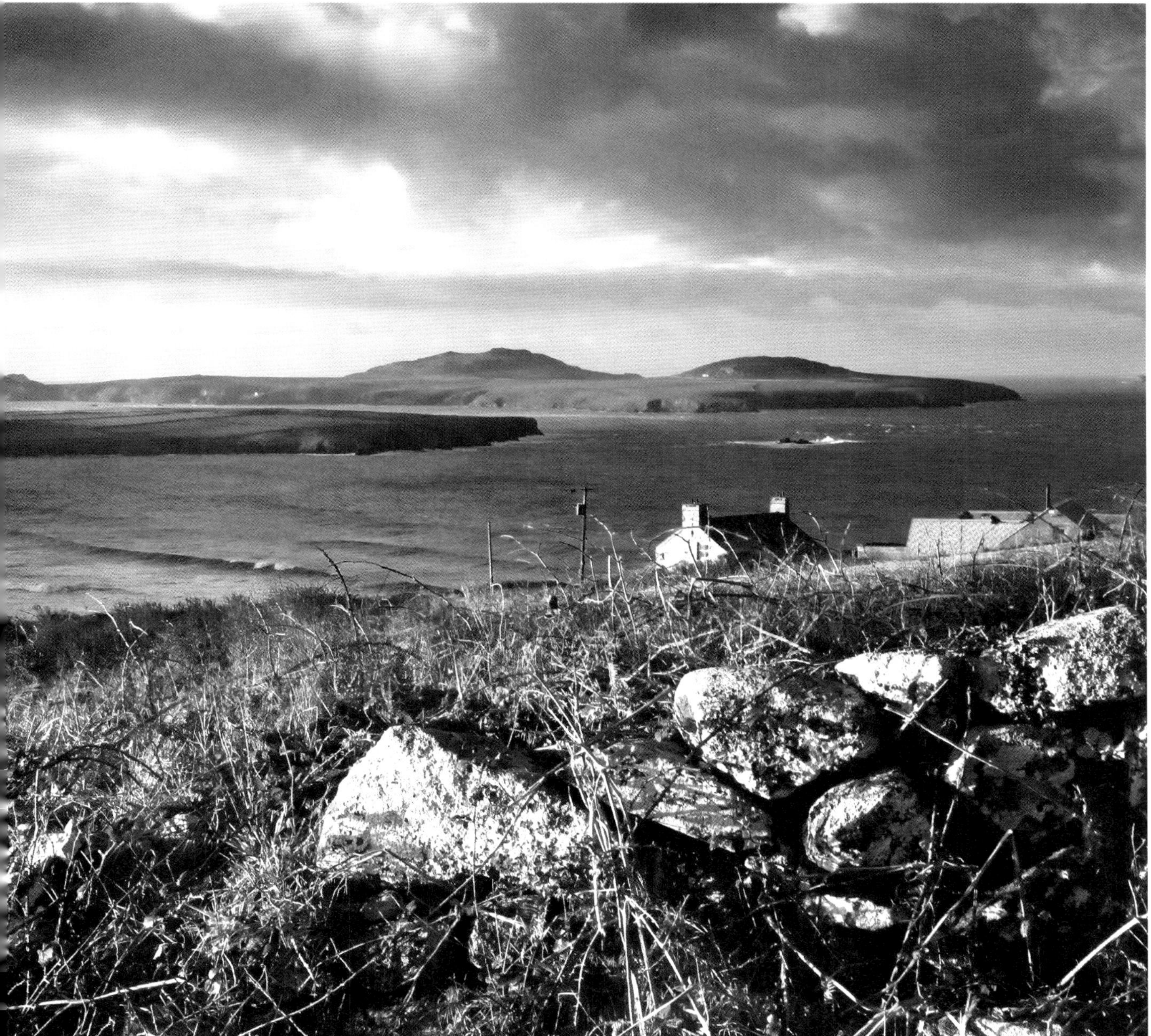

Whitesands Bay and Ramsey Island

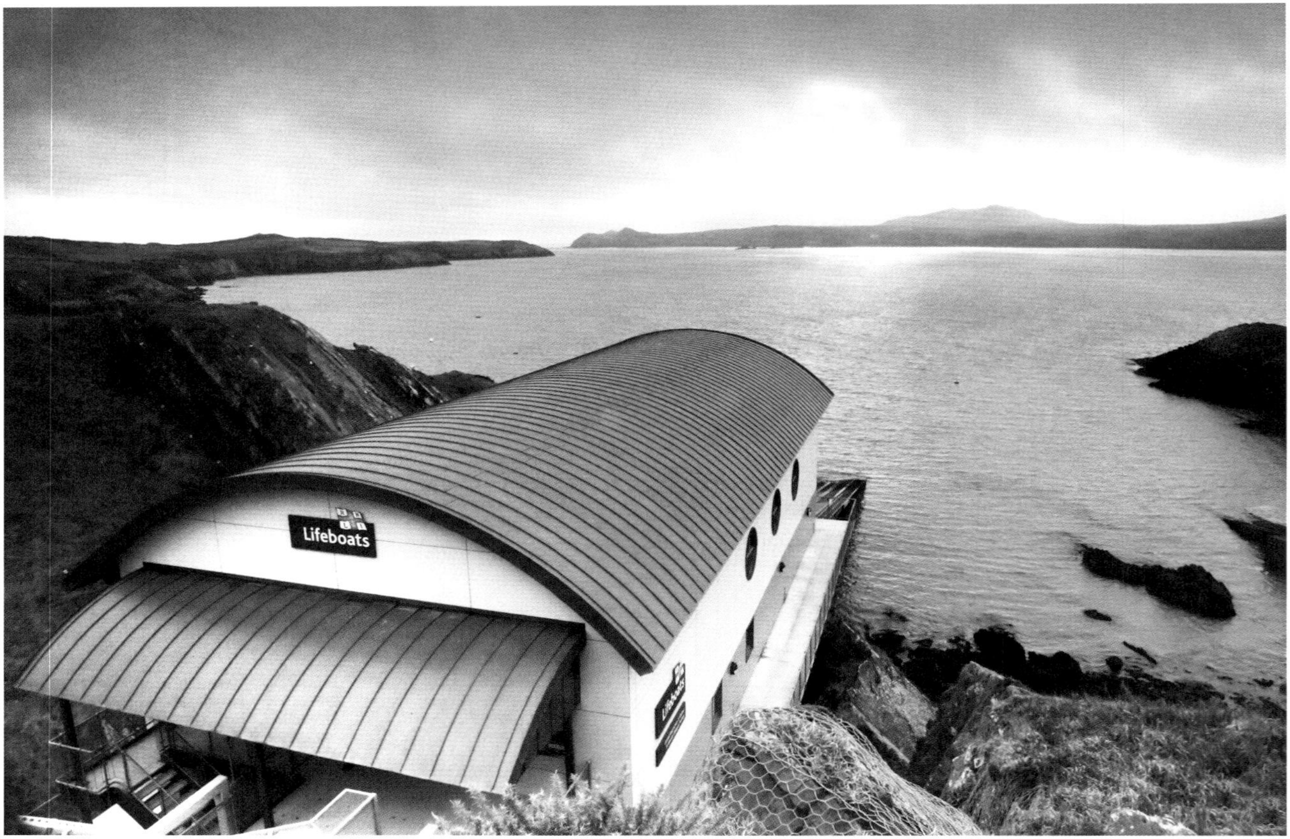
Lifeboats

The generations of St Davids folk who have staffed this lifeboat service are a breed apart, all of them defined by a willingness to put their lives on the line without reward to save others.

Dai John is the St Davids RNLI Coxswain. He has 30 years' service under his belt. His crew is 28 in total. Dai and his mechanic, Mike Phillips, are both full-time, but everyone else is a volunteer. Mike Chant and Will Chant continue the RNLI custom of families following the previous generation into the service, operational since 1869. Mike is a musician and Deputy Mayor; Ellen Evans is still a rarity in Britain's lifeboat service – one of two female crewmembers in a predominantly male calling. Her day job is manager of the restaurant St Davids Kitchen. Judd Kohler usually skippers the Ramsay pleasure boat trips and Will runs a B&B. They are everyday heroes, understated and part of the cement that binds our seafaring communities.

The Lifeboat Station mess room window must boast one of the most glorious views from an office anywhere in Britain – the wide expanse of the channel between the Pembrokeshire Coast and Ramsey Island. Today it looks like a painting; tomorrow it will frame the most violent night.

Much of Britain will be carousing in the last days before Christmas, a seemingly endless round of office parties and drunken nights. Christmas for the lifeboat crew is always tempered by the knowledge that the pager could go at any time, so celebrations are cautious and spent wisely. No one can timetable when a ship will sink or a trawler will radio in distress. There are no days off or bank holidays here. Just another day watching the waves, hoping all will be well.

There is a metropolitan conceit that no one carries out any work without reward, that community no longer exists and that we are obsessed with pecuniary pursuits. But this couldn't be further from the truth on the St Davids Peninsula, and for that matter, up and down the length of the country. We are a nation connected by the spirit of voluntary work, and perhaps at its pinnacle are those who put their lives on the line to save others at sea.

Dai says everyone has different reasons for volunteering. Ellen says it's about being part of a group endeavour, that volunteering gives you freedom. Dai agrees the psychology of freely giving your time seems to be a common theme among the team at St Davids. Many of the RNLI crew have worked or still work on the sea – they have been fishermen or boatmen and spent their lives around the coast. Their experience is not spoken of but is quietly understood.

Like the National Trust, the RNLI is funded by donations and fund-raising. Two of Britain's most successful organisations rely on volunteers and generosity.

The Lifeboat Station and its Tamar-class vessel are among the newest in the country. The vessel *Norah Wortley* cost £2.7 million and was funded with a bequest. Its home, the new lifeboat station, cost £10 million. Its huge grey edifice sits low beneath the cliff, towering above the retired red zinc station alongside. Inside the hangar, sitting high undercover

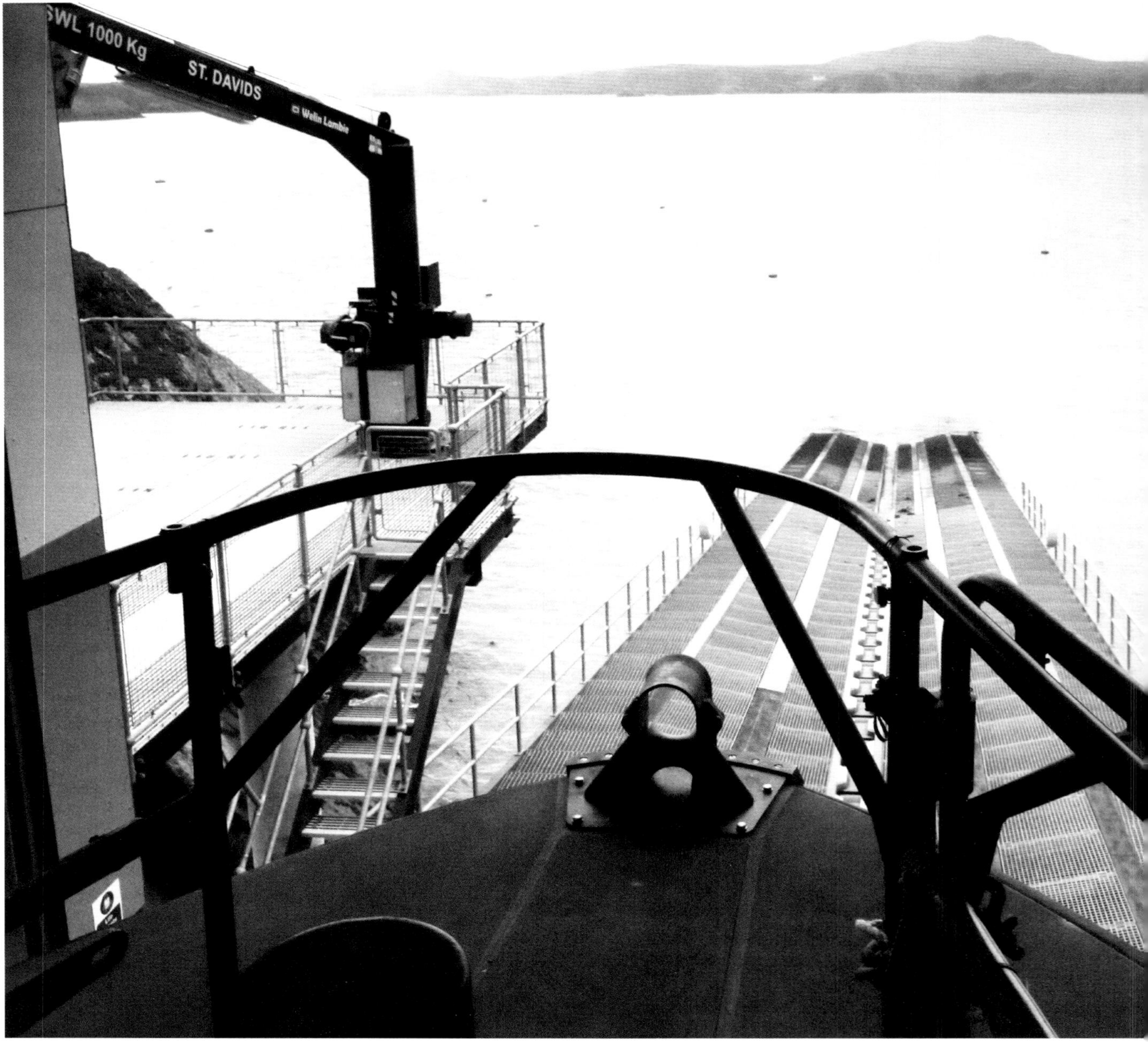
SWL 1000 Kg
ST. DAVIDS
Welin Lambie

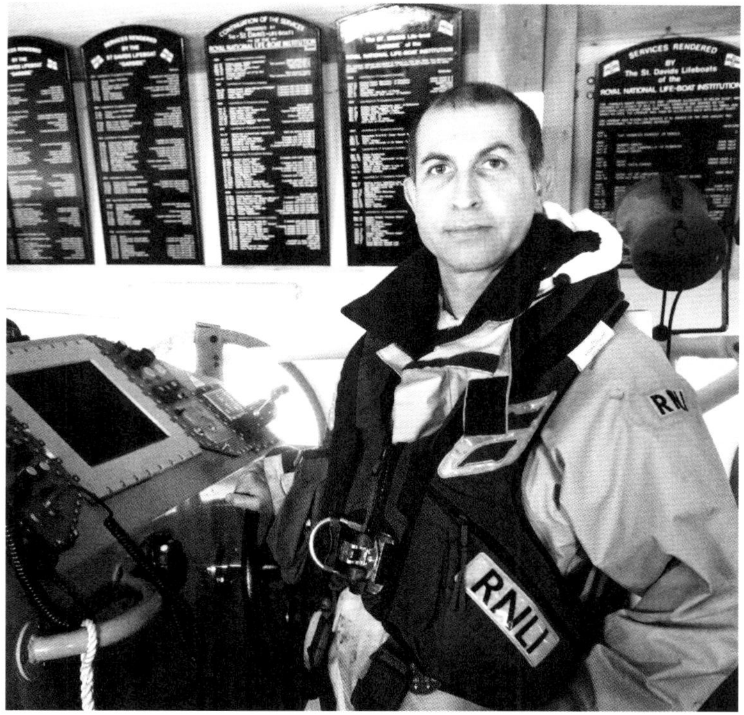
SERVICES RENDERED
BY
The St. Davids Lifeboats
of the
ROYAL NATIONAL LIFE-BOAT INSTITUTION
RNLI
RNLI

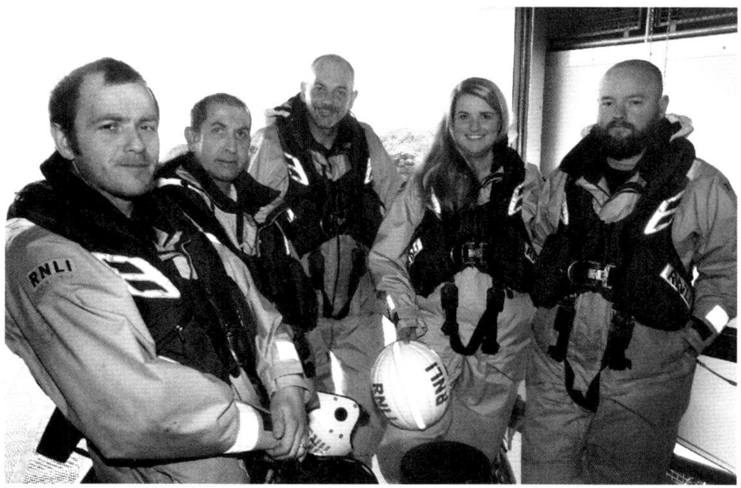
RNLI
RNLI

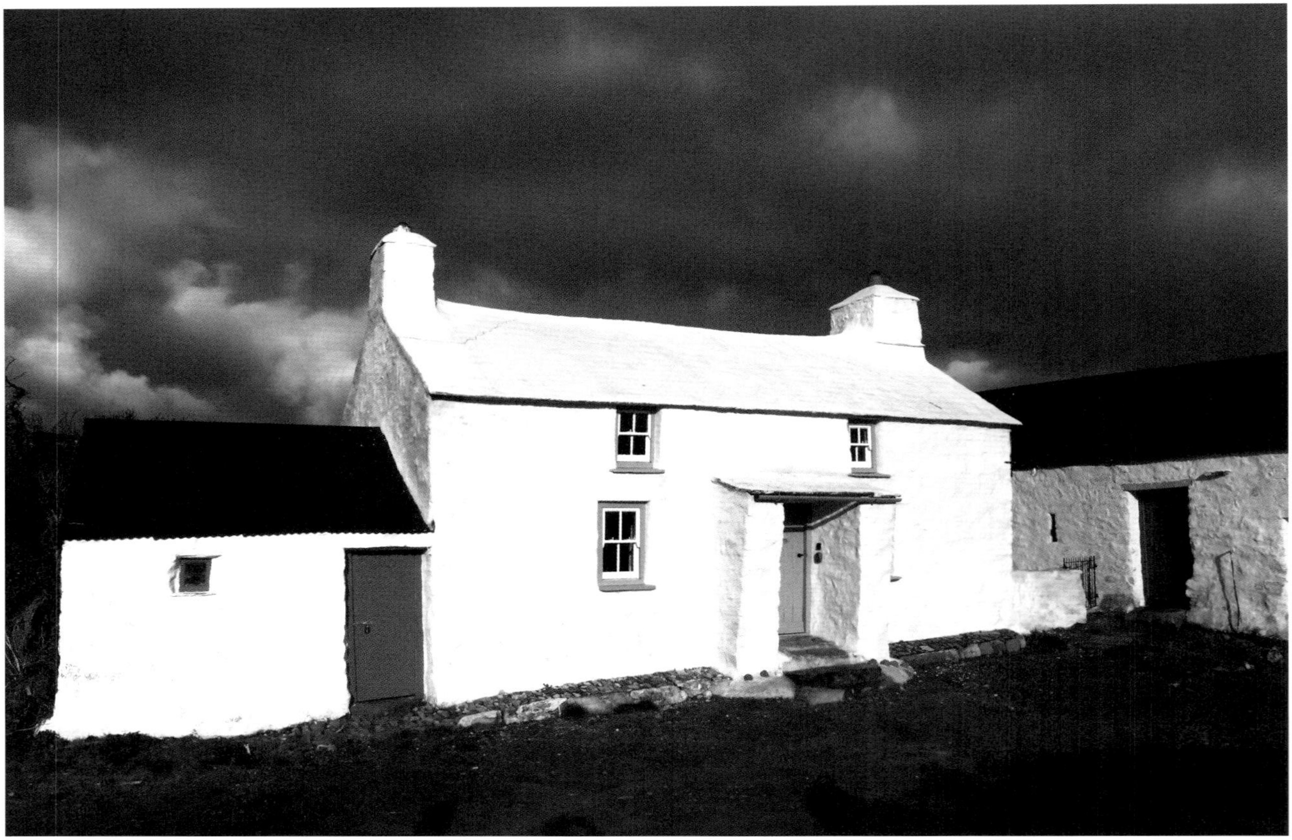

112 Treleddyd Fawr, near St Davids

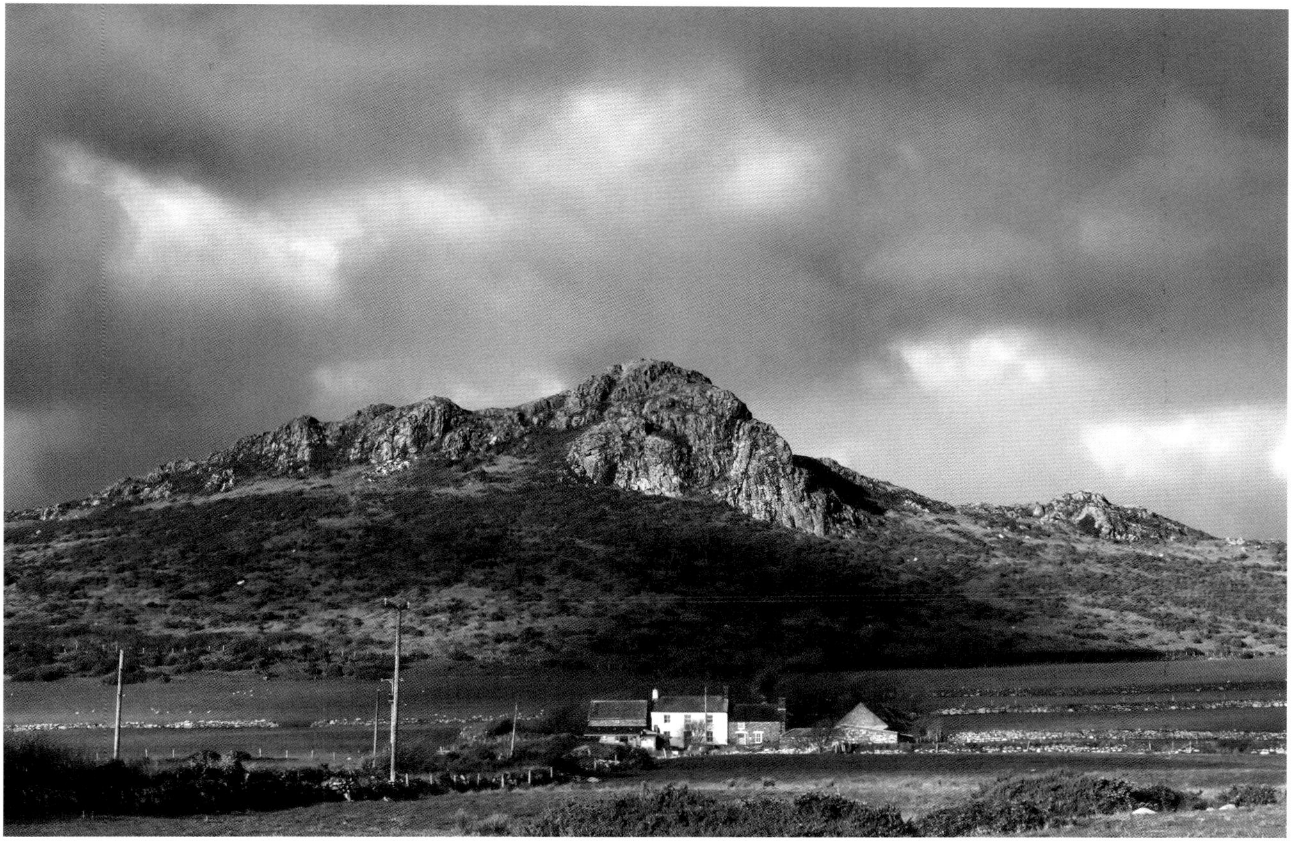

Carn Llidi, near St Davids

at the top of the slip, the new vessel looks like something out of science fiction; huge, loaded with technology and seemingly invincible. Its range is 250 miles, enough to power across the Irish Sea. It is the stealth bomber of sea rescue. The vessel is made of carbon-reinforced plastic, capable of 26 knots and is more racing car than lifeboat. The endless list of technological advances adds up to the simple maxim that the crew can reach an emergency faster, further away and more safely than ever before.

Dai's worst shouts include a Russian sailor washed overboard in a force 11 storm. The lifeboat searched for 9 hours in 35 foot waves. On another mission he was involved in a rescue of five people from the trawler *Western Bell*, 27 miles off Pembrokeshire. The length of the shout took its toll both mentally and physically – the lifeboat's own crew were injured, sustaining broken ribs.

This Christmas they will celebrate as all families do, but no lifeboat crewman or woman ever really relaxes or totally switches off. The world's cargo, passenger and fishing boats will continue to ply the seas off Pembrokeshire and no one can order the weather to take a few days off. The RNLI will be here to answer any call to service.

Beyond the harsh wind of the coast, St Davids Cathedral nestles in the valley, hidden from storms. The bell rings out three o'clock across empty grounds, startling the crows from their pulpits in the leafless trees. The River Alun, close to bursting its banks, carries a foaming yellow scum on its raucous race outside the Cathedral walls.

The monastic brotherhood St David founded was an austere order that required its followers to observe a selfless and simple life. They refrained from eating meat or drinking beer. After celebrating mass and saying their prayers, they cultivated the fields and kept bees. They fed and clothed the poor and needy and their impoverished lives stand in stark contrast to the former splendour of the Bishop's Palace beside the Cathedral. What feasts must the now ruined palace have boasted before it lost its slates and glass? It is a headless and decayed testament to a once wealthy church, powerful and dominant across this land. Formerly the finest medieval Bishop's palace in Wales, its majesty and power is still evident in its scale and its stone.

Pope Calixtus II declared two pilgrimages to St Davids were the equivalent of one to Rome. The faithful came throughout the Middle Ages. Vast wealth was raised from the pilgrims and the list of visitors to Pembrokeshire included William the Conqueror in 1077, Henry II in 1171 and Edward I in 1284. But by the 19th century the age of pilgrimage had long passed and St Davids was described as neglected and in decline.

The Cathedral door clunks heavily, but its thud is too distant to disturb the organist practicing Christmas carols and anthems. The sharp, pungent smell of a newly-felled Christmas tree at the entrance mingles with the warmth of candles and wood polish to greet visitors. The Cathedral is built on a slope, so visitors arriving have an uphill walk along its slate and stone flags in the centre nave towards the altar. The path to redemption is not a flat road.

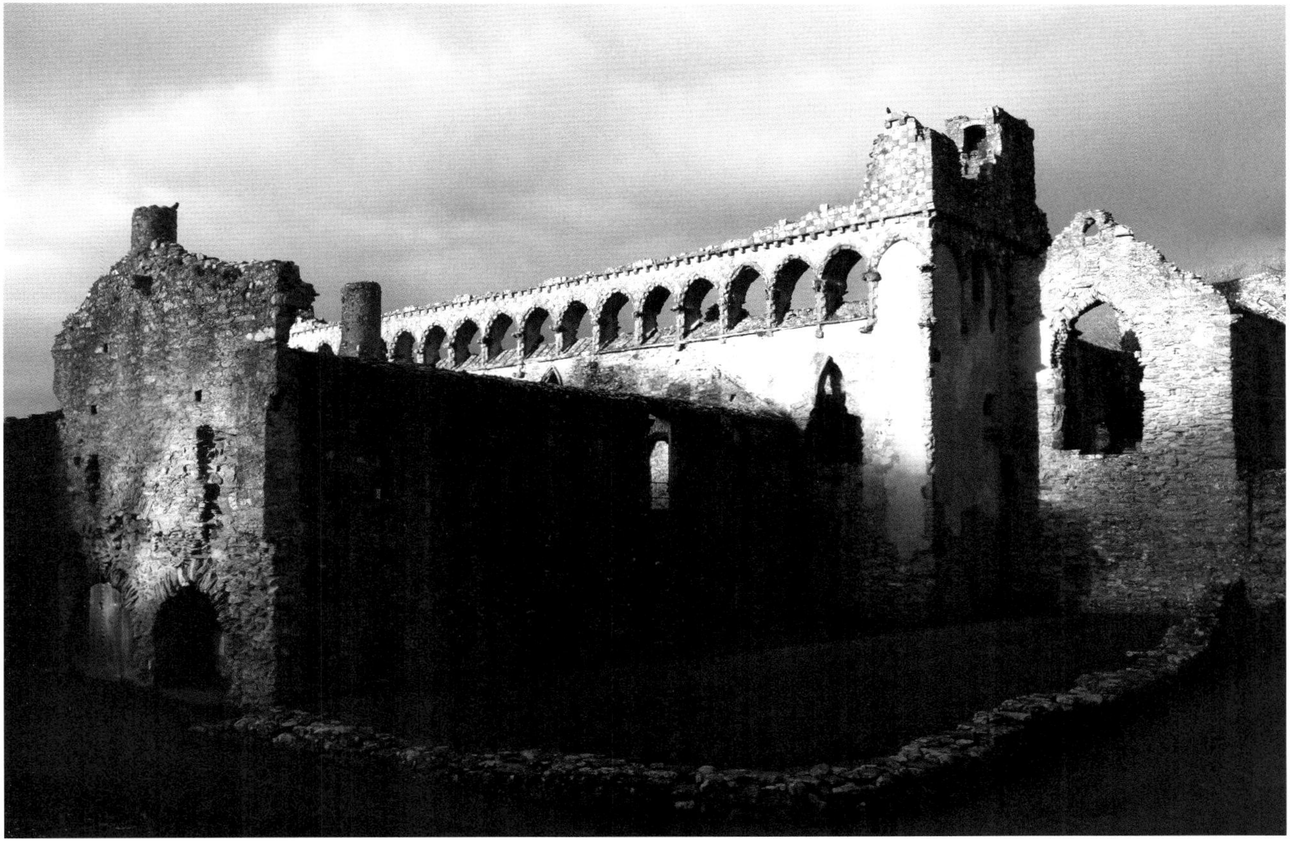

Bishops Palace, St Davids

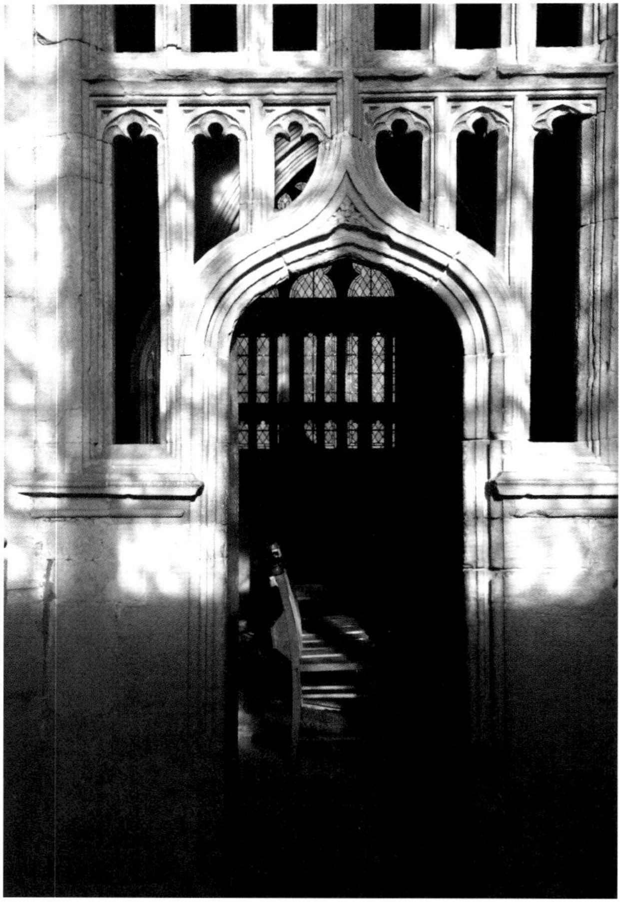

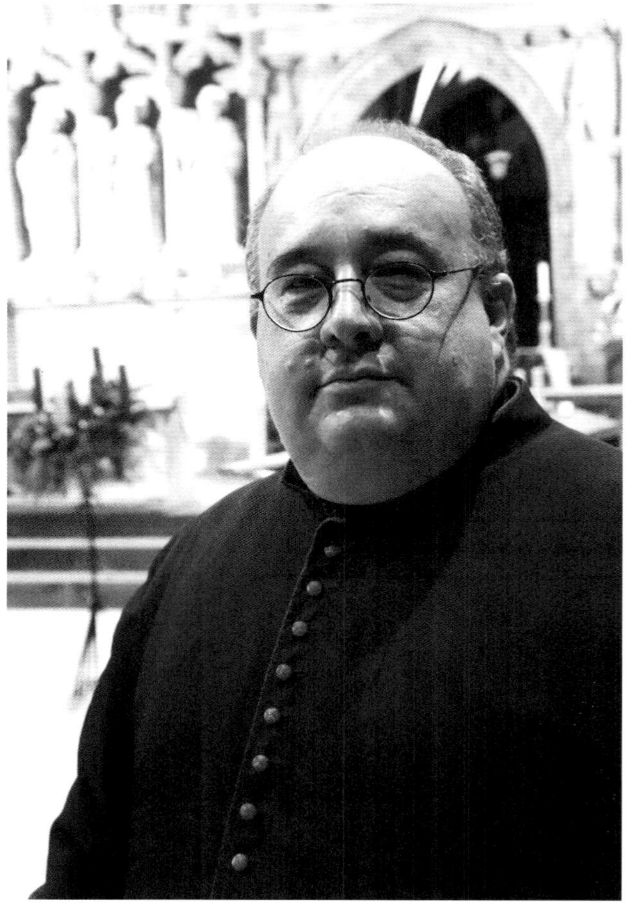

 The Archdeacon of Carmarthen, Dorrien Davies

The Assistant Director of Music, Simon Pearce, starts and pauses again, adjusting a flute stop and flicking over a sheet of music, unaware of his appreciative audience. There are a handful of visitors wandering around the Cathedral, some staring at memorials to long-forgotten bishops, others sitting in the pews looking up at the intricate wooden ceiling carved from Irish oak. Those who've read their guidebooks will know that poor foundations and a 13th century earthquake caused the walls on the west end to lean outwards, and so the Cathedral builders constructed a wooden ceiling rather than one of heavier stone.

The Cathedral will greet 800 worshippers to celebrate the Festival of Nine Lessons and Carols and a similar number for a New Year's Day concert later in the week. This is a place of worship, a tourist attraction and a concert venue. The Cathedral day is one of crowded hours.

The Archdeacon of Carmarthen, Dorrien Davies, is changing into his vestments in an anteroom off the nave. Evening service begins in a few moments in the choir stalls, hidden below the organ. Dorrien looks like a medieval monk, devout and all in black. He and the Canon's Verger process into the choir stalls and in moments the words and plainchant of evening prayer echo around the walls of an almost empty cathedral, as they have done for a thousand years. There is something unnerving about unaccompanied singing in the half-light. I have now walked back in time to any moment in the last 500 years and found a monk singing to the glory of God. There is no one else present. A pigeon trapped inside the Cathedral pecks at the red stained glass, trying to escape. Its clattering movements are out of time with the verses of the gospel and the responses.

After 20 minutes the service ends and the two worshippers process out of the choir stalls with their hymn books under their arms.

Dorrien sits behind his desk in the anteroom in the few minutes before preparations begin for the next service. He says, 'We worship for the glory of God, as clergy have always done in St Davids. We hold services for God, not man. It makes no difference if there are a hundred in the congregation or none.'

We are told we live in an increasingly secular society, but tonight he expects a full cathedral for the service; almost a third of the population of St Davids will brave the cold and the dark on a December night. I ask him why, when congregations are dwindling, so many still come to this particular service:

'Some come because they always have,' Dorrien says. 'Their grandparents and their parents came, so they come too. They will be reacquainted in memory for a moment tonight. They will suppress a sob during the old carols and remember the old times.'

'Others come for the spectacle – the old parish church of Pembrokeshire resplendent, full of song and light. Others come because they yearn for the unchanging certainty in lives that are caught in the gale of change.'

Tonight they will all be united in a timeless ritual that comforts the soul.

'I think even in this secular age, people need it,' he goes on. 'I think we are all searching for holiness. Just as the medieval pilgrims came here in their holidays to find God, perhaps we all yearn for something beyond our busy, materialistic lives.'

Dorrien's faith is stronger than the storms of secularism raining down on Christianity. His is an unshakeable certainty, a strong, muscular religion. When he was a child, his grandmother told him of her memories of the great religious revival of 1905. The influence of those who lived through that revival and told their grandchildren is still strong in Wales.

'It was the Great War that stopped that religious revival in its tracks. A generation of men and women would abandon their faith, after the unspeakable loss of the First World War.'

But Dorrien is comfortable being challenged and fighting for his faith, as the monks here always did. He is proud of the Cathedral and its work. Cathedrals are the success stories of the diocese – they are still here when so many of the branch offices have closed. He is part of the fabric, as familiar to the congregation as the statues and the stones. The Cathedral is the centerpiece of St Davids, but it's a community that is changing. Many of the houses are now second homes. The old resident families who once provided for the church, its choristers, flower arrangers, its worshippers and guides, are slowly disappearing.

We talk about what the pilgrims who came here in the Cathedral's heyday might have witnessed:

'The medieval pilgrims who came to St Davids found a cathedral that was their Disneyland. The building's magnificent scale, exquisite stone and wood carvings, the stained glass, the smell of candles and burning incense, the rich music and the words of

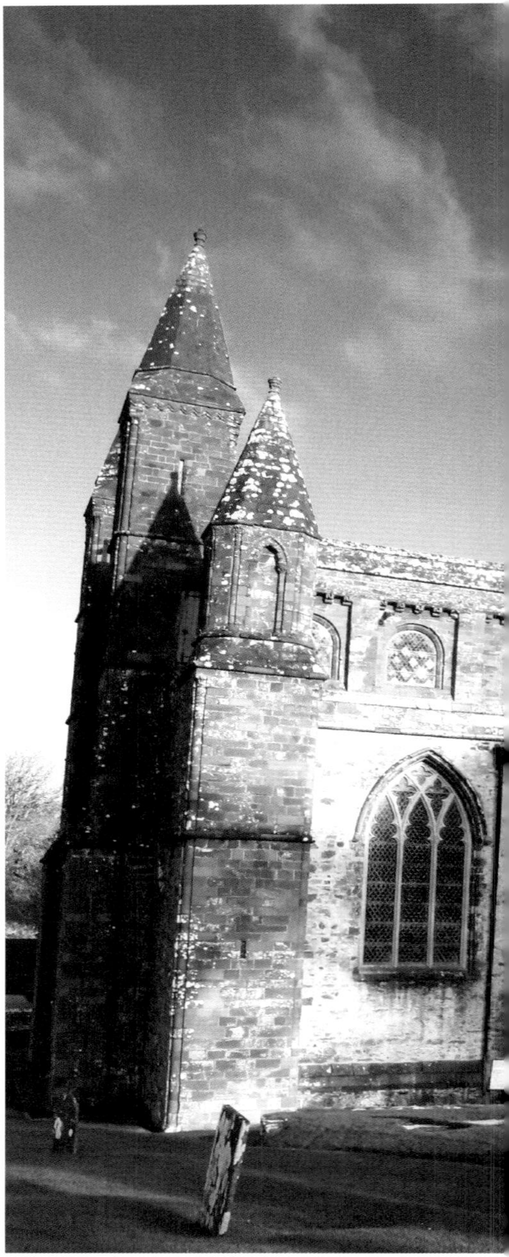

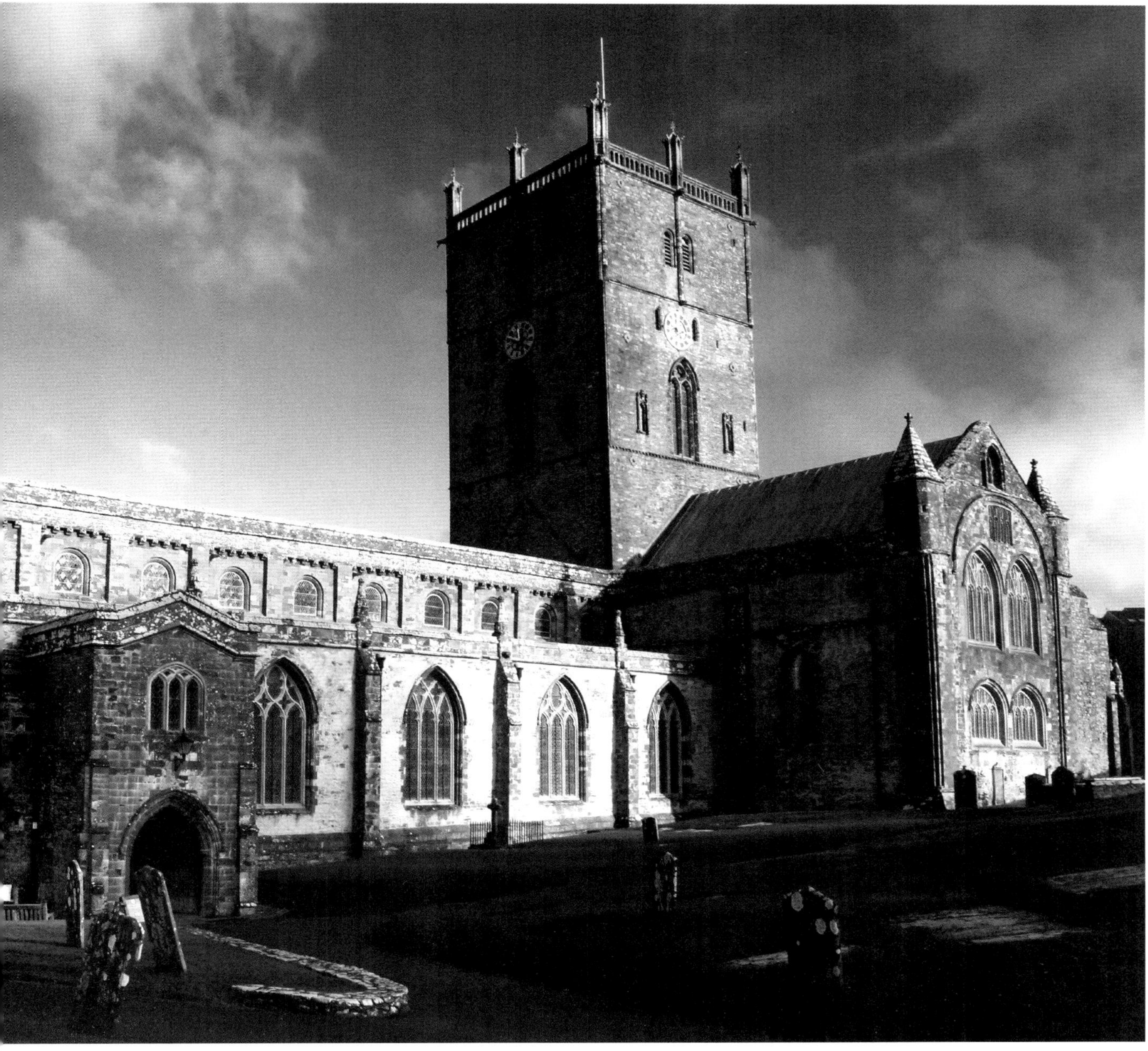

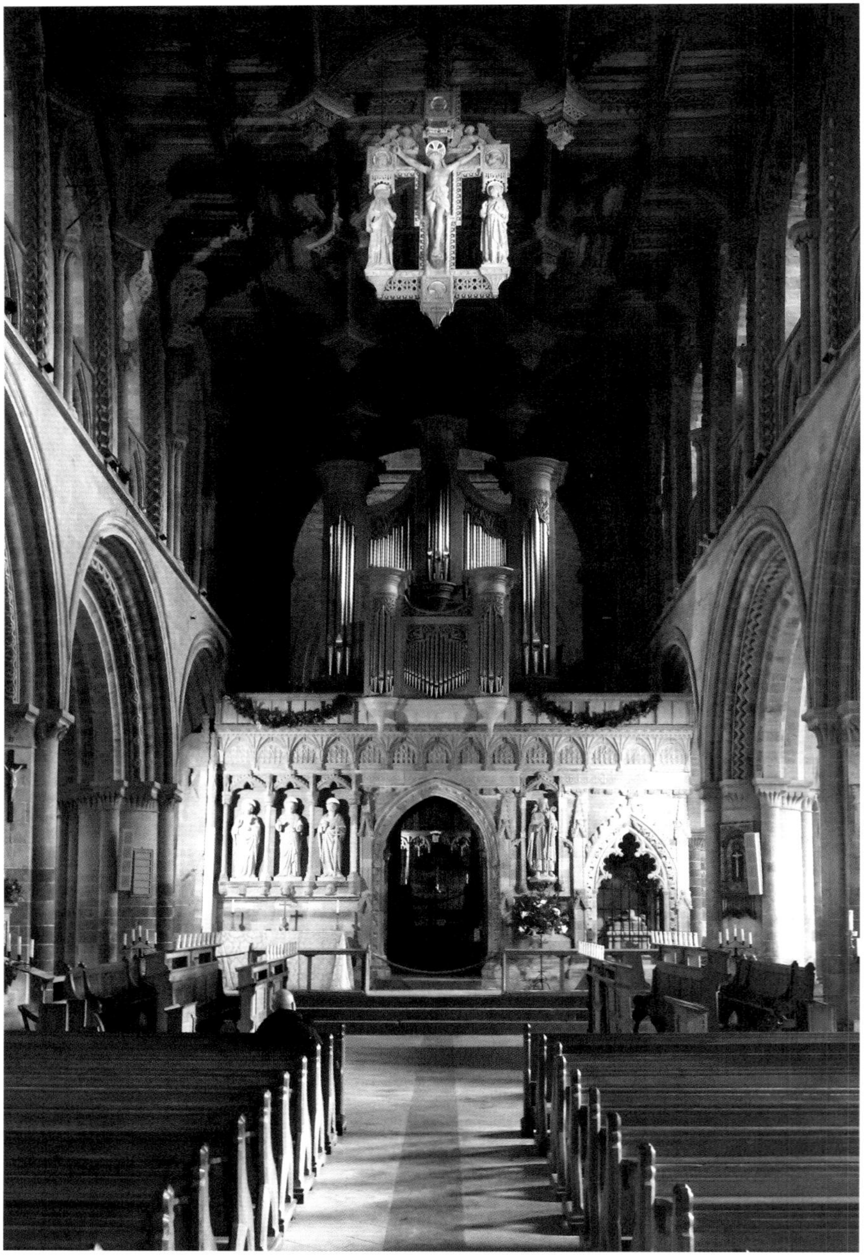

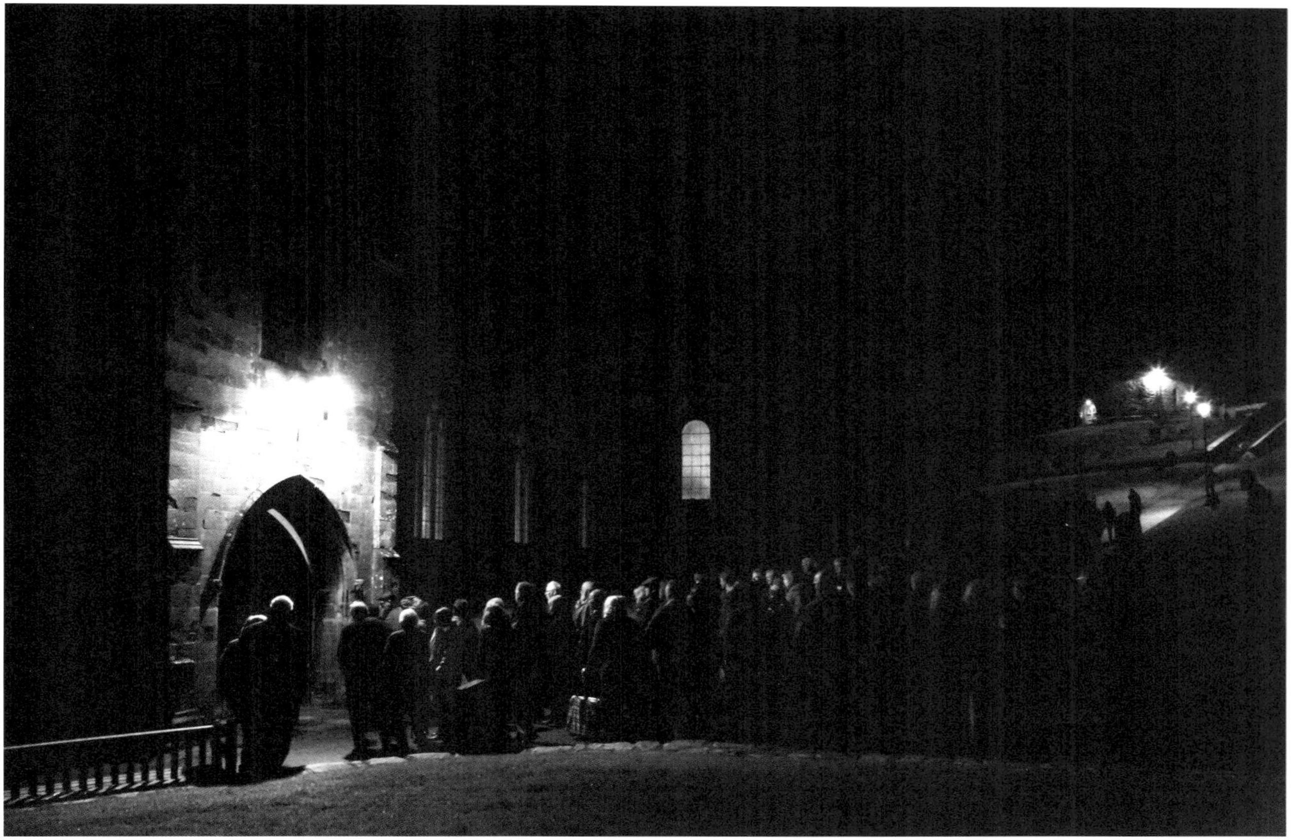

praise must have seemed like a glimpse of heaven, or at least another world.'

Dorrien too seems from another world; a kinder, gentler society, where everyone knows one another. He is a cleric who will always visit his congregation and have time for a cup of tea and another slice of cake. Soon he will leave his duties here for pastures new and another flock. I wonder what he will miss about working at the Cathedral. His eyes moisten and, despite his promotion, this clearly marks the end of a love affair.

'This place is our collective history and our conscience,' says Dorrien, 'St Davids is the story of Wales; it's the story of our county and our country. This is the cradle of our history. No one ever comes to this Cathedral unaffected by this place. They may not like it, but the Cathedral always provokes a reaction. I believe no one can come here and sit through a service and be unaffected by its sense of spirituality – God permeates everything in this Cathedral.'

Darkness is settling around St Davids and Lizzie Albery, the new Canons' Verger, lights the last of the candles on the choir stalls ready for the service of Nine Lessons and Carols. The congregation is already queuing to enter and each worshipper is given a candle to hold as they collect their order of service.

The bass-notes of the organ vibrate the flagstones and rattle the windows as J.S. Bach's Sinfonia from *Christmas Oratorio* floats down the centre nave. The electric lights of the Cathedral are switched off and the congregation, now numbering hundreds of worshippers, is bathed in the soft glow of candlelight, the small flames dancing in the draughts.

This is the sight that might have greeted those medieval pilgrims, an awe-inspiring rally of a large crowd, a sea of flickering lights and, emanating from the shadows, the most beautiful music to behold. Who could come here and not be moved?

After the silence of anticipation, in the far darkness beside the high altar, a solo treble voice sings the first notes of the processional hymn:

Once in royal David's city
Stood a lowly cattle shed,
Where a mother laid her Baby
In a manger for His bed:
Mary was that mother mild,
Jesus Christ, her little Child.

From the darkness, the choir emerges singing in four-part harmony. The words of C.F. Alexander were written in another century, but are familiar to the shadowed congregation who don't need to look down at their hymn books. Tonight we are gathered in this ancient place to sing the old carols together.

Dorrien, processing behind the choir as they slowly make their way along the length of the nave, nods as he passes each pew. He will know virtually everyone here.

The Cathedral Choir is unique in Britain in that its top line consists of girls aged from 8-18. Once the preserve of men, this is now a mixed endeavour. The choir has toured the world. There is also a Boys'

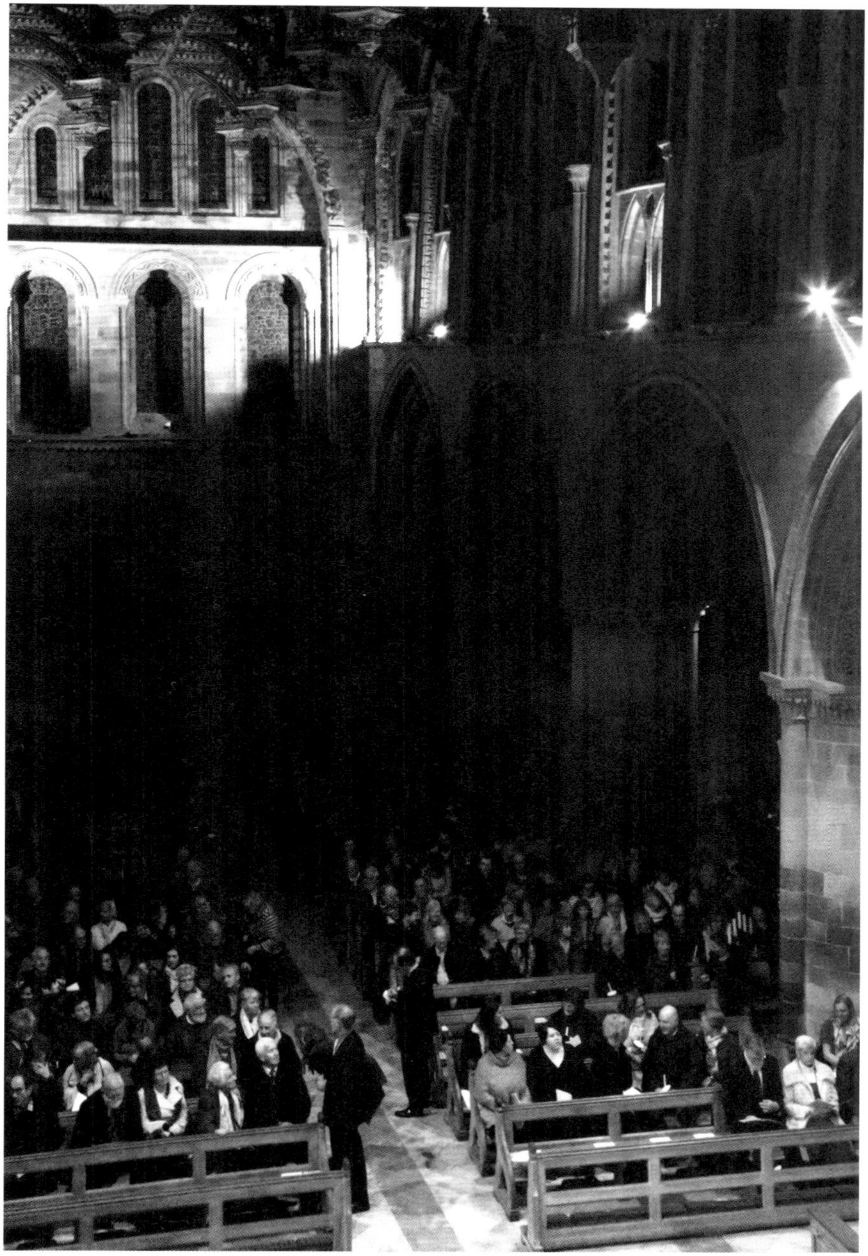

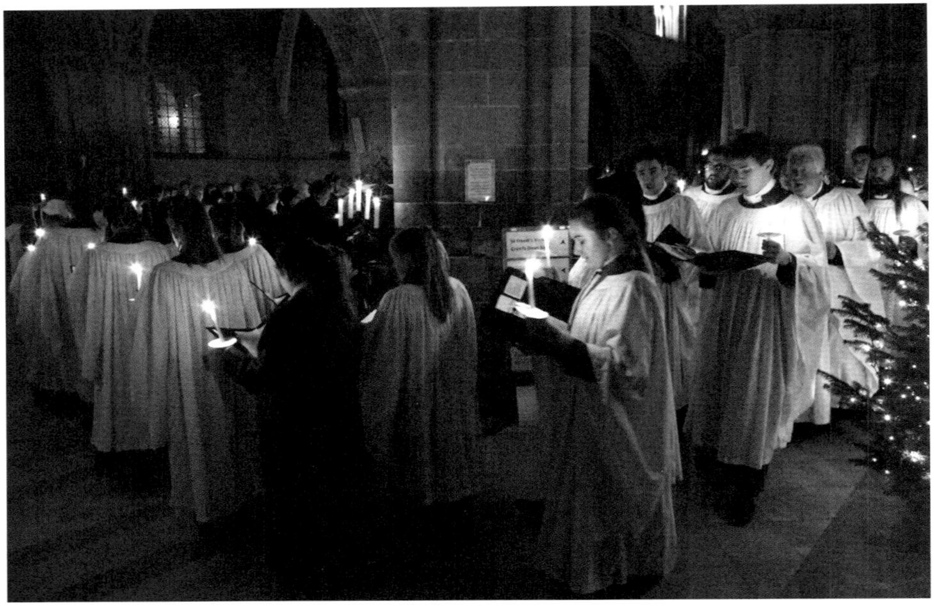

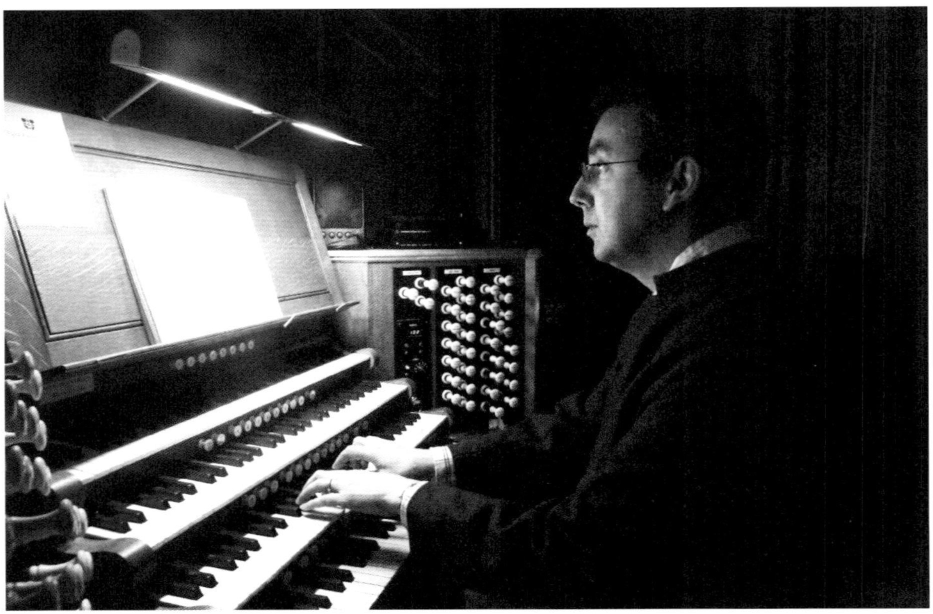

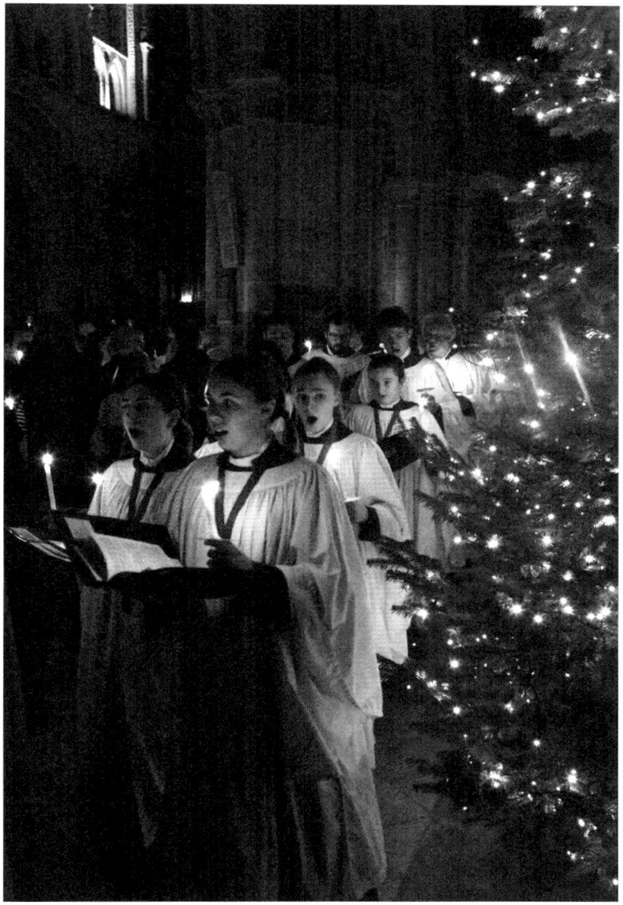

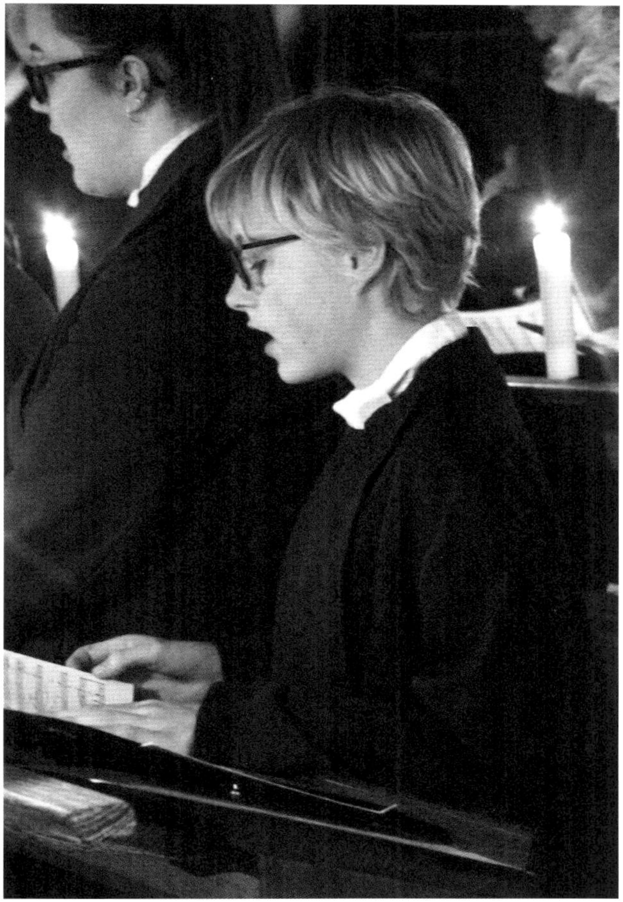

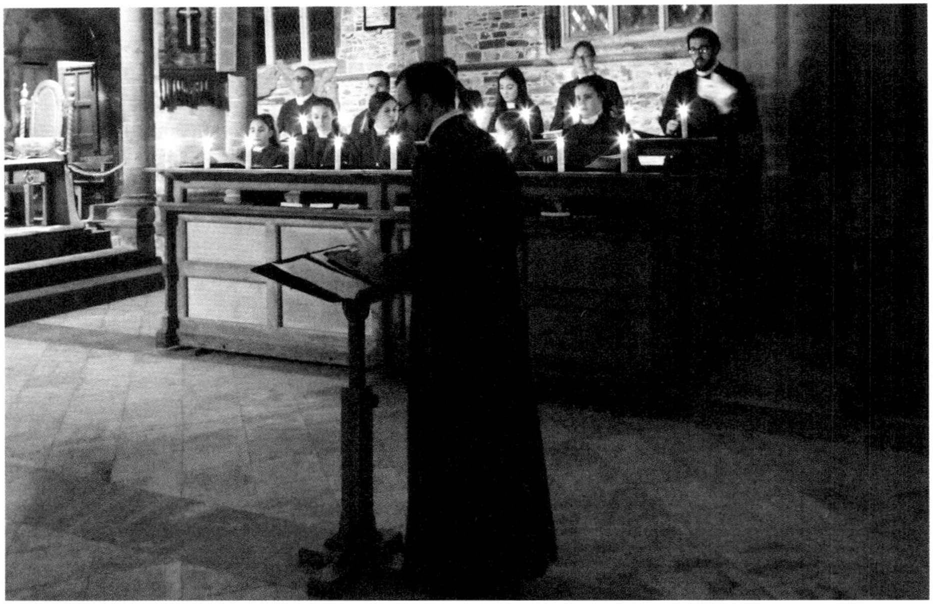

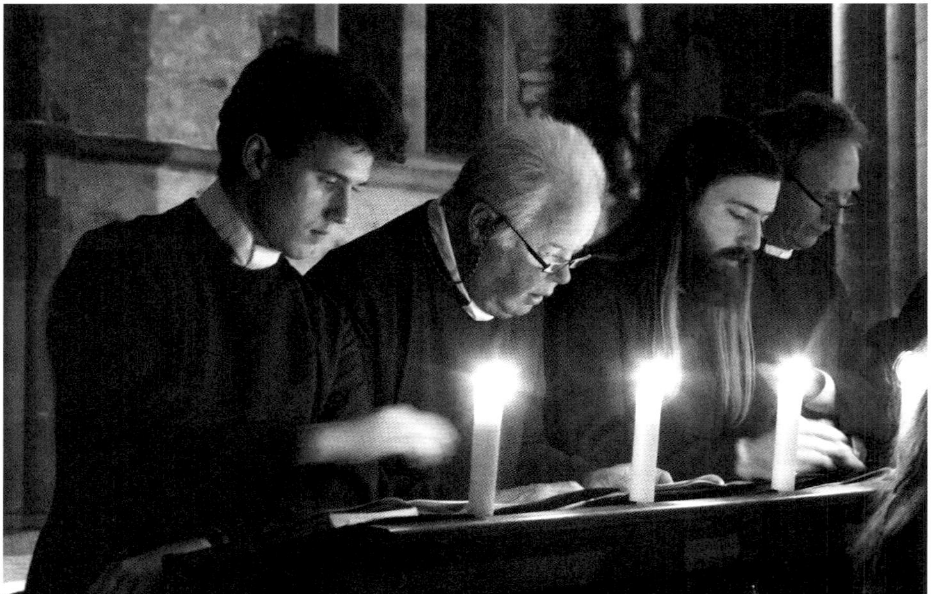

Choir and Junior School Choir for primary school children drawn from across the county. This couldn't be further from the technology obsessed popular perception of children. The professional discipline and standard of musicianship is a credit to Simon Pearce and Oliver Waterer, Organist and Master of Choristers. In a small community on the furthest periphery of Pembrokeshire, they have inspired excellence.

The congregation is shy and uncertain singing some of the carols, but the choir, like their monastery forbears, sound out the stanzas with bell-like confidence. We are watching another world, a community confident in its music. We are observers of a performance as old as the ages.

The choir sings the words of Christina Rossetti:

In the bleak midwinter,
Frosty wind made moan,
Earth stood hard as iron,
Water like a stone;
Snow had fallen, snow on snow,
Snow on snow,
In the bleak midwinter, long ago.

The composer Harold Darke's notes hang heavy in the air. The most powerful moment in music is the silence in between the sounds. In those silences, you'll hear the thoughts and prayers of those who gather here.

Some worshippers sing a few lines then stop to remember, others are too moved to join in. Worshippers will perhaps recall last year, another life, or hope for a time to come. Tonight is the marking of time passed or time to come. In these familiar carols, we return, we wish, we forget, or perhaps, the notes fill the hours and block out life's noise; one hymn but hundreds of different stories.

In a world that is increasingly obsessed with selfish individuality, there is something soothing about joining a group of strangers in a common endeavour that is older than all of us. In this ancient place, the cares of the world disappear for a moment. This Cathedral has known war and worry and survived. The preoccupations of the present seem trivial when measured against its scarred centuries.

On a cold winter's night, hundreds of people have gathered here. The music and candlelight are enchanting, but so too are the quieter moments. There is something enduring and vital about the human desire for somewhere to stop and think. St Davids is home now, as it has always been, to those who come here to find peace. Between the verses, I imagine my father's deep bass voice singing his favourite descants and remember Christmases long past.

St David is said to have told his followers to 'do the little things'. On the edge of Britain, in a world where some feel disengaged and helpless to shape events, his words aren't such a bad maxim to live by. Do the little things.

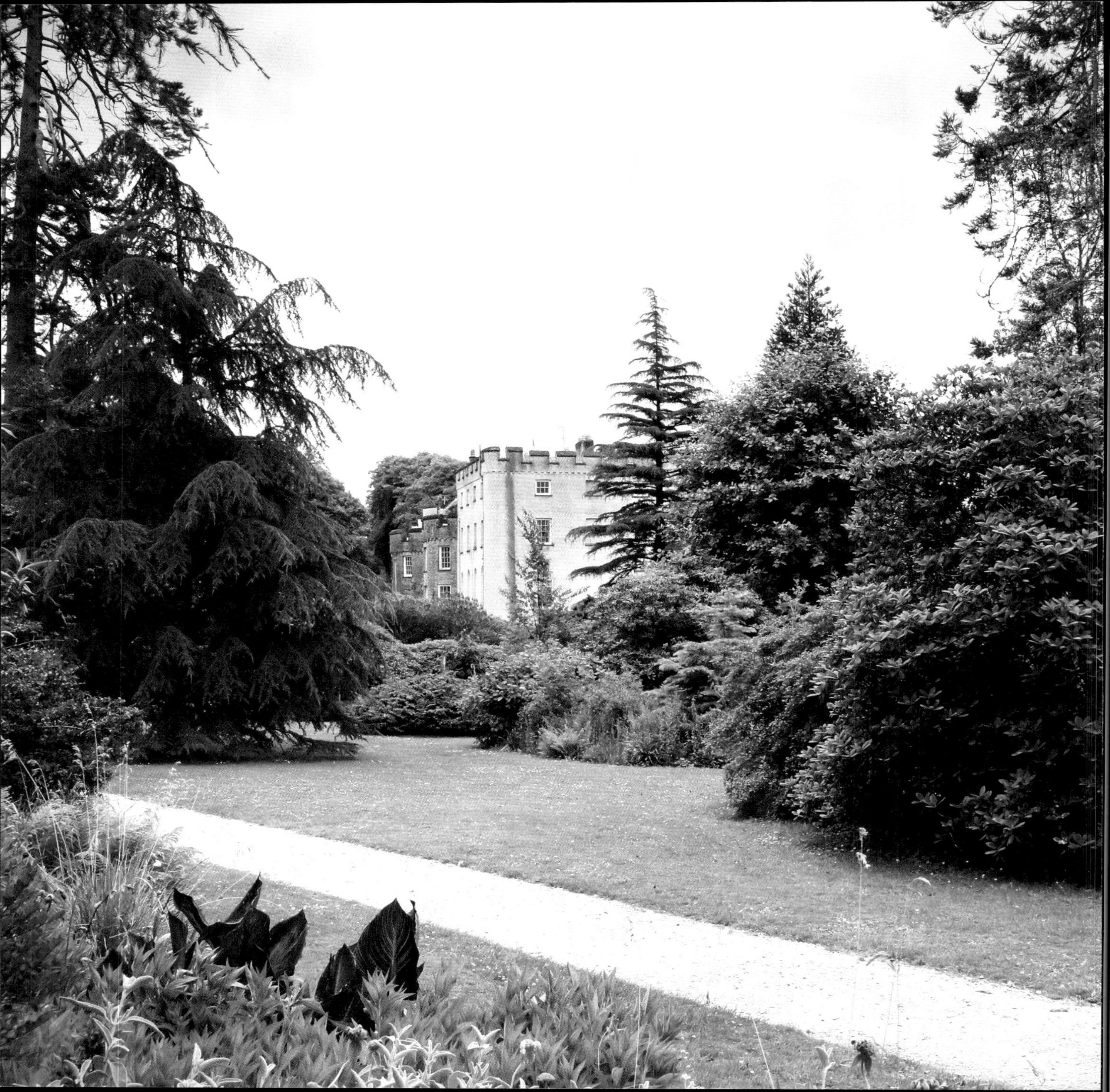

Picton

Castle and Gardens

We are a cosmopolitan bunch of 10 visitors who gather outside the entrance of Picton Castle for the two o'clock tour; among us are Dutch, French, Americans and Germans enjoying an unseasonably sunny week in June. The Welsh flag dangles on a pole from the battlements and flutters far above us, the red dragon perhaps unsure if the foundations below are more English than Welsh.

The majority of visitors to Picton wander around the gardens only and miss the chance to explore the castle. Many others simply call at Maria's courtyard restaurant for lunch in magnificent surroundings. Wales has a hundred castles to choose from – terrifying fortresses marked by history, more modest tumps reclaimed by the grass and, most of them, roofless and ruined. Picton has kept its roof and is more stately home than stronghold. You won't need your imagination to wonder about the splendour of how aristocratic Pembrokeshire once lived; it's all still here to see, as if the family has popped out for a moment.

So many stately homes that are open to the public have been restored to showroom perfection or are too perfect to touch, but Picton is comfortable in its imperfections and more relaxed for its informality. You won't find any DO NOT SIT HERE signs left on the sofas or a sprig of sharp holly on the chairs. You can touch what you want and sit where you want, which on a warm day is a welcome invitation.

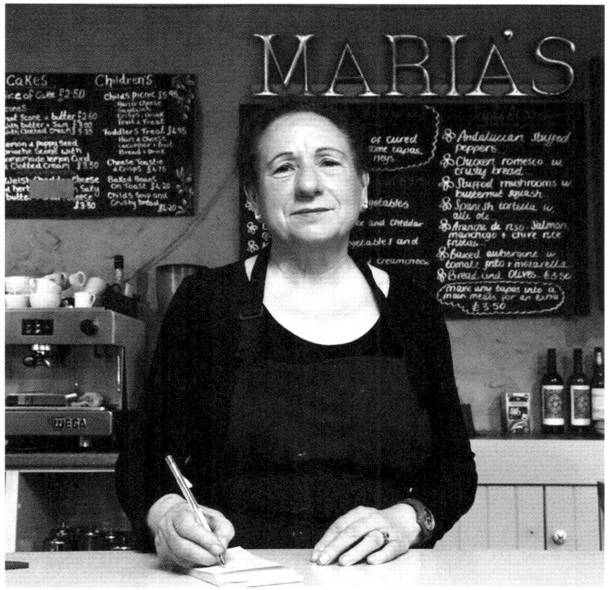

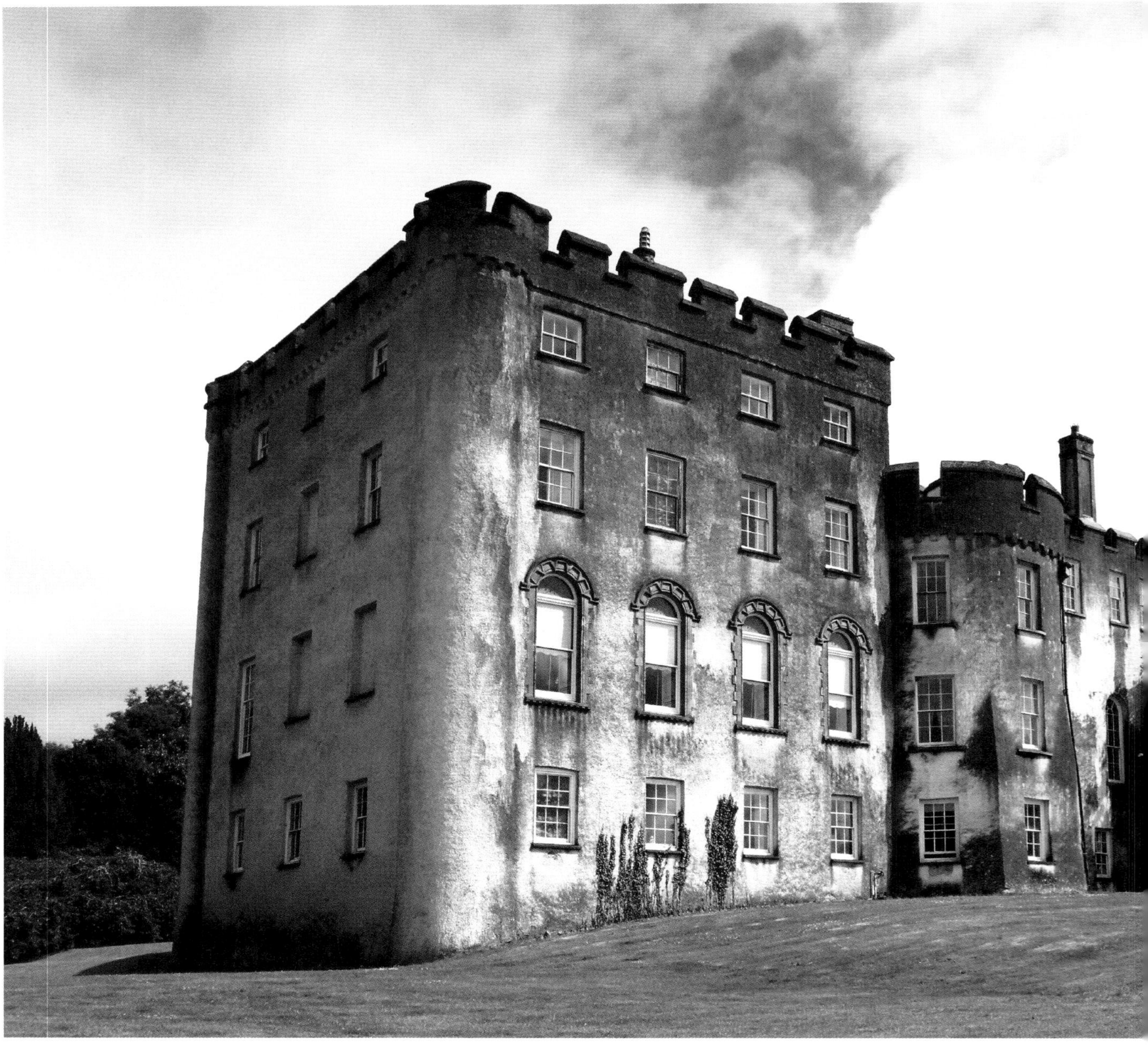

130 Picton Castle and Gardens

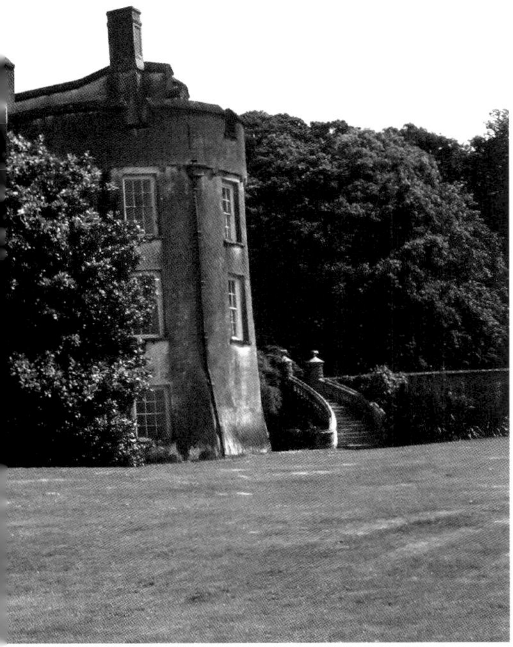

Our tour guide is Dai Evans, the Director of the Picton Trust now charged with maintaining the castle and gardens. The building's ruinous upkeep and death duties made its last occupants, the Philipps family, flee for the warmth and affordability of more modest arrangements. Now Picton is open to all.

'I'm afraid there is to be no filming of the contents of our tour, less the light-fingered spy the contents of the castle on the internet – but still photographs are acceptable,' we are told. Our appetites are whetted and the camera-laden, waterproof-wearing gathering advance to the double-fronted doors to begin our invasion.

Picton looks very little like other Welsh castles, being much rebuilt. This is an Irish castle in Wales. Its drum towers give away its ancient foundations, but behind them an extension from 1790 offers more generous country house living in place of the older, more austere lodging in the original stronghold.

If you put a pin in the map of Pembrokeshire, Picton wouldn't be far off the centre. It sits near the upper reaches of the River Cleddau that was previously the transport network of these parts. In the age before decent roads and railways, goods and passengers would have been transported to Picton by boat and then collected by horse and carriage for the short final journey. Romantic paintings depicting the river in close proximity to the castle are an older form of artistic photoshopping – the water was never within sight of Picton's lawns. But for all its position in the heart of Pembrokeshire, Picton's enemies were not the English but the marauding Welsh. Picton is on the fault line between the anglicised south of the

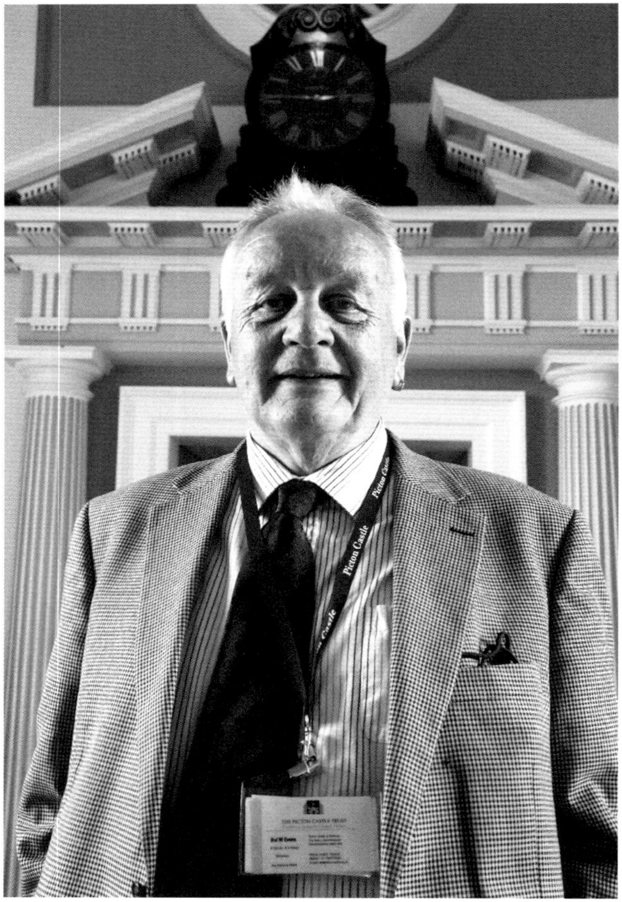
Picton Castle

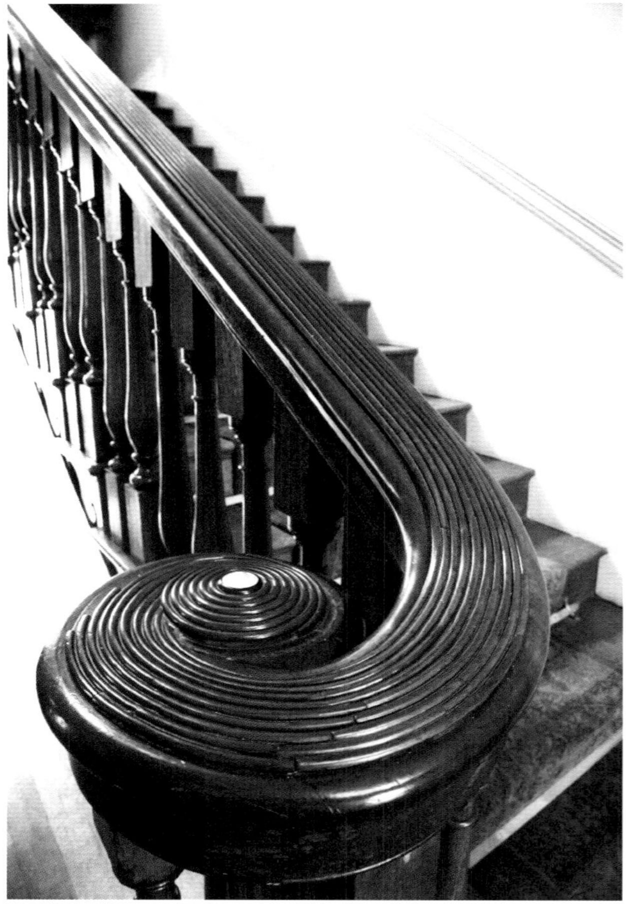

county and the Welsh north. The castle sits on what is known as the Landsker, the imaginary line across the county marking the rich flatlands of the farms of the south and the hard, mountainous living of the north. This was the front line on the map, the marker between order and disorder.

Richard Fenton, writing *A Historical Tour through Pembrokeshire* in 1811, arrived at Picton by boat and a congested and busy waterway:

'I repass Lawrenny, where large vessels take in coal and culm brought them in barges...but the place is likely to be much injured in a few years, unless gentlemen in power...will prevent vessels throwing their ballast into the channel, thereby choking the passage. Gliding up gently with the tide, I enter the eastern Cleddau, and landing opposite to Landshipping quay, at the place where passengers take the ferry boat, walk up through the beautiful woods to Picton.'

Today's visitors arrive through the seemingly endless and enchanting lanes of farms and woodland that make up the Picton Estate. After many turns in the road, much forest and a long way off the main road, Picton sits seemingly in the middle of nowhere, the centre of a beguiling maze.

You enter Picton Castle from the 1820 circular carriage drive, but we are arriving through what was once the first floor, the original castle entrance buried beneath us at ground level. This later mountain of earth, piled up and gravel topped, allowed the castle's guests to alight from their carriages and walk straight into Picton's palatial first floor rooms, rather than climb winding stone steps up the inside of the drum tower.

Picton's entrance, flanked by carved stone faces, narrows at first – its Great Hall entices from a distance but will reveal itself in full later in our tour. We turn almost immediately left and into the intimacy of the Library, built into the womb of the round tower. This is one of the castle's smallest rooms. The thick walls, once lit only by arrow slits, were hammered out to make windows to read by and look out onto the vast estate. The whiff of furniture polish, old leather book coverings, damp pages and well-used armchairs hangs in the air. This circular room in a turret must have challenged the craftsmen who transformed the building from a dark defensive bastion into a more luxurious home. Lined by its circular glass-front bookshelves, this is a civilised oasis of learning where archers would have stood. The inlaid wooden floor and complex joinery was the work of the carpenter James Rich. He too designed the hidden cupboards beside the bookshelves, though we will never know if they held restorative brandy or risqué literature.

I would love to sit here now on one of the inviting armchairs and take a leather bound volume from the shelves. The view from the windows stares across the fields. How much reading would anyone have done in such beguiling surroundings? The crackle of logs in the grate and the sound of swallows would accompany the hours. Will anyone build libraries like this in our new age of eBooks and the internet? For many, shelves of books have become unnecessary.

Who ordered each book? Who last turned their pages and what occupied their thoughts as they looked up from the text? Books are our memory and our witness, not only of their own words printed on yellowing pages in fading covers but also the keepers of each reader's thoughts and time. This room whispers with twice the volume of its library's stories.

A bible from 1616 is the oldest book in its collection. Sir Erasmus Philipps was the scholarly collector who sought out many of these volumes. His own life is the stuff of tragedy and drama, as his untimely end in a hunting accident, sliding off his horse into the River Avon.

Picton's rich heart is the double height galleried Great Hall, complete with organ. A painting hanging here taunts the castle's trustees. Picton's roof, walls and windows are on borrowed time and in need of considerable investment. What is held to be an original painting of Renoir stares out across the room – its sale at auction would fund the fabric of the castle and keep it safe for another generation – but its authenticity is at issue. Without the experts' formal agreement of its provenance, it remains hanging in its peeling surroundings.

Sir Henry Cheere of Norwich created the fireplaces, so large that our entire tour party could hide within them. Cheere's carvings either side of the fire were inspired by Bacchus, the Greek god of wine. Those unchanging faces must have watched centuries of hospitality. Before death duties and declining fortunes took their toll, Picton's occupants clearly lived well, even if the principal rooms were reserved for rare occasions. Picton Estate's wealth was derived from patronage, inheritance, good marriages, farmland, mineral exploitation and the East India Company, but this was a family that shared the proceeds of wealth too, as well as acquiring it.

Picton has been home to many of the country's notable players. Good Sir John Philipps, as he was known, was a life-long patron of the Society for Promoting Christian Knowledge that distributed devotional books, sponsored two editions of the Welsh bible and founded 95 charity schools. This was a time long before free state education and the impact of these endeavours was so profound that Catherine the Great sent envoys to learn from Wales.

The stairs to the first floor wind beneath the 1750 Snetzer organ and Minstrels' Gallery and lead to the bedroom of the last chatelaine, Lady Marion. The bedroom occupies the space in the tower above the Library. Its hand-painted murals on the doors and yellowing ceiling have seen better days. The en-suite bathroom is a civilising touch in a castle turret, unless you were the under gardener whose duty it was to collect the waste from the long drop garderobe.

The Chapel for family and servants separates Lady Marion's bedroom from the sleeping quarters of the last master of the house, Hon. Hanning Philipps. Our tour party exchange looks and hushed words on viewing the separate bedroom arrangements of the Welsh aristocracy, though the women in the group, perhaps sleeping with snorers, seem to approve.

Our party gathers on the Minstrels' Gallery beside the organ to look down on the portraits and grand

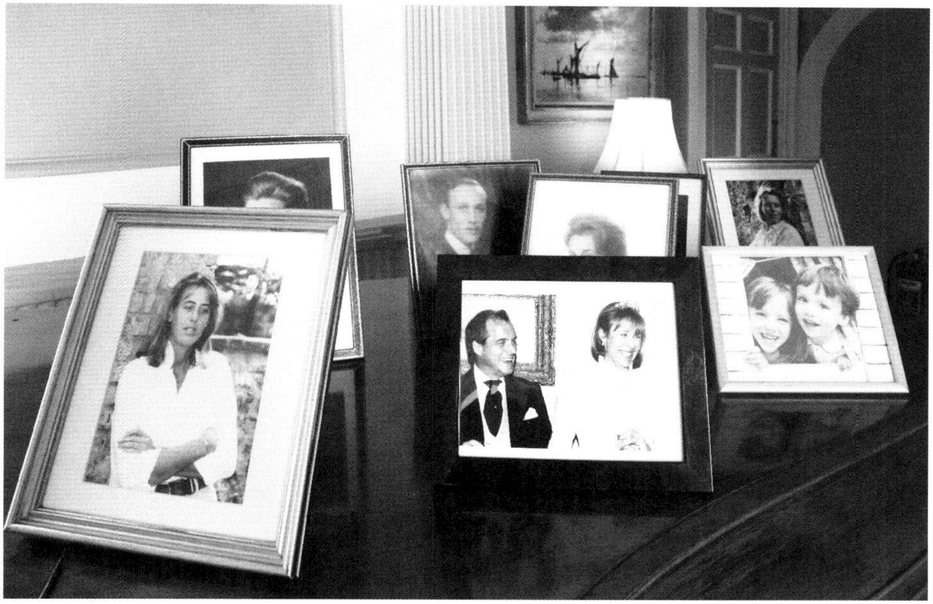

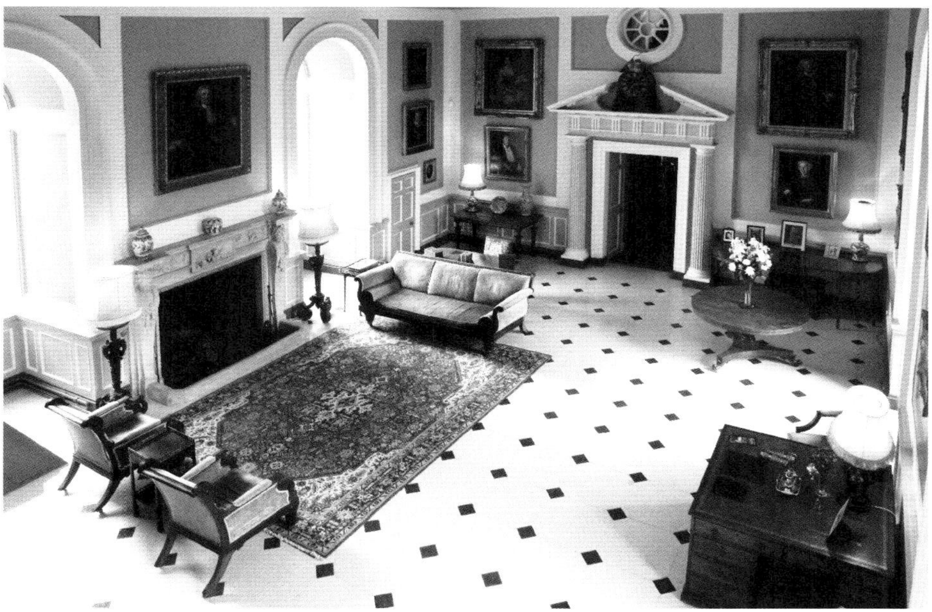

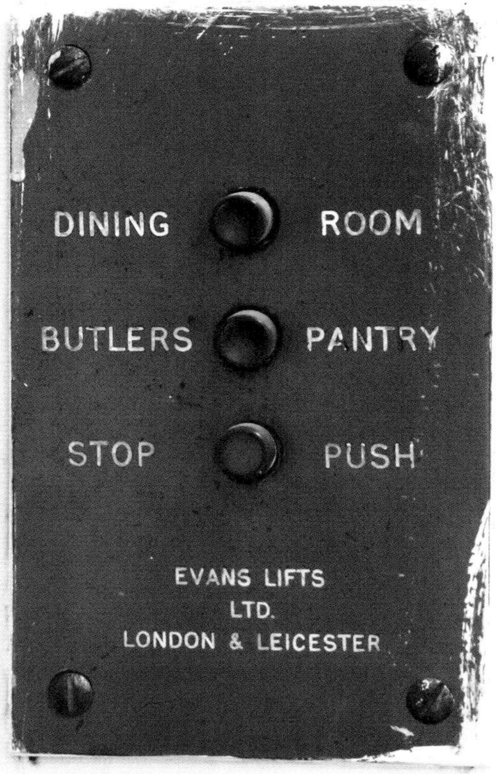
DINING ROOM
BUTLERS PANTRY
STOP PUSH
EVANS LIFTS
LTD.
LONDON & LEICESTER

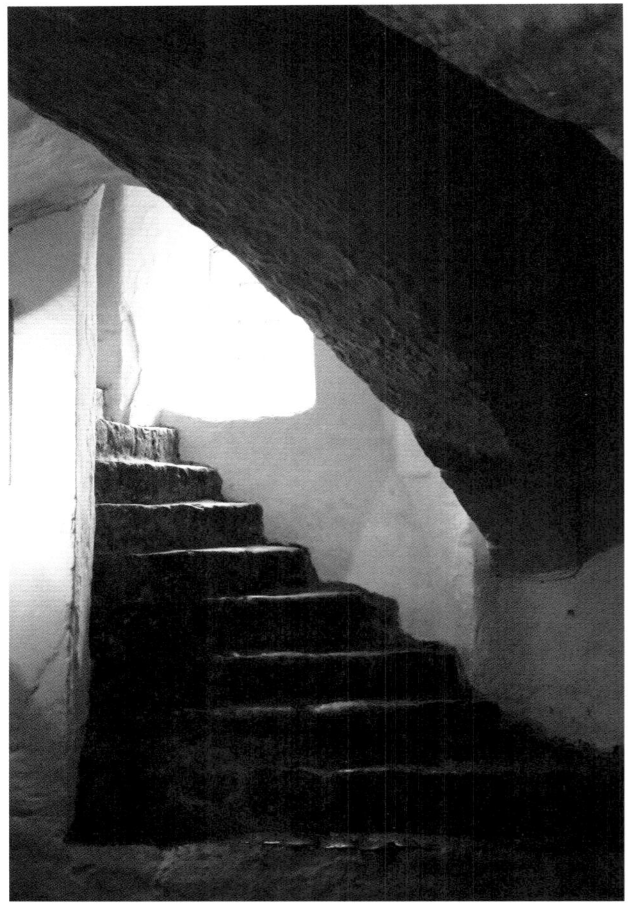

piano in the Great Hall below. In medieval times this was the entertaining and banqueting space. Down the stairs, back on the ground floor and through the Great Hall lie the newer rooms of Picton, built in the 1790s. A grand staircase, dining room, drawing room and bedrooms in the new extension marked the architectural transition from austere fortification to stately home.

The white and gold drawing room is too tempting for some of our weary party, who immediately take the opportunity to sit down after the exertions of the tour. After the double height of the Great Hall, the low ceiling of the drawing room offers an intimacy and informality. The Rococo panels frame four British poets and philosophers, perhaps to remind guests of how high-minded and well-read their hosts were.

We shuffle out into the corridor to view the display cabinets of Swansea porcelain, the watercolour of Augustus John and the beguiling portrait of the notorious London courtesan Teresia Constantia Phillips. According to her own book, she was debauched at the age of 13 by the Earl of Chesterfield, and she went on to write what would now be called a 'kiss and tell' account of her life in order to blackmail her many influential lovers. It was the best seller of 1748 and she signed every copy she sold.

The longcase clock chimes the half hour as precisely as the day it was made in Haverfordwest two centuries ago. We pause before entering the dining room to look at the vast tapestry made by Gobelins in the 18th century. It was bought by Lord Milford in 1928 with the winnings of his horse, Flamingo, in the 2,000 Guineas.

The splendid white and blue decoration was commissioned by Lord Milford in the 1790s. The plaster designs were already out of date by the time it was constructed but are no less impressive for that. In a familiar act of recycling, the marble chimneypiece came from the old solar tower, which was demolished to make way for these rooms. The Queen had lunch here on a recent visit to Pembrokeshire. Towering over the dining table are some of the portraits of the family; Sir James Erasmus Philipps, whose exhausted wife bore him 13 children, and Lady Walpole, wife of Britain's first Prime Minister and niece of Sir Erasmus Philipps.

The drawing room next door silences our group for a moment, much taken with the grandeur of the chandelier. The portrait over the fireplace is perhaps another work in a familiar Picton pattern of mistaken art provenance. This is the oldest painting in the castle. Lord Milford bought what he thought was a full-length portrait of Queen Elizabeth I by the 16th-century painter Sir Anthonis Mor, but it is thought not to be the Queen, instead perhaps a study of a woman of high rank. Whoever she is, she still commands the room. We each take turns to sit in the armchair in which the most recent Queen Elizabeth sat and look around the salmon walls, exquisite furniture and deep picture windows framing views of the lawns. Royal patronage of Picton didn't stop with the present Queen; Prince Charles stayed here when he was a student at Aberystwyth University. The estate's vast acreage and distance from Fleet Street's prying eyes must have been a welcome retreat.

We know some of Picton's great chapters, some of its illustrious former residents and its royal connections, but much of Picton's story is a puzzle. Historians don't have a full picture of the life and times of the castle and gardens or all of the occupants who lived here. The curse of so many grand houses struck Picton too – a fire in 1934 destroyed many of its records and a good deal of the fabric. What remains is remodelled and refashioned, sometimes by whim but sometimes necessity. The retention over centuries of so much wealth and so many treasures owes much to inheritance, sound investment and the fact that Picton has remained in the ownership of only three famous Pembrokeshire families since 1300.

That's the end of our tour of the aristocratic quarters of Picton – we've seen paintings, tapestries, carvings and carpets; we've done the upstairs and the gracious living. Our tour party jokes that what we're now about to see is the place where perhaps most of us would have spent our time, had we worked here. We step slowly downstairs to the service quarters into a colder, darker world. The afternoon sun that flooded in through the wide windows of the upstairs rooms is rationed in these quarters. There are no carpets down here.

This is where the first period of the castle's history was set and where guests would have originally arrived: low torchlight, no windows, stone spiral staircases and vaulted cellars. This is more as you would imagine a castle interior. The empty corridor would have been home to huge wine cellars, bustling servants' quarters and the steaming kitchen, all now long gone.

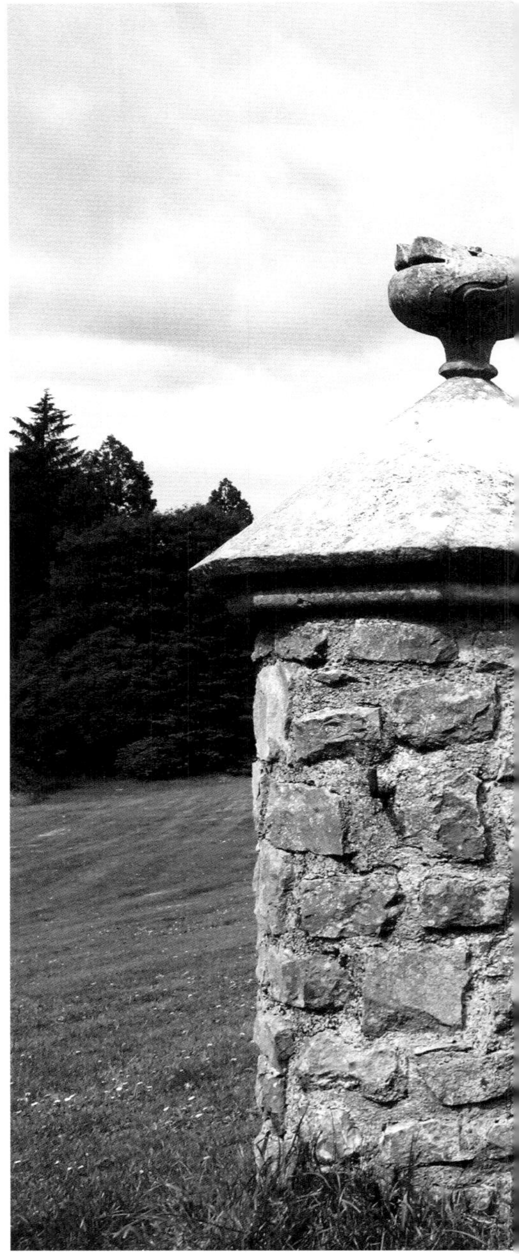

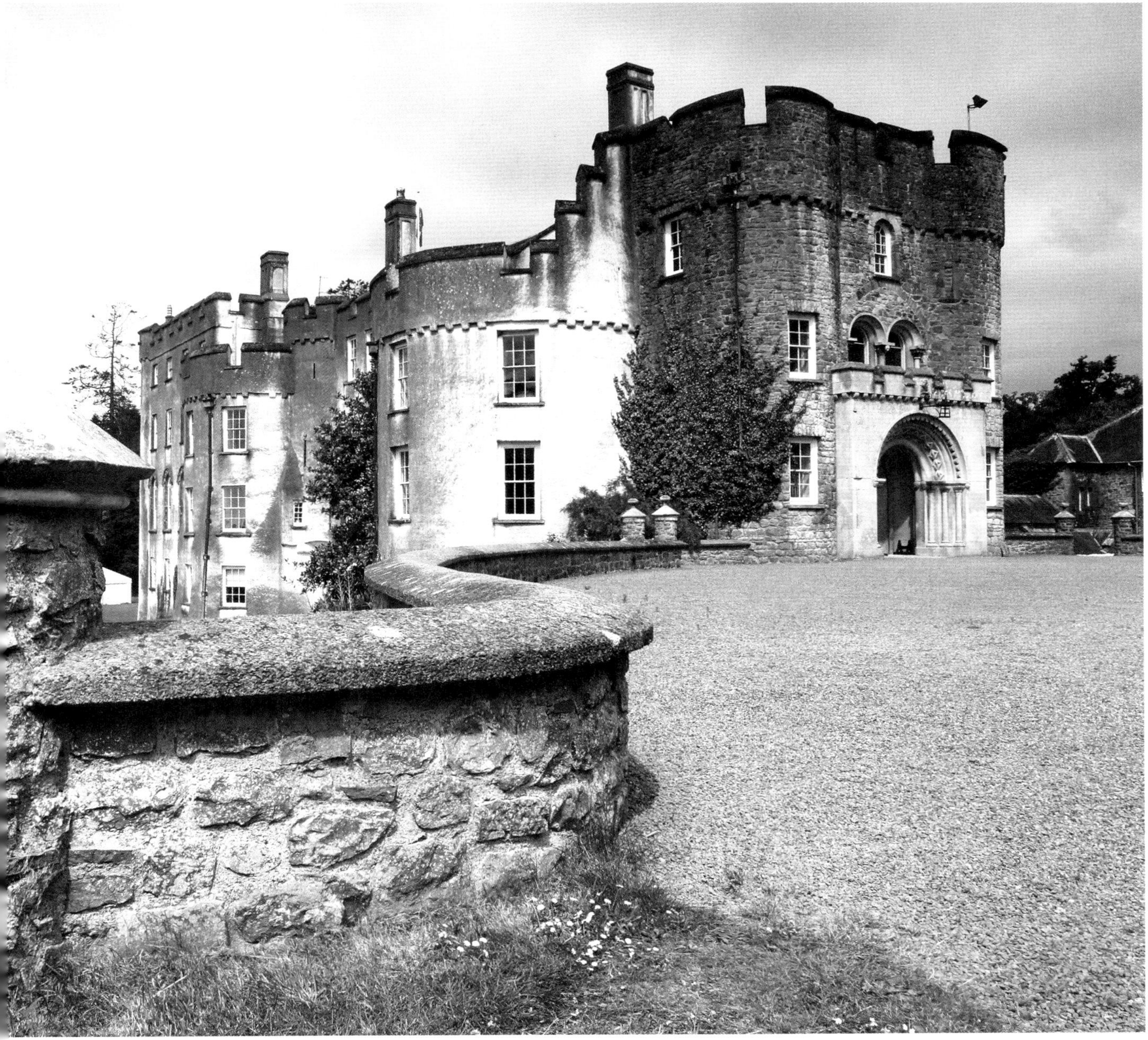

But in their place, an inkling of Victorian and Edwardian Picton, a rich collection of implements and tools from domestic life that might have been familiar to those who would have worked here in the kitchen and laundry.

As many as 23 or 24 servants were employed below stairs in Victorian times. In the age that gave the world industrialisation and consumer goods, Picton's collection of housekeeping equipment offers an idea of the heady times in which the staff here operated and how the workplace was changing in the face of new technology. The kitchen collection includes an early electric toaster – its metal frame has no earth lead – which must have livened up breakfast times. The laundry display has familiar washboards and mangles to scrub and dry the clothes, but also an early petrol-powered clothes iron that curiously never captured consumers' imaginations. In an age before health and safety legislation or widespread product testing, working life below stairs here must have been a sometimes dangerous occupation.

A murder hole set in the stone wall above us, through which hot sand would have been poured onto unwelcome visitors below, briefly captivates our youngest tour members before our party is let out of the thick drum tower door and back into the afternoon sun. After our hour in such close proximity, bunched tightly to listen to our castle guide, the grounds of Picton's gardens appear even more enormous; we will not bump into each other for the rest of the day.

The afternoon sky has become blue and hot while we've been inside the cool of the castle. The soaring temperatures will have tempted many visitors in Pembrokeshire to the beaches, leaving Picton's extensive acres quiet. The castle's rear wall is covered in scaffolding. Beneath her leaking Welsh slates, dressed stone walls and peeling windows, Picton is just about keeping up appearances. In the sunshine swallows swoop down on gnats hovering above the lawn. They can't believe their good fortune in finding such generous accommodation. The castle walls glow pink, like an unsteady old actress applying too much blusher.

Much like the castle, the landscape of Picton is a tapestry of garden styles, each owing a little to different centuries. The gardens are of national significance and recognised by the Royal Horticultural Society. A map of the Picton Estate drawn in 1746 details exquisite Baroque gardens in the front of the castle, but changing fashion and the cost of maintenance saw them grubbed up.

Richard Fenton's account describes them in 1811:

'The gardens...of vast extent and luxuriously cropped, and the hot houses and hot walls occupy an immense space; nor is the conservatory ill-stocked. No desert can be better or amply furnished than that of Picton, which exhibits a profusion of the richest fruit of every kind the whole season round.'

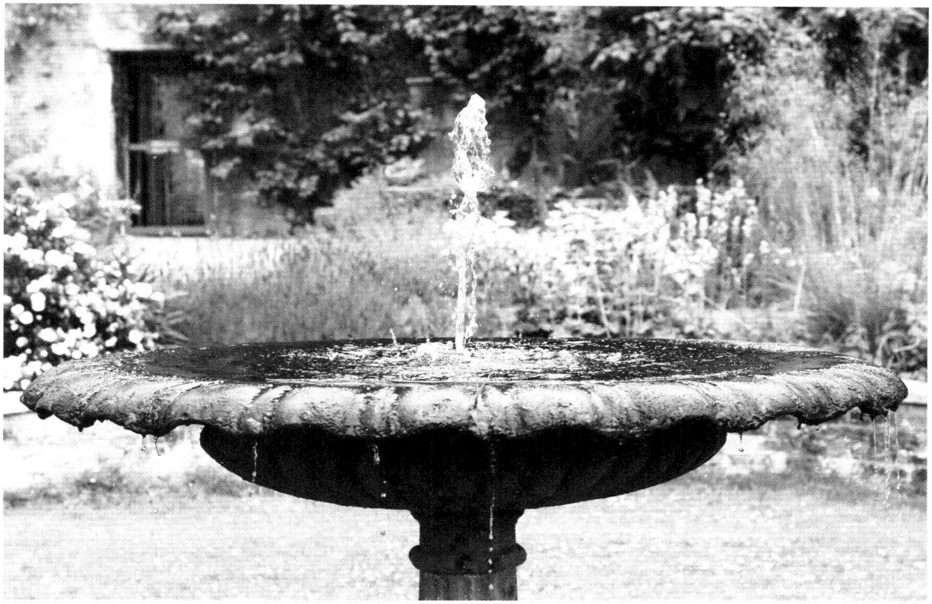

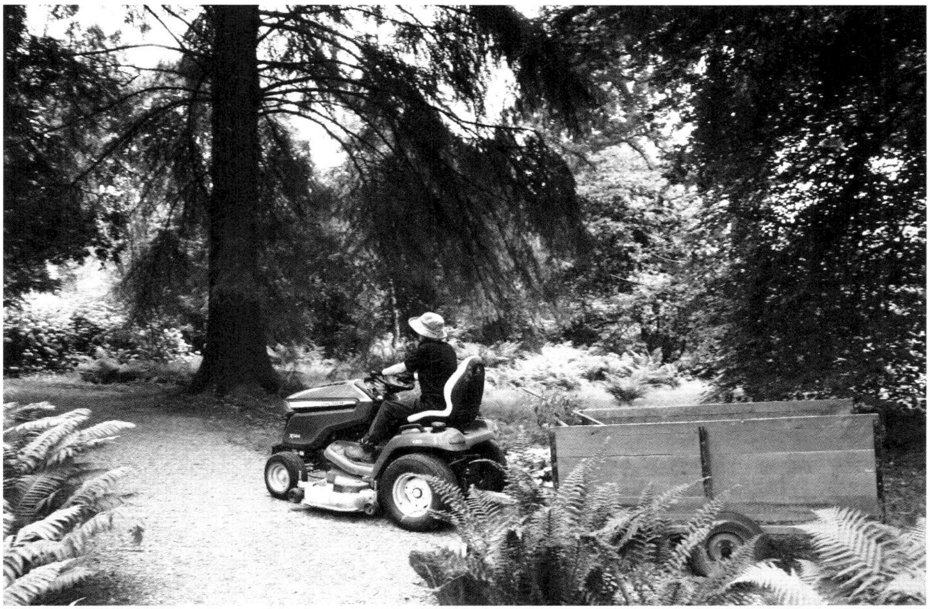

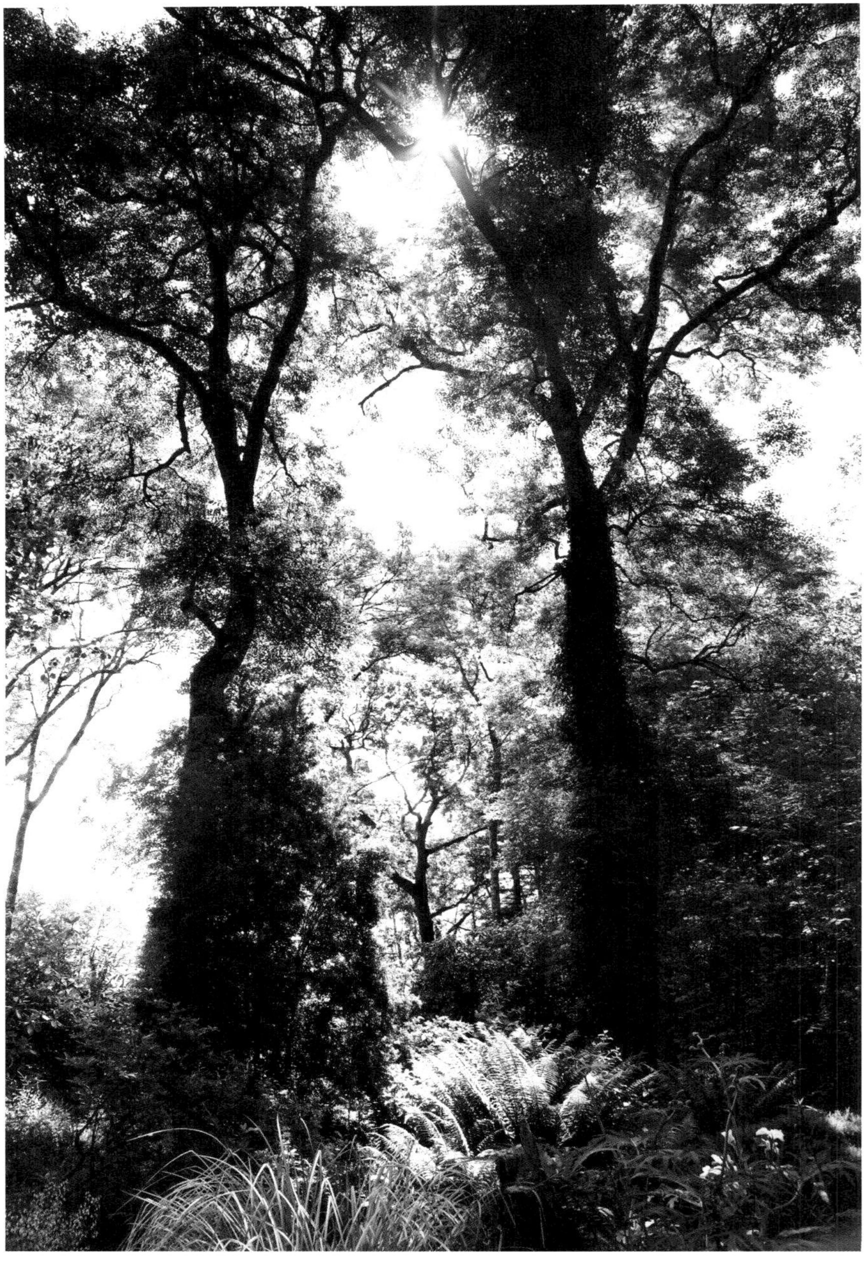

The present grounds were redeveloped and replanted from 1954 by Lady Marion Philipps and Hon. Hanning Philipps. They were indebted to their Victorian forebears, who loved laurels. Lady Marion relates that these were:

'so dull to look at – but at least provided the protection needed by more special and fascinating flowering shrubs.'

Picton's present owes all to its past – even its plants.

Hanning and Marion brought back specimens from all over the world to plant at Picton. Along with their Head Gardener, Leo Ekkes, they reshaped today's 40 acres into one of the most beautiful collections in Wales.

The woodland garden is almost empty of visitors, perhaps deterred from the dappled darkness of the tree canopy shielding the sunlight. Squirrels and ground-nesting birds complain noisily at my ambling intrusion into their territory. Deep within its forestry, the ice house, once the repository for that essential ingredient for impressive puddings, lies overgrown and fenced in to keep away the inquisitive from its precarious stones.

After the wilderness of the woodland, the order, shelter and warmth of the walled garden sweltering in full sun. The impressive gates and gateposts frame a horticultural treat, with fountain, pond and heaving borders worthy of a painting. Half a dozen visitors slow their walk to pause to hold a stem or stoop and smell a bloom before ambling past more shrubs, each step infused with changing scents. The fountain whispers water onto the stone beneath, the only sound to break the swallows' song. A listless dragonfly competes for attention with white lilies stretching open on the pond's flat surface.

The walled garden was constructed in the 1800s; it supplied the castle with food and flowers and kept a small army employed.

The garden's pink brick walls are crumbling and close to collapse. The ancient structure that breaks the Atlantic's wind, warms the air and changes the climate is fast wearying of Welsh winters. The wealth that once built this place is no more and now it is the kindness of strangers who it's hoped will fund its restoration.

One side of the walled garden was once home to the glasshouses, which would have incubated fruit, vines and tomatoes tricked into growing quickly on artificially warmed walls. In front of its ruined perimeter are the herb borders where Picton's medicinal and culinary herbs were nurtured.

Volunteers weed, plant and prune under the watchful eye of Head Gardener Roddy Milne. He has grand ambitions to see the glasshouses, walls and gardener's bothy restored. It will be a great sadness if Picton's story decays further, having survived so many centuries.

Here wormwood grows to strengthen digestion, sweet woodruff to heal the skin, Solomon's seal for strong bones, silverweed to heal cramp, vervain for depression, yellow flag taken for toothache, agrimony for diabetes and evening primrose to aid arthritis. All of them waving gently beside passing feet remind us of half-forgotten remedies from not so long ago. The volunteers add their signatures to

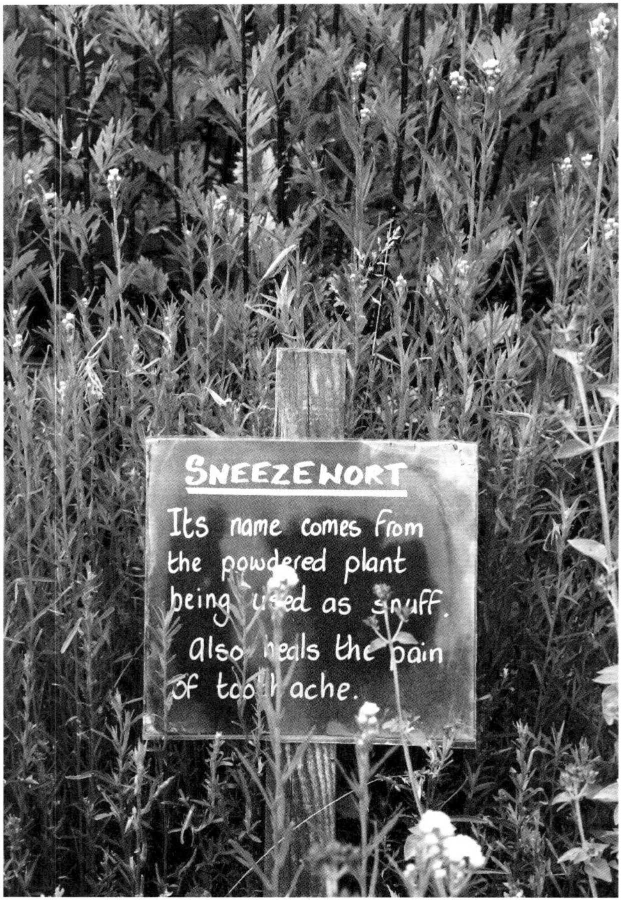
SNEEZEWORT
Its name comes from
the powdered plant
being used as snuff.
Also heals the pain
of toothache.

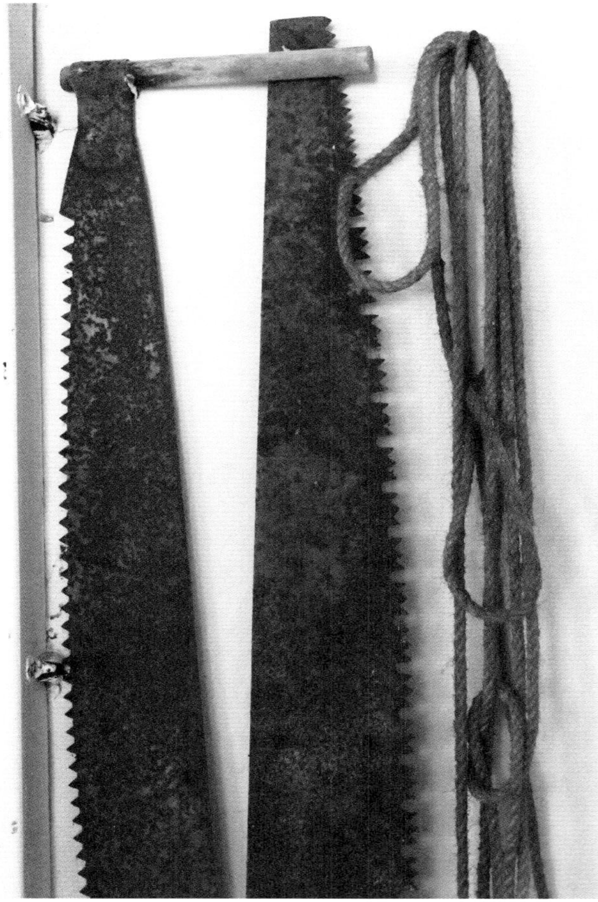

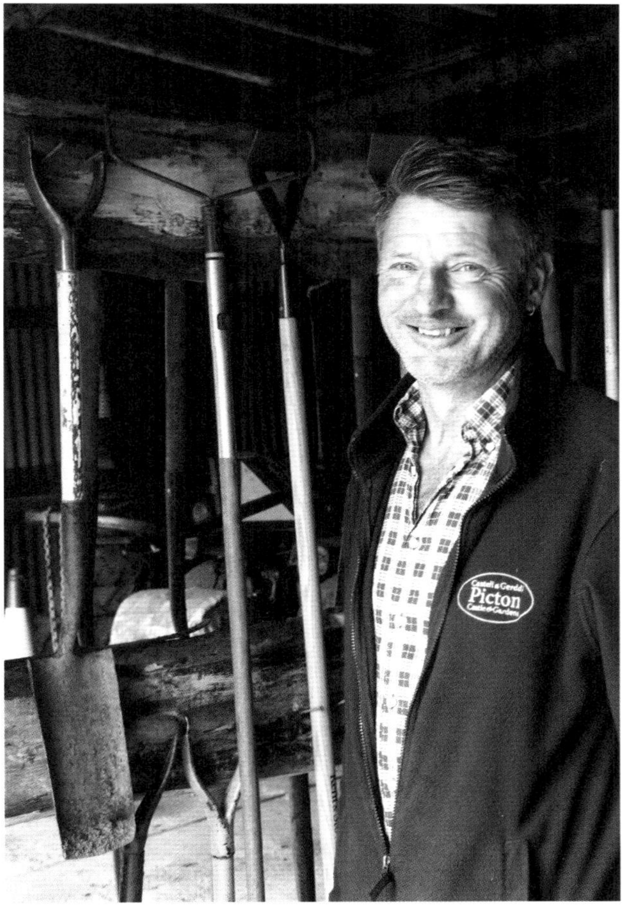

the story of one of Wales' most influential estates, and so it lives on.

This is a unique place. Not one of those tidied up heritage houses restored beyond honesty, but a home where you might still bump into the family that once lived here. I hope Picton retains the damp patches and a little of the rot in the window frames. Its struggle to keep going and putting on a brave face earns a deep affection and a better understanding of what it takes to keep a show like this on the road. I have fallen in love with its charming decline.

Volunteers weed, plant and prune under the watchful eye of Head Gardener Roddy Milne. He has grand ambitions to see the glasshouses, walls and gardener's bothy restored.

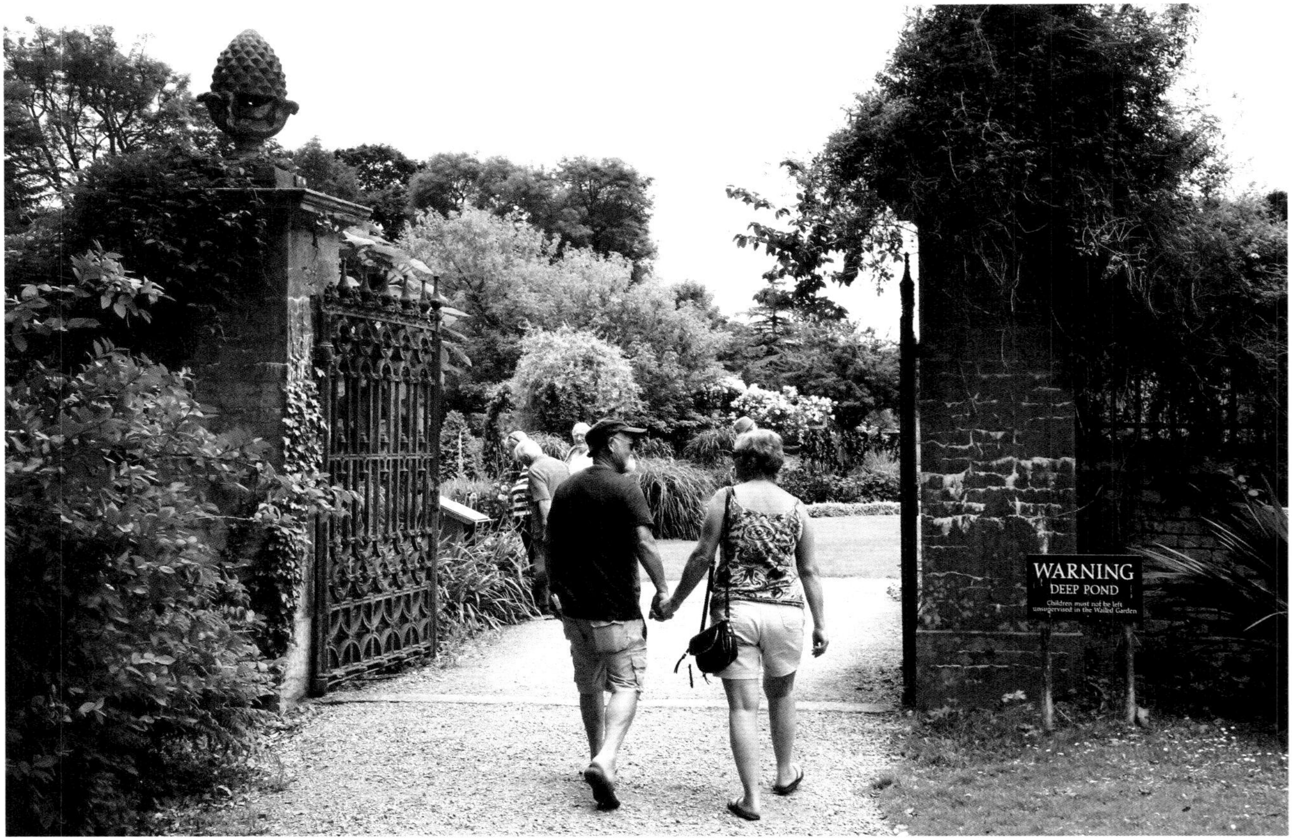
WARNING
DEEP POND
Children must not be left
unsupervised in the Walled Garden

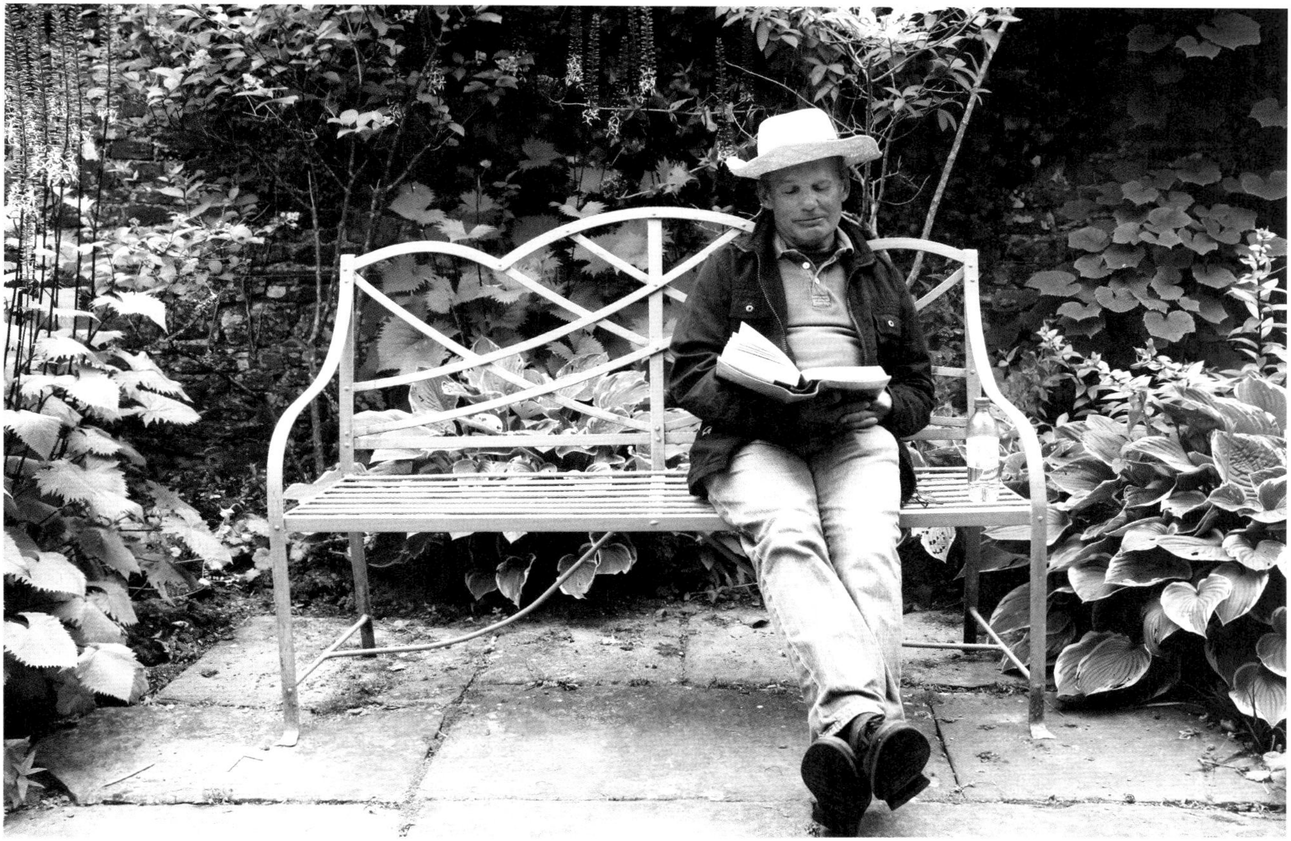

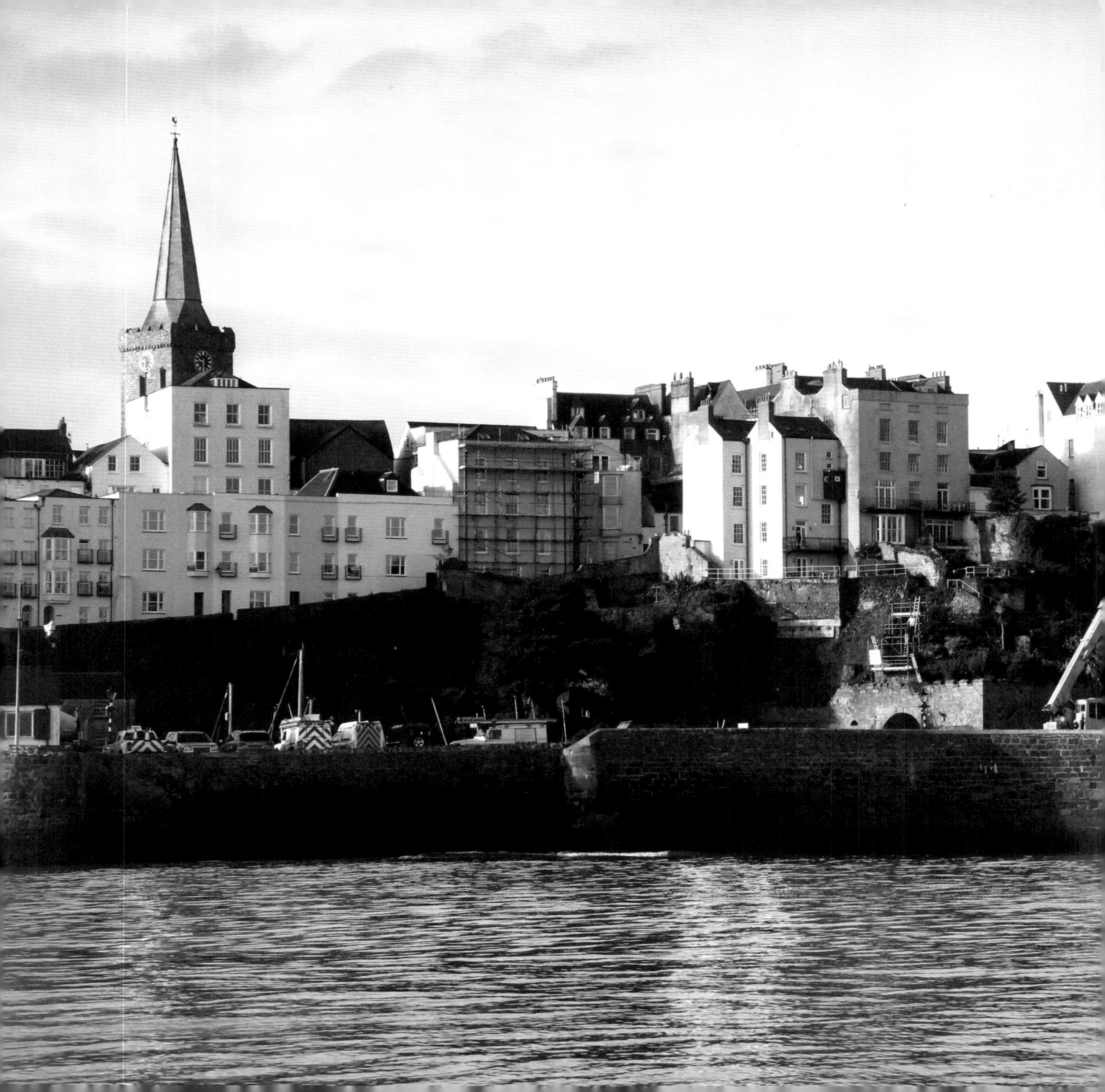

Tenby

High tide in the harbour

It's early in the morning in October and the town's beaches are almost empty. The summer's visitors who carpeted the sands have gone home to work and school and Pembrokeshire is settling down to autumn's quieter life.

Tenby yachts and fishing boats are rising slowly in unison with the incoming tide. Their mooring ropes are strung out from their bows like spaghetti tied to iron rings, rusting in the stones of the harbour wall.

Tenby is an enigma. So many of Britain's seaside resorts have fallen into decline, victims of a generation's love affair with the Costas and guaranteed sun. For decades the tourists came to take these waters, enjoy the fresh air and the saucy postcard connotations of a break by the sea. Then the cheap package holidays came. We stopped being an industrial, organised workforce and our inclination to patronise those familiar holiday resorts of childhood declined too. Many of us are now freelance and self-employed citizens of the world, more familiar with Barcelona than Bangor, more frequent visitors to Spain than Swansea. Fewer holidays, both parents working and the rise of the Internet have forced places like Tenby to change.

The Tenby of my childhood was a rather unsophisticated destination that depended on dry weather. If it rained, and it did often, you were reduced to walking the streets and lingering in cafés. You'll hear many stories of sour-faced landladies pushing out their customers into the drizzle. There was almost contempt for the punters; 'they had always come and so they always would' was the mindset. Then the cut-priced foreign holidays took off. Suddenly it was cool in school to brag about going to Spain and having a tan. If you were tanned from a holiday in Pembrokeshire in my school days, it was more likely from the wind than the sun.

Factory fortnight and its hordes of holidaying railway passengers flooding coastal towns disappeared with the closure of the mines. A regular, predictable tide of business slowly seeped away and the old certainties were over. Tenby, like many other resorts, had to reinvent itself. The customers who once booked into a hotel or a B&B and were content to toddle down the corridor to queue for the bathroom have gone; the tourists who now come on holiday expect their accommodation to be as comfortable as their home, with en-suite rooms and Wi-Fi. They are also unpredictable clients. They won't book their holidays months beforehand – they wait to see the week's weather forecast and then go online to check availability and find the best deal.

For Tenby, this new type of clientele has been the great challenge and opportunity of the last decade. The customer is king and has the world to choose from. Tenby and other resorts have had to rise to the test and, just as it has in the past, the town is benefiting from the uncertainty and inconvenience of foreign travel. The care-free days of quick check-ins at airports and hospitable welcomes in every country have disappeared, to be replaced with a more nervous world. Families with young children have to endure waiting times that take longer than flights, and fear of terrorism stalks the sunshine too. For the fading coastal attractions of Britain, their proximity, safety and familiarity have been their salvation. A new generation is discovering the simplicity of paddling in the rock-pools on a last minute long weekend. Tenby is on the up. The B&Bs are being refitted, the restaurants are upping their game, and a seafront hotel has been converted into retirement apartments.

Yet there is still confusion and disagreement as to how Tenby should sell itself. Is this the hen and stag night destination for a cheap, beer-fuelled blow out, or should the town appeal to families and pitch more up-market? Maybe, Janus-like, it can be many things to many people. For my money, I love Tenby out of season, quiet on a mid-week morning like today, when the sound of the gulls echoes around the amphitheatre of the harbour, the smell of wet sand stings your nostrils and fishermen and walkers wander past the boats.

Many of the boatmen that worked on dolphin spotting, sea safaris and fishing trips throughout the summer now revert to their winter schedule; cleaning, fixing and painting vessels, mending fishing nets and looking for another job to tide them through the season. The vessel *Caldey Island* makes its money taking summer trippers from Tenby to Caldey and back – a simple old-fashioned day out. Come autumn, this boat continues its service, making the short passage out of the harbour, passing the lifeboat stations, old and new, and into Carmarthen Bay towards the island, just off the Pembrokeshire coast. She'll carry the post and parcels, as well as passengers who live on the island or those who have business there.

The skipper, Alan Thomas, is a distinguished looking man, surely descended from the pirates who once roamed these waters; his white, close-cropped beard, small earring and weathered face speak of someone who lives outside every day of every year. He has sailed here since childhood and moves seamlessly from steering wheel to ropes, hopping on and off the boat from deck to harbour with the agility of a much younger man. Without raising his voice, he oversees the seemingly impossible task of lowering a vehicle onto his boat deck before a further cargo of waiting foot passengers. They are an eclectic gathering. The harbour's few walkers come to a standstill as a small crane smokes into action and wheezes loudly as it lifts one of Caldey's more cumbersome cargos. The Land Rover is to be

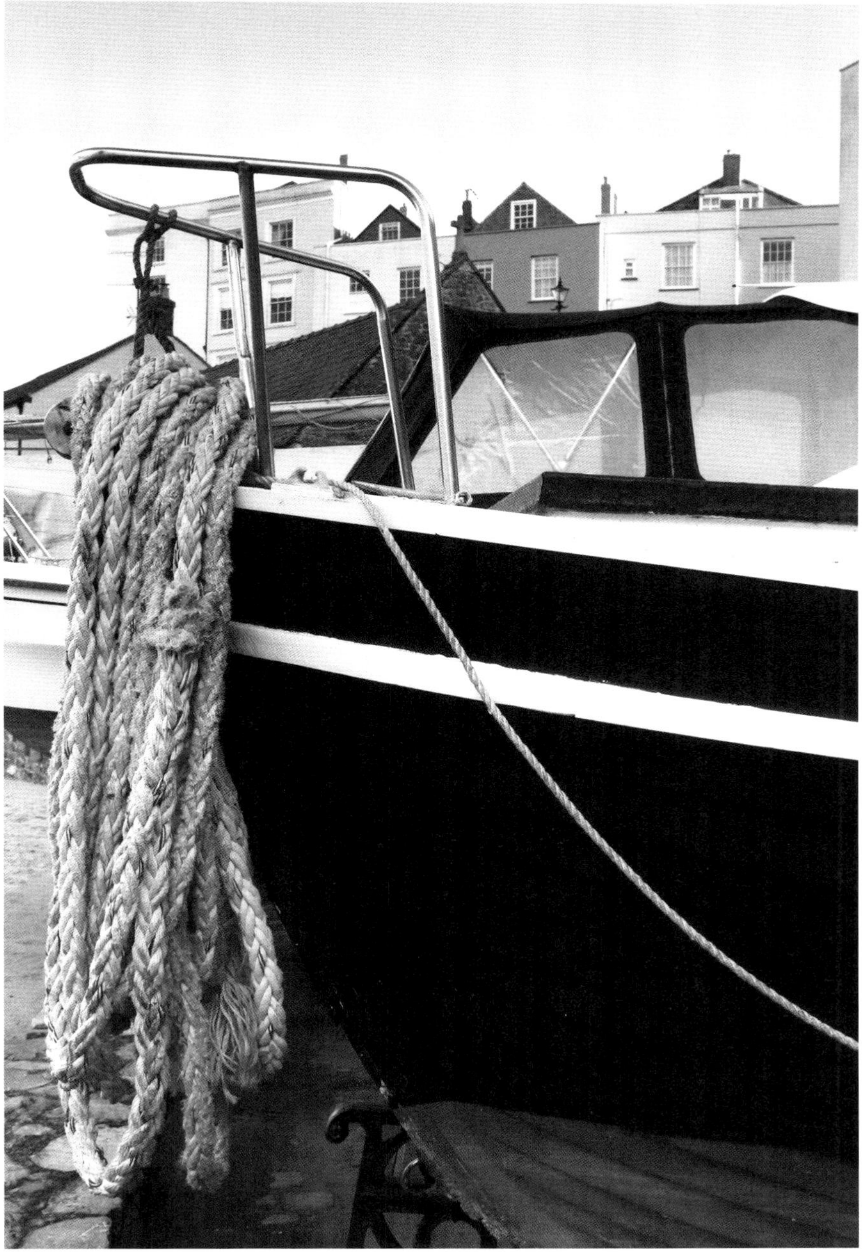

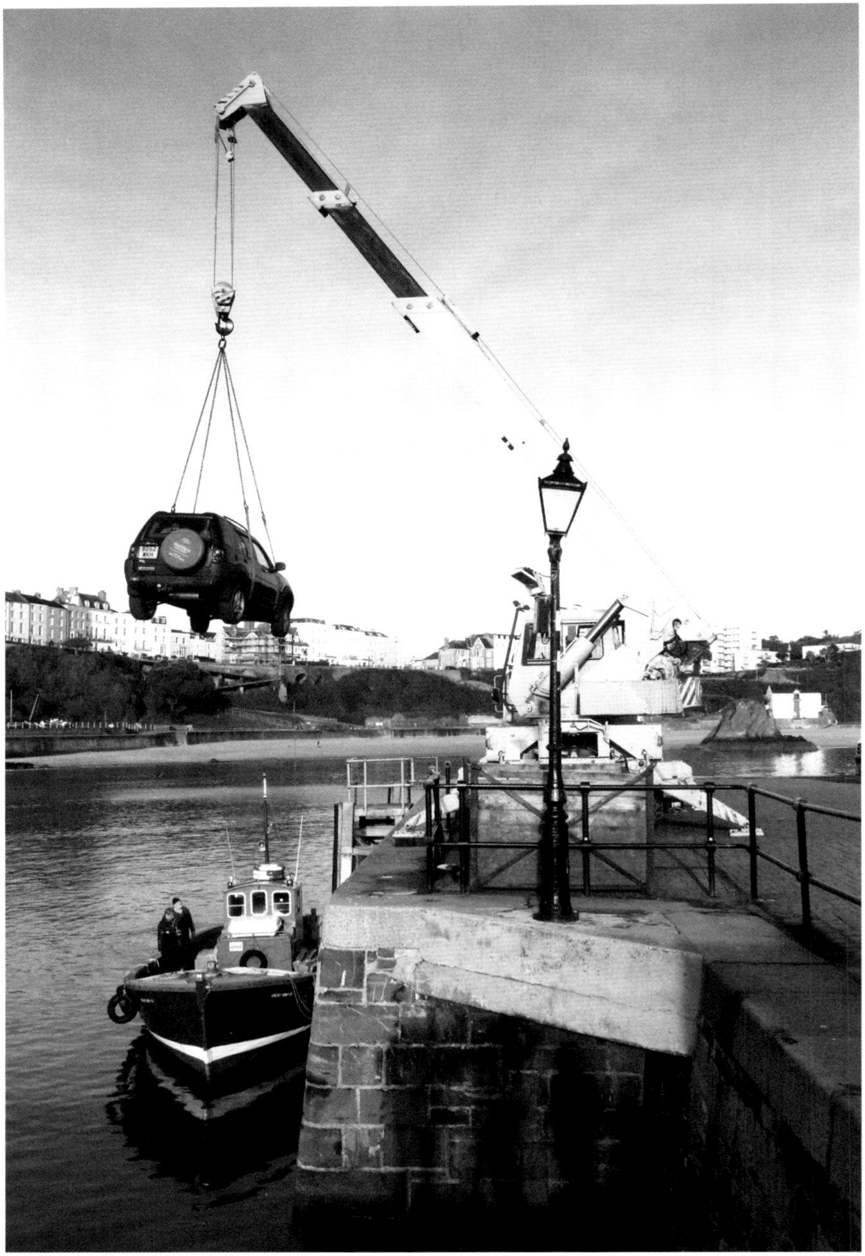

shipped to the island and its new home. The vessel isn't much wider than the vehicle and in a deft operation that sees all-comers stand and stare, Alan Thomas directs as the vehicle is lifted using chains and a cradle, then swung out over the water and gently lowered. Everything needed on Caldey Island, however difficult, has to be transported this way.

Among the passengers lining up on the quay are two beekeepers carrying a small bag containing a smoker, hive tool and bee brush. They are making their way to their single hive on the island. They say it's been a dismal summer and honey production was much greater in the warm spring. This will be one of their last visits to the island – they'll treat for Varroa and place mouse guards on the entrance to the hive, leave some food and hope a harsh winter doesn't kill off too many of their bees.

Beside them, three electrical engineers in their Western Power Distribution overalls are returning to Caldey to complete their work to replace ageing telegraph poles that carry the mains supply across the island. Caldey is unusual for the Pembrokeshire Islands – it has an underwater power cable from the mainland to supply its energy. They are joined by two workers from Pembrokeshire Council care department, who are travelling to Caldey to construct an orthopaedic bed for Father Senan, one of the elderly monks at Caldey Abbey. This is their first and most unusual house call of the day. The bed was delivered earlier in the week and they are here simply to assemble it. They'll return on the lunchtime boat. My plan is to walk to one of the oldest buildings on Caldey – St Illtyd's Church on the far side of the island, beyond the abbey that is used by today's monastic community.

The ropes are slipped and the inboard engine clears its throat, all safely aboard, the best seats on the vessel taken by the Land Rover. The passengers lean against the wheelhouse or the stern as the boat moves dead slow, away from the wet stone steps of the harbour wall. The incoming tide will raise the anchored fishing boats and yachts for another two hours, hide most of the sand on the beach, then slip gently away again, leaving the shore dry and the boats sitting on their keels. Tenby's fine square houses shine in the morning's autumn sun. At high tide there can be few finer places to stand and stare than this ancient port.

By road and rail, it seems to take forever to get to the western-most corners of Wales. But in the great age of ocean travel it was perfectly placed for the Atlantic and the Irish Sea. Tenby was a shelter in the storms and a natural place to settle for traders.

Tenby was the town where my grandparents did their weekly shop. In a time before having your groceries delivered after clicking online, they spent Saturdays driving around the town, calling into each shop – a 50-year unchanging ritual, often with me sitting in the back of the Morris Minor in my shorts and Start-rite shoes. There were no supermarkets then, so the odyssey, with both of them in their best clothes, would begin parked on yellow lines above the harbour to pop into WHSmith to pay the paper bill and collect *The Shooting Times* and *Woman's Weekly*. Then, my long-suffering grandfather, waiting outside in the car and overheating in his three-piece tweed suit, would be motioned on by my grandmother, wearing a huge hat and a white Gannex raincoat made popular by Prime Minister Harold Wilson, to drive 10 yards to the fruit and veg shop.

'Mrs Jenkins. How are you, what can I get you?' was the constant refrain from each shopkeeper. Gran had known most of them for decades, yet they remained on formal terms. In Pembrokeshire, this was still the age of deference; the informality of the 1960s had yet to arrive. Next it was the Star General Store in the square. Gran would take in her eggs to sell to the shop and emerge with whatever goods she needed. My grandfather, close to expiring, would be told to double park outside, until her signal came to help with carrying her laden wicker baskets – there were no plastic bags.

The butcher's premises were on the narrowest of streets and our call there would bring the town to a halt for ten minutes. After impatient hooting from motorists queuing behind us, I would be handed the week's meat, which would include a parcel of bones for the corgi. This entire expedition would end with our departure through the Five Arches gateway – holding my breath as we squeezed through the tight passage, emerging into the daylight like victorious gladiators. Double yellow lines, one way systems and multi-storey car parks were an anathema to my grandparents. They reasoned that they were simply innovations meant for the visitors.

Tenby wasn't always a peaceful place given over to shopping and pleasure. The town was fought over with the Normans in the 12th century and this Norman-controlled 'Little England beyond Wales' saw Tenby thrive as an important harbour.

The cycle of war and peace continued, with Tenby being attacked and sacked by the Welsh army of Maredudd ap Gruffydd and Rhys ap Gruffydd in 1153 and 1187, and again by Llywelyn ap Gruffudd in 1260. This final onslaught prompted William de Valence, 1st Earl of Pembroke to build the town's outer walls in the late 13th century. Fear of a second Spanish Armada in the 16th century saw the Five Arches built. Sitting in the back of my grandparents' car, I always feared my grandfather would misjudge the Five Arches and demolish a historic landmark that had survived centuries of conflict.

My grandparents' Tenby had become a tourist destination. They could just remember commercial ships in the harbour, but their lifetime saw the trade vessels quickly disappear. Traders who had come from Bristol and Ireland, France, Spain and Portugal with cargos of wool, skins, canvas, coal and oil were a fading memory. The Portuguese crew that delivered the first oranges in Wales was all part of a long era of international trade that would come to an end. Tenby's new story would be the pursuit of pleasure and its dominant commodity would be tourism. But that long memory of international commerce runs deep.

From the harbour, Tenby looks like a wealthy, well-heeled town perhaps having more in common with Mediterranean communities than other Welsh settlements, but its prosperity has been historically cyclical and transient. In the English Civil War the town backed the wrong side, declaring its support for the Royalists, and only a few years later an outbreak

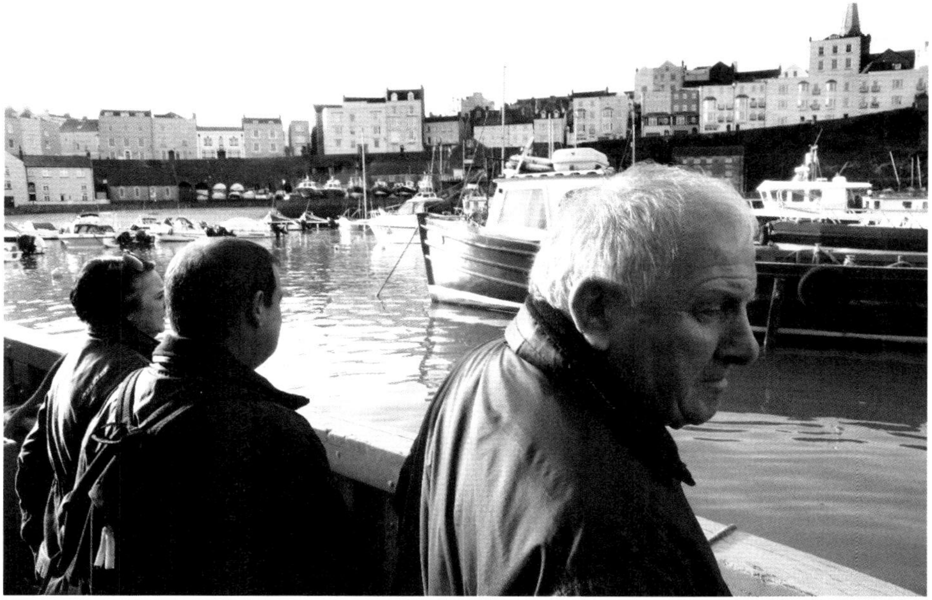

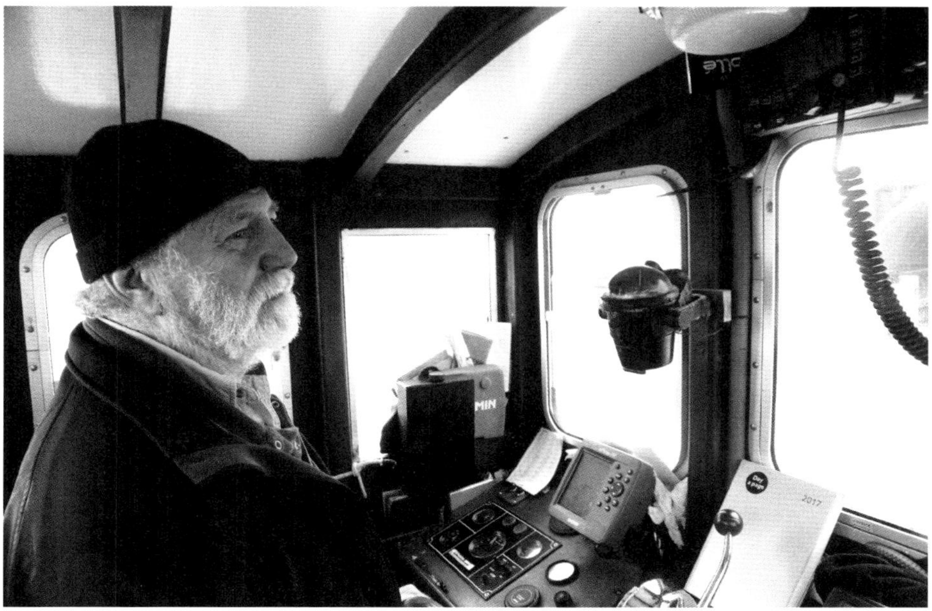
MIN

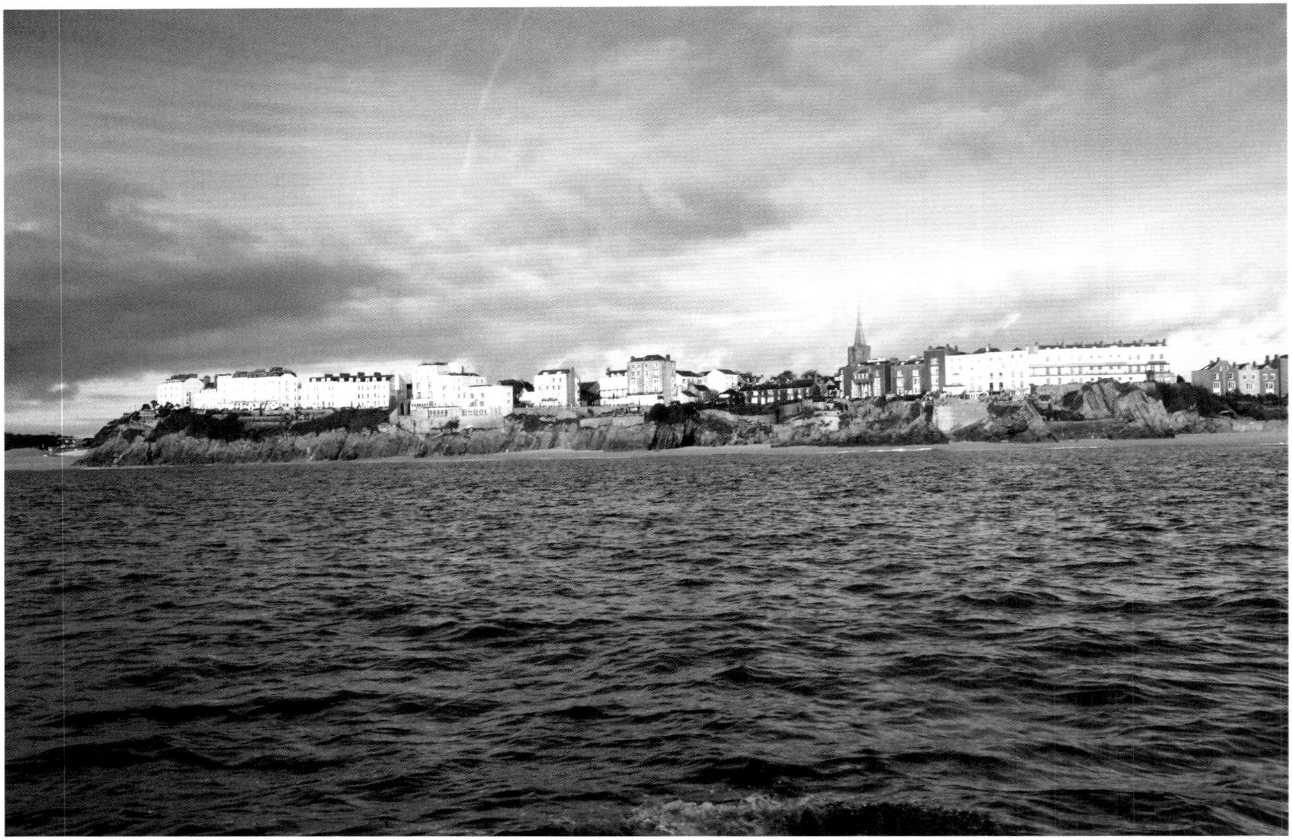

of plague killed half the beleaguered population. The town fell into decline and ruin. At the end of the 18th century, John Wesley visited and wrote:

'Two thirds of the old town is in ruins or has entirely vanished. Pigs roam among the abandoned houses and Tenby presents a dismal spectacle.'

It was to be another war that delivered Tenby from terminal decline. Napoleon's European domination put paid to the British aristocracy's Grand Tours to the war-torn continent. So instead, the rich spent their money closer to home. The entrepreneur and MP Sir William Paxton saw an opportunity in the market and Tenby's ebbing fortunes were reversed with his considerable investment. The town became an attractive destination to enjoy the waters. Salt water sea bathing became all the rage and Paxton created a 'fashionable bathing establishment suitable for the highest society'. Even after the Battle of Trafalgar reopened Europe for holidays once more, Tenby's place in the affections of wealthy travellers was assured.

Morning sunshine has brought out dozens of walkers, wandering the beaches and harbour walls. The timeless attraction of simply watching the waves is more enticing than ever. Who needs an excuse to sit and watch a harbour at work and the tide washing a weary world? Idle meandering shouldn't be underestimated in Tenby – it has a long track record

Tenby was also home to the Welsh artist Gwen John.

of producing worthwhile endeavours.

The man who gave the world the equals sign was born here. Robert Recorde was a physician and mathematician born in Tenby in 1510. He rose to become the doctor of King Edward VI. Became Controller of the Royal Mint and Comptroller of Mines and Monies in Ireland, but ended his days a broken man, sued for defamation and dying in debt.

Tenby was also home to the Welsh artist Gwen John. Overshadowed during her life by her brother Augustus, her reputation bloomed after her days. Following her mother's premature death in 1884, the family moved to Tenby. She and her brother often went to the beach to sketch the constantly changing clouds and sea. She wrote:

'I would often make rapid drawings of beached gulls, shells and fish on stray pieces of paper'.

Augustus was born in Tenby in 1878 and became one of the leading lights in Post-Impressionist art, lauded for his figure drawings and later for a new technique of sketching with oil. He was mentioned in the same breath as Gaugin and Matisse and his portraits captured an instantaneous attitude in his sitters. The Tenby seascape may have even sharpened his genius – in the summer of 1897, Augustus suffered a serious head injury when he dived into the sea and hit his head on concealed rocks. Rather than ruining his talent, his injury and long recovery is said to have galvanised his art.

Our voyage begins at walking speed towards Caldey Island. A lone yacht is making gentle progress on the horizon and a power boat speeds past us, creating an enormous bow wave for our boat to cut through. Past the two lifeboat stations now – Castle Hill, high on its rock, St Catherine's Island, St Mary's Church spire and North Beach disappear, and then the broad sweep of South Beach comes into view, its big houses and hotels peering from the cliff top. Above the throb of the engine, the distant boom of the army training range sounds a few miles beyond Giltar Point.

Anna is going to visit her parents on Caldey. She grew up on the island, but these days she runs her own business in Tenby. Her parents, Blackie and Suzanne, have lived on Caldey for all of Anne's life. The school she attended on the island has long since closed. She says:

'On Caldey you have to have something to do. Dad is the farmer, the refuse collector and the boat hand. Mum helps in the perfume shop and anywhere else that needs an extra pair of hands. It's in the nature of island life – everyone has to muck in to make it all work.'

Our boat's maritime chart shows unseen memorials to Tenby's violent past. Bowman's Point is on the mainland behind us, Man of War Roads is the stretch of water to the side of Caldey, and on the island itself, Jones Bay is named after John Paul Jones, the founder of the American Navy.

Tenby gets smaller in our wake and the island before us grows larger with each chugging minute of our journey. On Caldey's distant jetty a handful of passengers are lined up waiting for our boat. A few of them will go shopping in Tenby and a couple of overnight guests, perhaps clergy who have been staying in the monastic guesthouse, are waiting to return home.

The sea is almost flat. The gentle swell of the waves calms as we approach the lee of the island and Priory Bay. We will disembark on the jetty wall at high tide to save using the island's amphibious vehicle. At low tide, it transports passengers a few metres out to sea to transfer to the waiting boat anchored in deeper water. A low tide boat-to-boat transfer at sea using the amphibious vehicle is an altogether more precarious operation.

Anna's father, Blackie, is waiting to meet his daughter. Big-bearded and sweatered, the island's boatman stands on the concrete for the boat to almost kiss the jetty before catching the ropes and tying the vessel bow and stern and helping to unload the passengers and goods. A blast of the engine in neutral and the ignition is killed, a momentary silence, before Caldey's jetty crane roars into life, accompanied by a black cloud of diesel smoke and stink. The Land Rover starts to be lifted from the deck like a toy and placed on the concrete, ready for its new life offshore.

Our fellow passengers, so intimate for a short time, leaning or sitting beside each other, now walk quickly up the slope away from the dangling vehicle and towards the road to the village and their different tasks. The beekeepers are thankful that the warming day will find their bees in kinder mood after yesterday's enforced incarceration in driving rain. The council's bed builders check the departure time of the next boat before walking to the monastery.

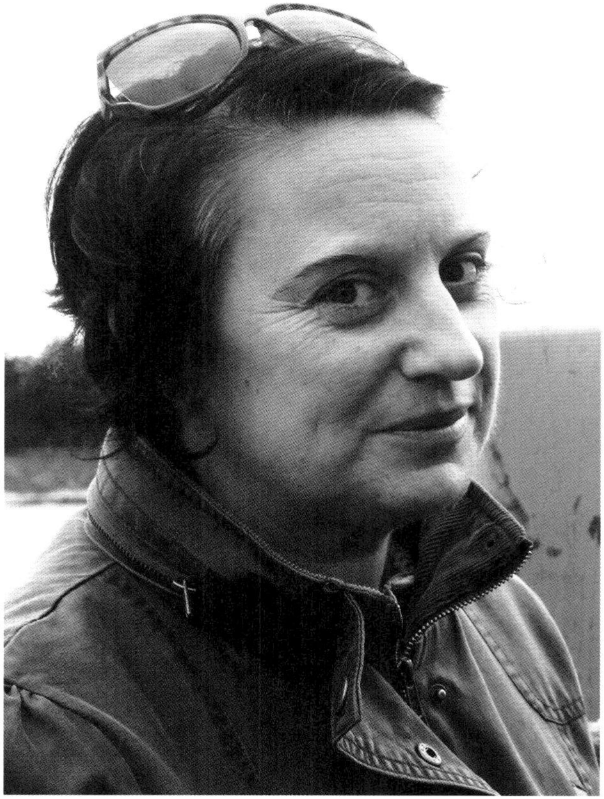

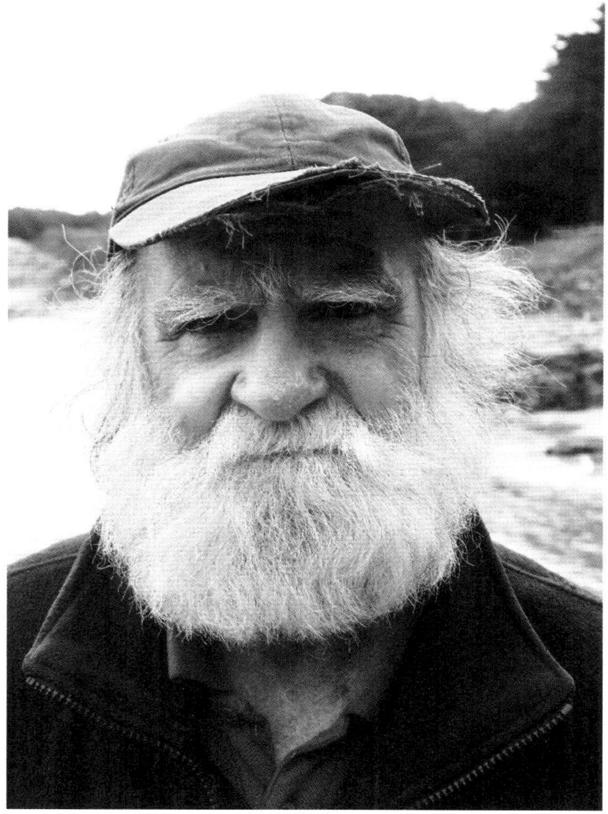

Anna Bolton and her father Blackie

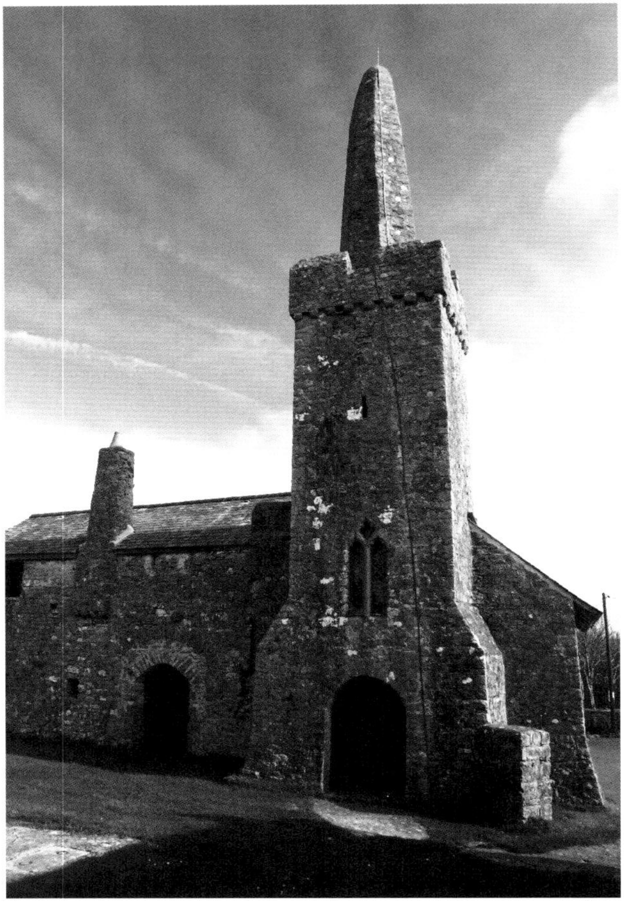

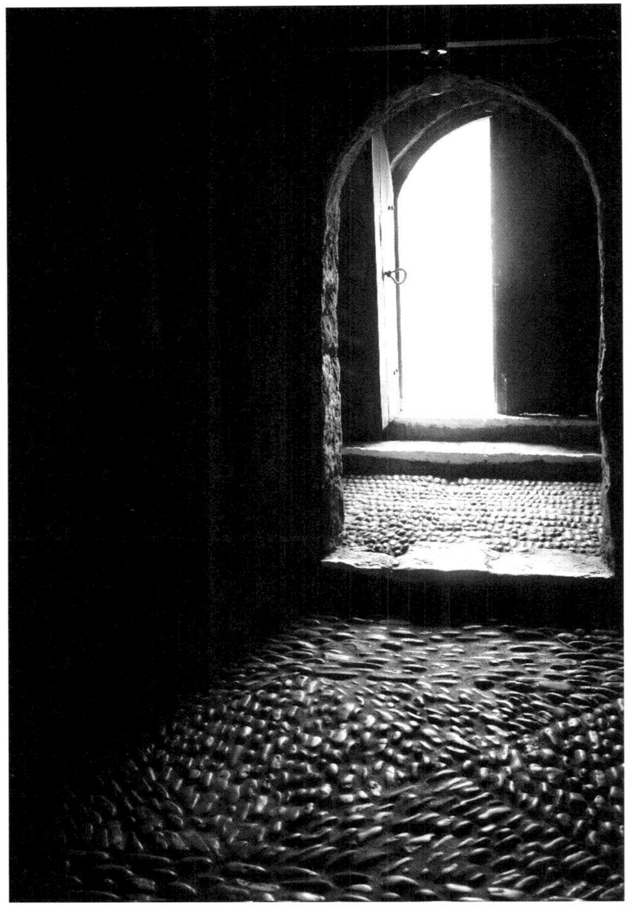

The electrical engineers lift their tools off the boat and, like the bees, they are no doubt grateful not to be battling the weather conditions.

The vessel collects its new passengers and their luggage and as quickly as it arrived the engine is fired up, ropes are slipped astern and the boat moves away from the jetty, riding higher in the water this time, rid of its heavy load. The jetty echoes for a moment to the thrum of the engine as it pushes its way back through the waves, becoming small on the water as its sonorous notes are lost in the island's birdsong.

Past the sugar sand of Priory Bay now, there are no footprints yet on its small length of beach. The village square, hiding beneath the abbey, is edged by low white buildings. There are a few cottages to rent, the café is closed up for winter and the gift shop is dark now until the spring. The Post Office is open just for an hour to sort the arriving mail and parcels. The wide square lawn, covered by picnics and sunbathers all summer, is revived from yesterday's rain, its green stripes given one last cut before winter.

There was once a substantial farm on Caldey, but the challenges of small farms are exacerbated tenfold on an island. Moving livestock on and off boats is not for the faint-hearted. Finding people to work in farming is difficult enough on the mainland, but here it is almost impossible, the result being that Caldey's pastures are rented out for sheep and pony grazing.

Monks first came to Caldey in the 6th century, but Vikings may have brought this first monastic community to an end by the 10th century. Benedictines from St Dogmaels in north Pembrokeshire established a priory on the island in the 12th century and remained here until the Dissolution of the Monasteries in 1536. Their medieval priory is still standing. In more recent times, Anglican Benedictines bought Caldey in 1906 and built the current abbey. Their stay was short and troubled by financial problems and they sold up in 1925. Today's monks are Cistercians, originally from Belgium, but reasserting a long tradition of the Order in Wales.

I walk past the current monastic buildings and the cottages on the road to the lighthouse to explore the old Priory and St Illtyd's Church with its leaning tower. These are among the oldest buildings on Caldey. Their stone walls were quarried from the island. The Prior's Tower is thought to have been built as a fortified house. The monks' original vaulted stone chapel now forms the sanctuary of the larger church, with the spire built in the 14th century. The Priory is thought to occupy the site of the original Celtic monastery. The Caldey Stone standing near the altar at St Illtyd's was excavated in the grounds. Little is known of the history of this church and the monks who lived and worked here, but sitting in the brown wooden pews that line the pebble stone floor with the sun shining through the narrow windows, the quiet spirituality of the place is overwhelming.

A single votive candle burns to the side of the altar. Prayer cards scribbled by the faithful are left behind: 'Bring peace to this troubled world', 'Help Mum through her operation', 'Make me happy', 'Please bring my baby safely into this world'. The silence of the old priory ruins is broken only by

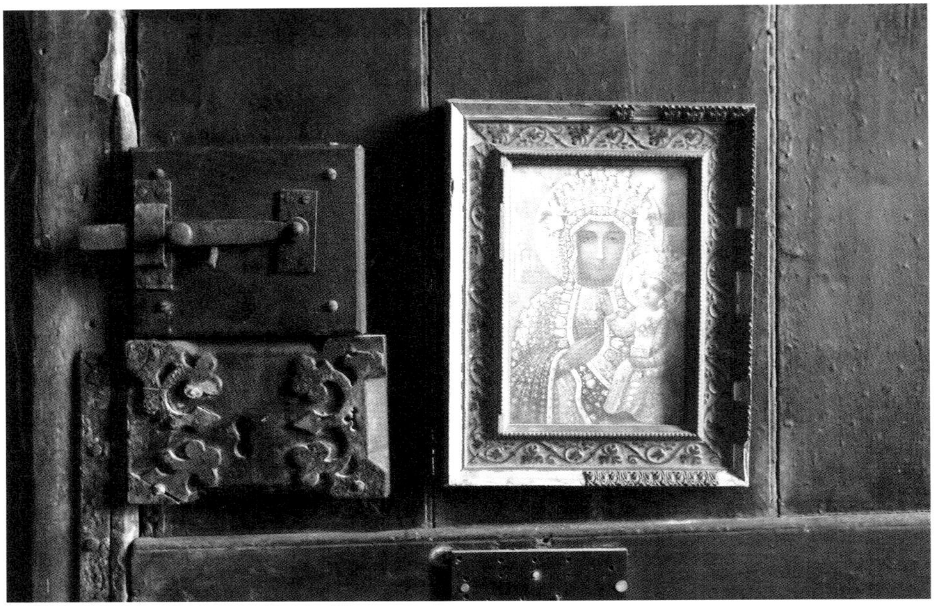

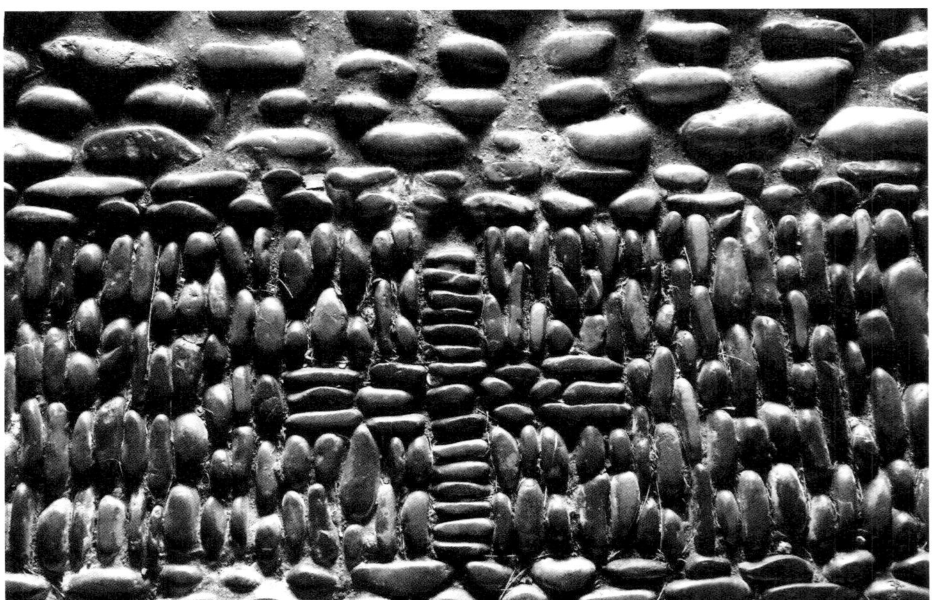

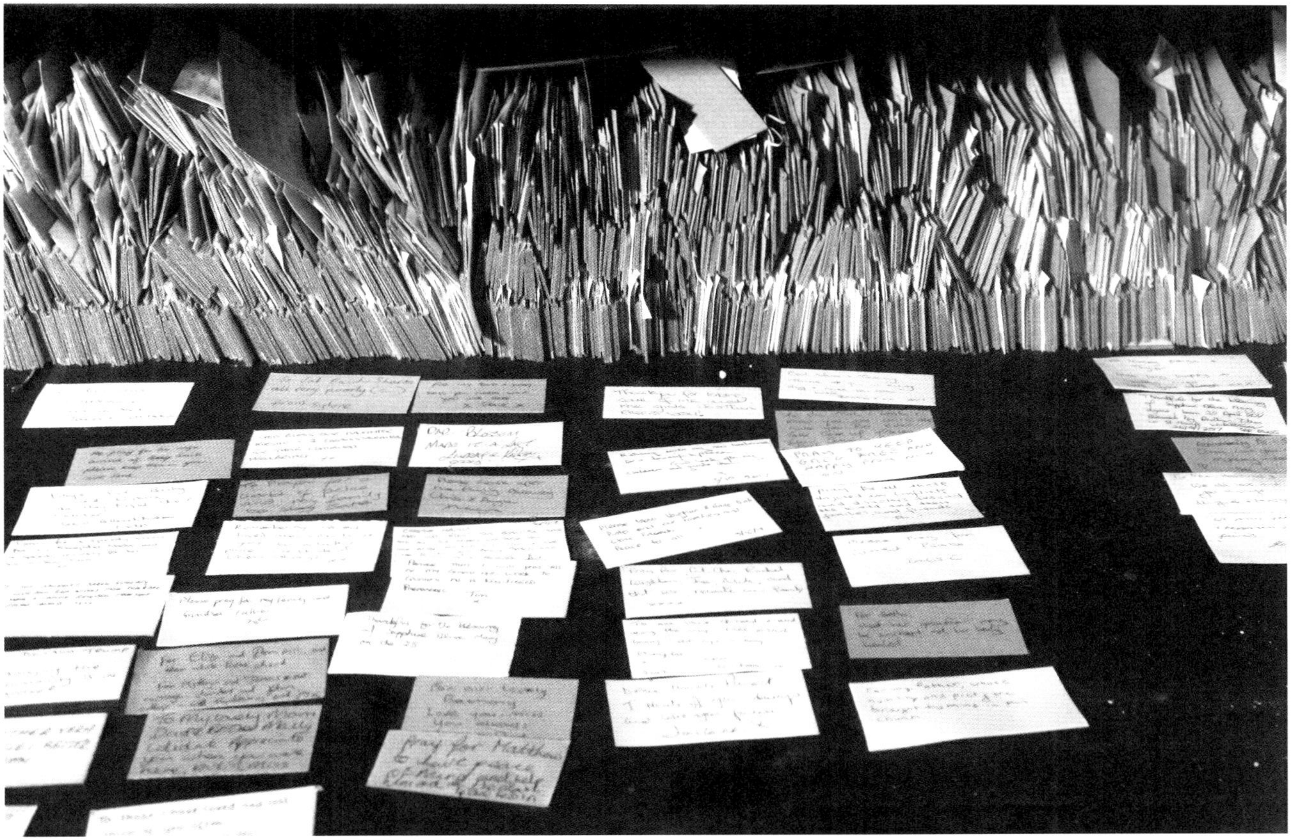

the metronomic clangs of the electrical engineers nearby, hammering the fittings into place on their new telegraph poles. For a moment the monastery bell clangs in the distance, calling the monks to the abbey church. The two sounds ring as one chorus – the call to prayer and the clangs of work.

Our day is done and, like the monastic hours, the tide timetable is demanding of our return. Already the jetty is busy with a handful of passengers returning to Tenby. They all arrive early, knowing this is the last service of the day and perhaps, if the weather is poor, the last of the week. The engineers are assembled, their telegraph poles renewed. The council bed builders have finished their task at the monastery, the bee keepers' jobs are complete and Anna has spent the day with her parents. A trailer full of sheep bound for the mainland waits quietly, unaware yet that their voyage begins with their undignified crane hoist towards heaven before being placed on the deck.

The boat draws near and the visitors clamber aboard. Evening creeps over the island and the monastery bell rings for Vespers.

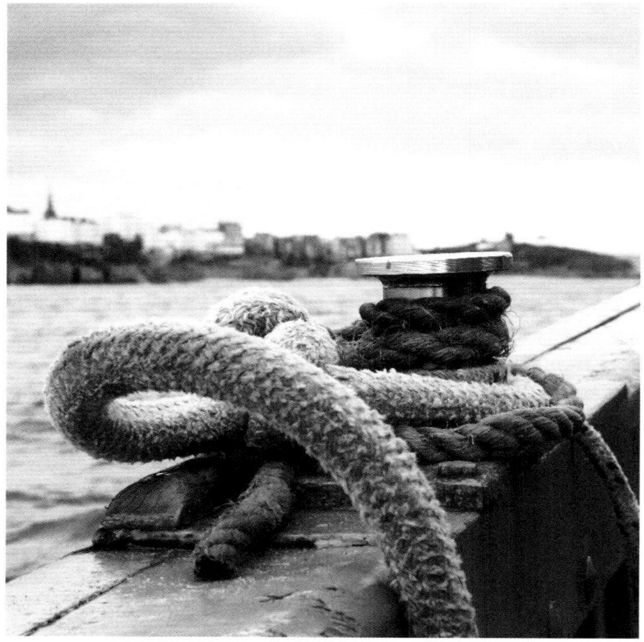

Our day is done and, like the monastic hours, the tide timetable is demanding of our return.

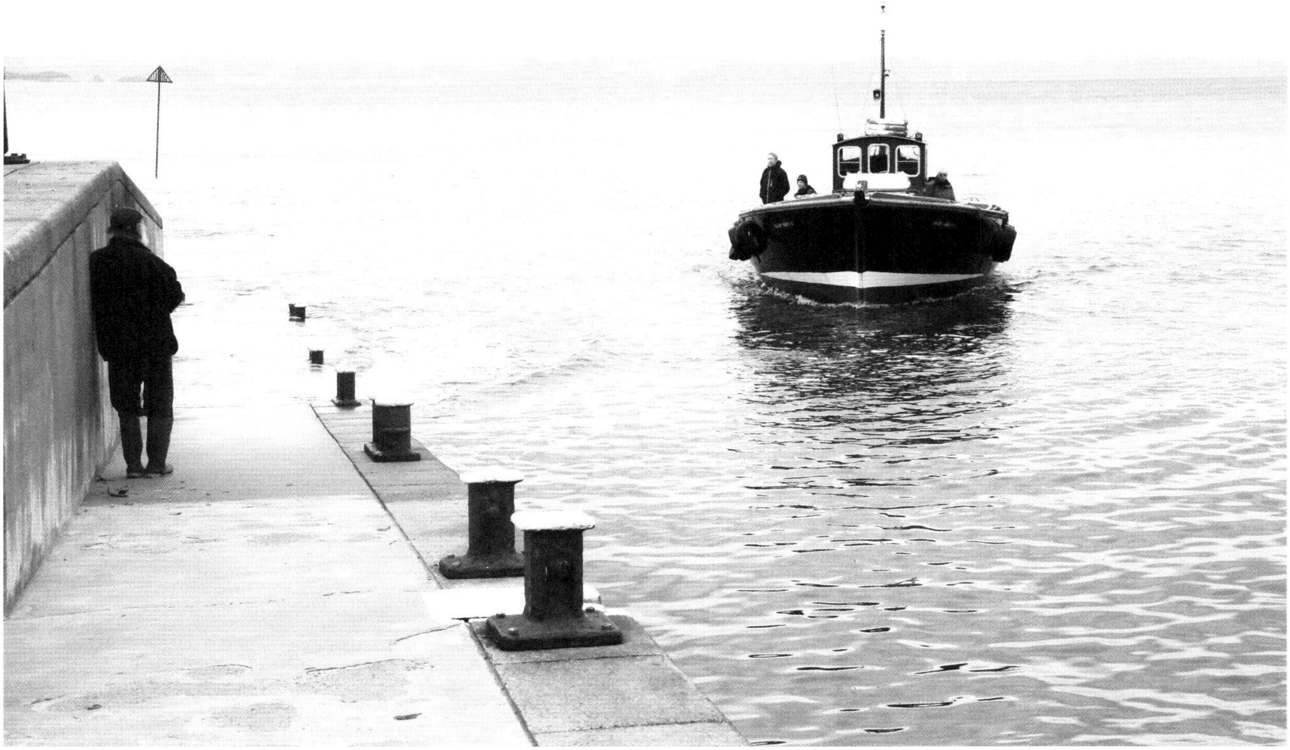

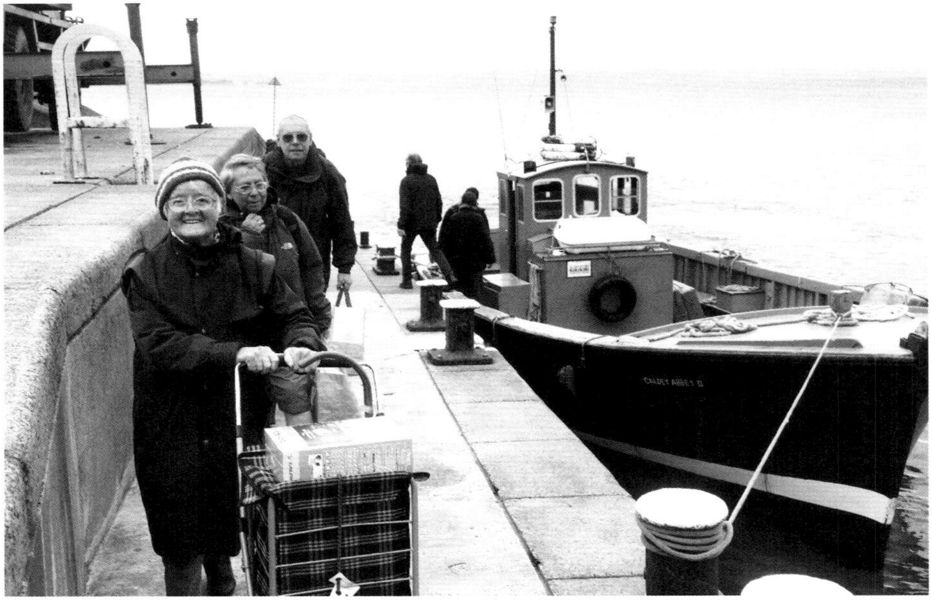
CALDEY ABBEY II

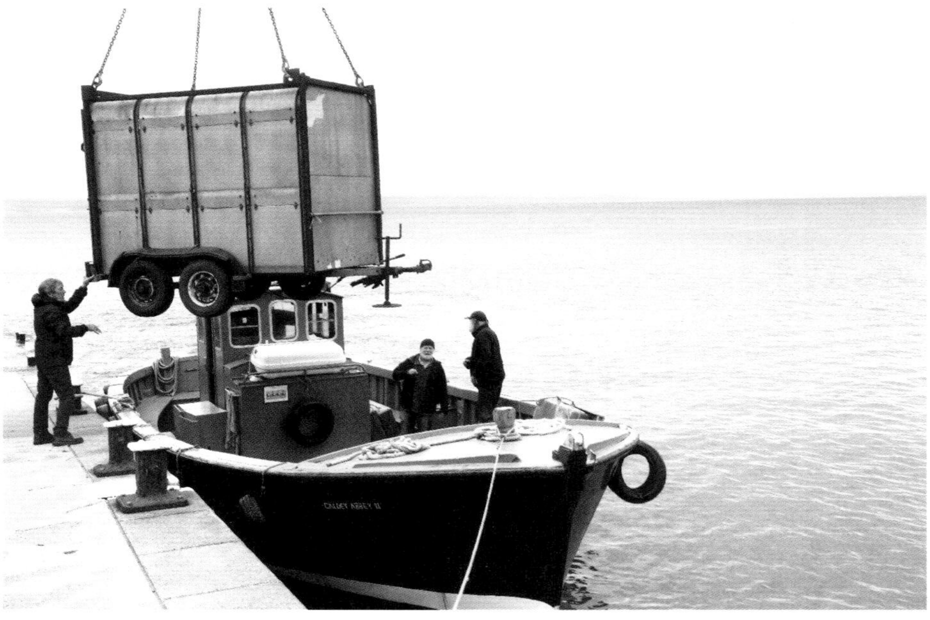
CALDEY ABBEY II

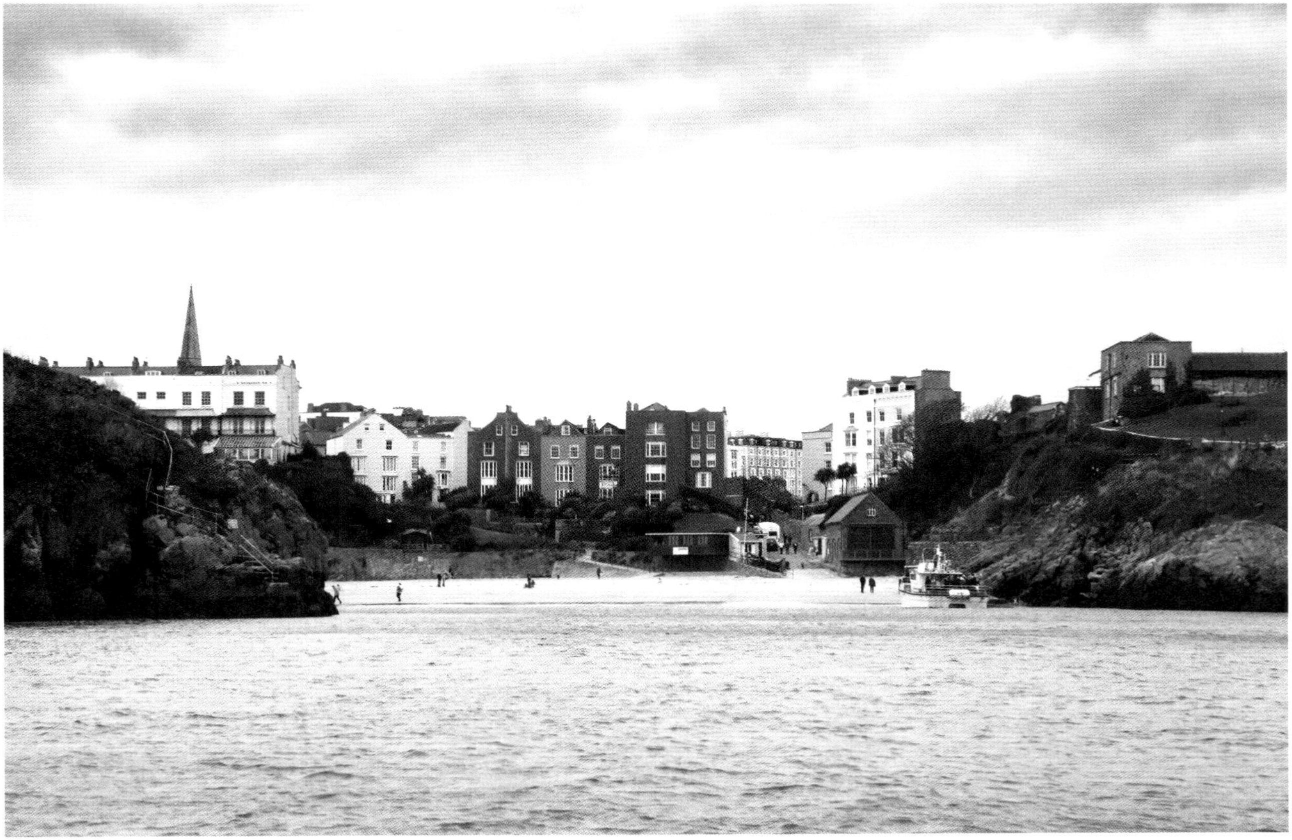

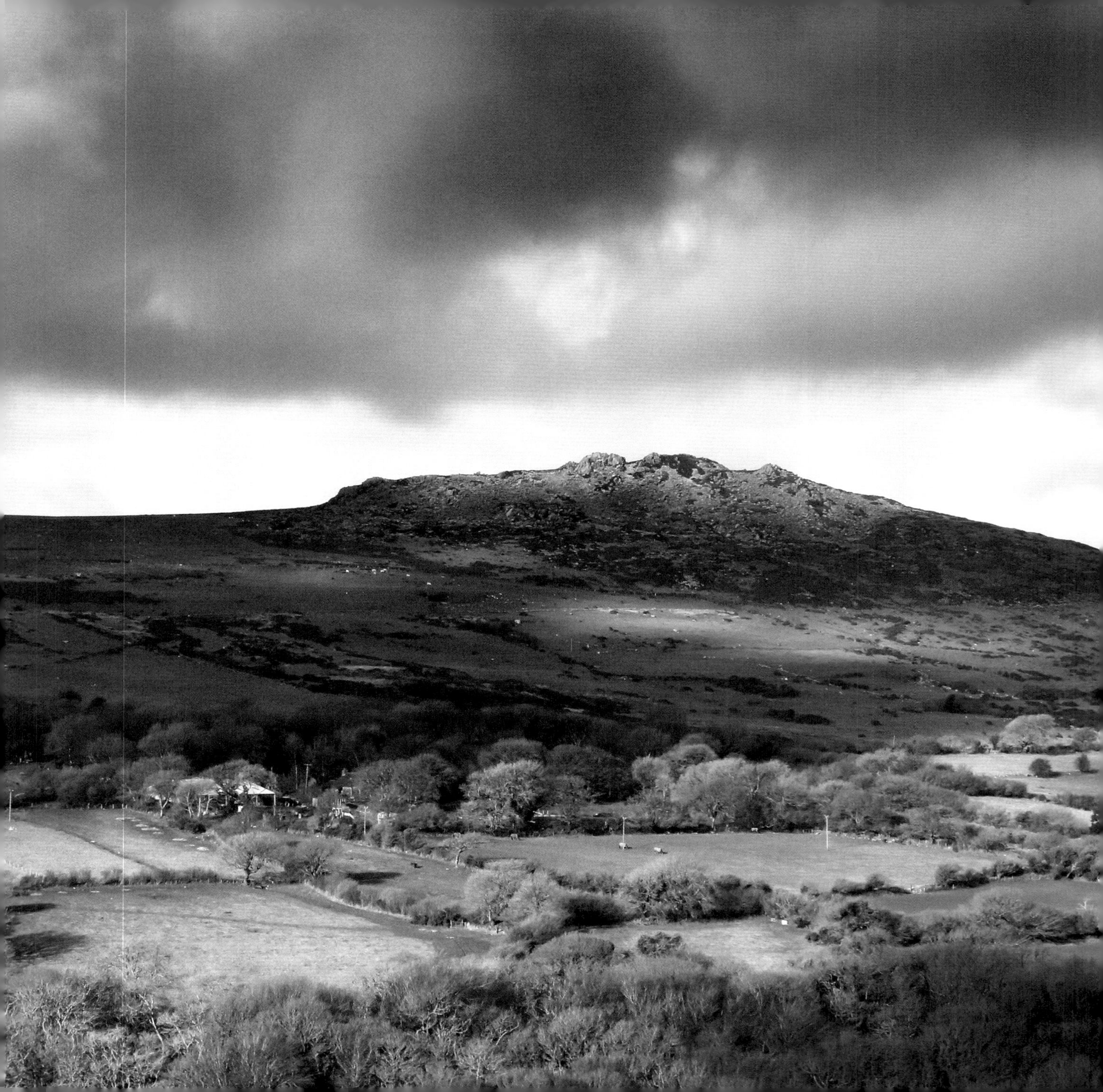

Preseli Hills

A long walk on a winter's day

The lane to Gernos Fach is half stream, half gravel and opening the farm gate entails a hop, skip and a jump between stones to keep your feet dry. November has clothed the highest mountain tops in the Preseli Hills in a light blanket of white. Below the snow line, the fields and roads are running with days of rain. It's a slow drive along the winding mile to the farmhouse, past the standing stone at Tafarn-y-Bwlch. From here you can look in any direction and see no sign of the 21st century: no pylons, no wind turbines, in fact, after a hundred yards, no sign of any road. This is north Pembrokeshire in the raw – pretty much unchanged for a hundred years. This rural idyll is a world away from the manicured villages and beautifully restored cottages of the Cotswolds. The poverty of upland farming and the unforgiving climate has, for the most part, deterred the improvers and the developers. What remains here are the isolated smallholdings whose occupants have made a Faustian pact to keep faith with a farming tradition that is essentially uneconomic, in return for living on the high altar of Pembrokeshire amidst some of the most glorious surroundings in Britain.

My affection for this part of the county began in childhood. We were a family whose roots were very much in the south of the county; we came to north Pembrokeshire for a treat. The Preseli Hills was a day out – a drive in Dad's Marina or Mum's Allegro. We came here for childhood picnics, three children from the town let loose to run in the mountains. We would spread the old tartan rug on damp grass and eat hard-boiled eggs, sandwiches and Welsh cakes, while our grandparents sat on deck chairs in their Sunday best. We would run up the hills, dispatched to look for shreds of sheep's wool left snagged on barbed wire. It was a clever ruse to exhaust three exhausting children.

My grandfather taught me to drive in the Preseli Hills. His lovely old Morris Minor took us up lanes to abandoned farms and forgotten fields and places we'd never seen before. We would spend hours lost in what felt like another country. When the sun baked the black roof, Grandpa would nod off beside me and leave me in charge. Even without his full attention the Morris' lethargic progress never countenanced the possibility of an accident. So for me, the Preseli

Hills offer a rich bank of treasured memories – it is a temple to a happy childhood and the simplicity of an uncomplicated life. This is also where I live now, the part of Pembrokeshire that I call home; that warming, settling, calming word 'home' that means the world to everyone, wherever you live. I have made my future in my past.

Gernos Fach cultivates old cars, vans and tractors in its front garden. Once-bright bodywork is slowly gathering lichen and moss, becoming part of the landscape with each passing season. You never know when something mechanical might come in handy again, so you keep it. When you have some land, very little is ever thrown away, it's just put to one side, just in case. This is not the usual prettified chocolate box notion of a country farmhouse, but a working business that has little time for aesthetics. It's cold up here, even in summer. Pleasant gardens and patios are the stuff of suburbia. Outside is for work, inside is for rest.

The squat house, rebuilt in 1887, hides behind what is thought to be the ancient original farmhouse and now the low, thick-walled stone cowshed. The adjacent house boasts a new porch to keep out the worst of the gales that race up from the lowlands. There are new hardwood windows to blunt the wind, a new roof and a wet room to wash off after farming. But essentially, this two-storey slate and stone home, hunched against the storms, is much as it was when it was built more than a century ago. The hall's flag floor and tongue-and-groove wooden walls lead to the snug, where beside the Rayburn sits the wooden skew – a Welsh high-backed settle offering the best seat in the house – and a comfortable armchair. The Rayburn rhythmically wheezes out its gentle warmth and a faint whiff of heating oil.

Lynne and Gwyndaf Rees are brothers. Gwyndaf came here as a little boy, along with his parents and his brother, John. Lynne was born at Gernos Fach. Their father, a blacksmith from Eglwyswrw, had served in France in the Second World War. He moved to the Preseli Hills with his wife in search of better health in the mountain air. The couple paid £800 for the property. The farm was also home to 100 sheep and a herd of dairy cows. The land amounted to some 50 acres. Mr and Mrs Rees milked their 15 cows by hand, taking the milk down the rough track in a churn balanced on the pedal of a push-bike to meet the milk tanker on the main road. As their fortunes improved, a neighbour from Crymych sold them a horse and cart.

The boys went to Preseli School, seven miles away. Their usual journey, in an age before heavy traffic or health and safety, would be hitching a lift in a neighbour's car. Seven or eight children would squash into one vehicle and be delivered to the school bus route. In the harsh winter of 1963 they lost nearly a term of lessons to the heavy snow. There are few hedges in the Preseli Hills and in the conditions it was impossible to distinguish between white field and white road, so the boys stayed at home.

The Rees family bought the adjacent farm in 1963 for £6000. They couldn't get a bank loan to buy another small farm with such unpromising land, so a private arrangement was made. Long before the dominance of the big banks, peer-to-peer lending was well-established here. They milked cows until 1976,

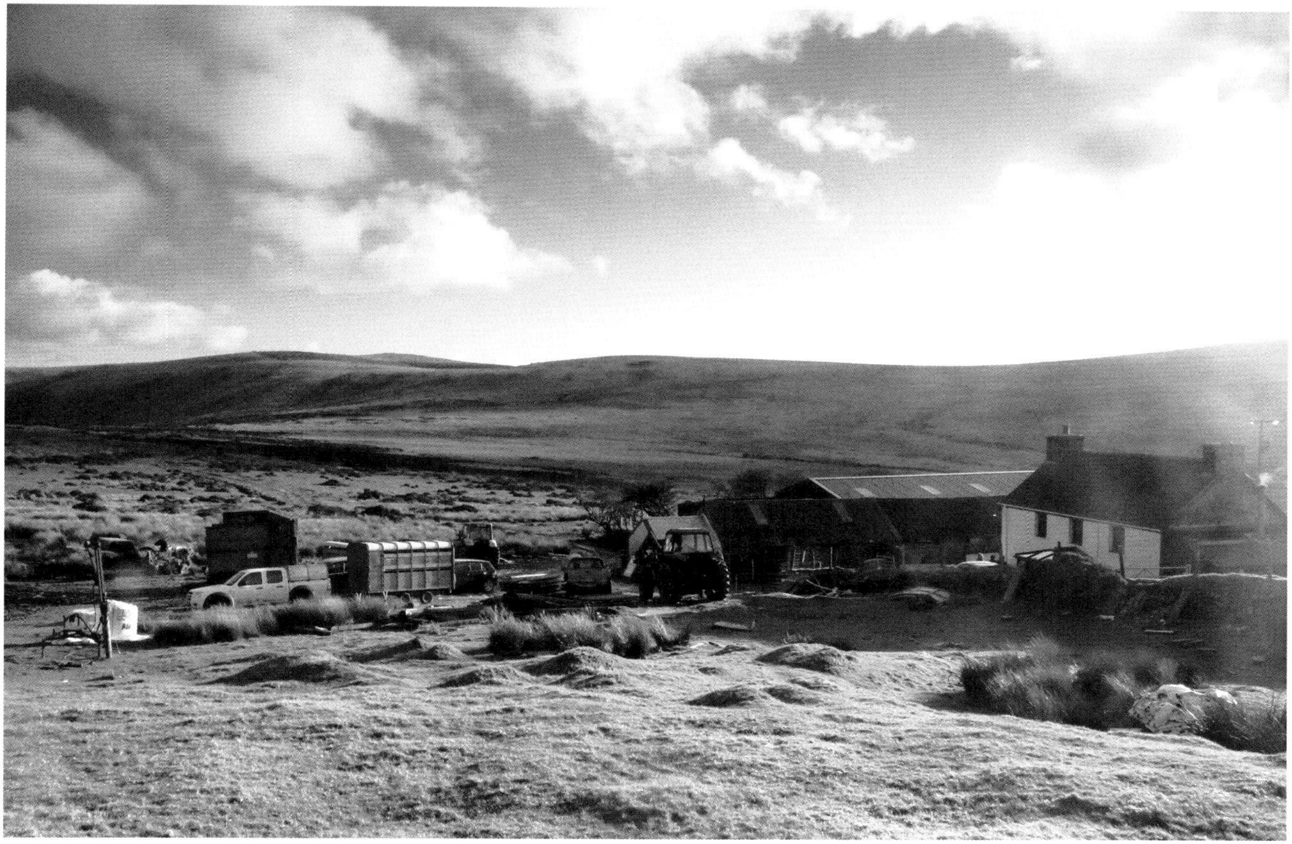

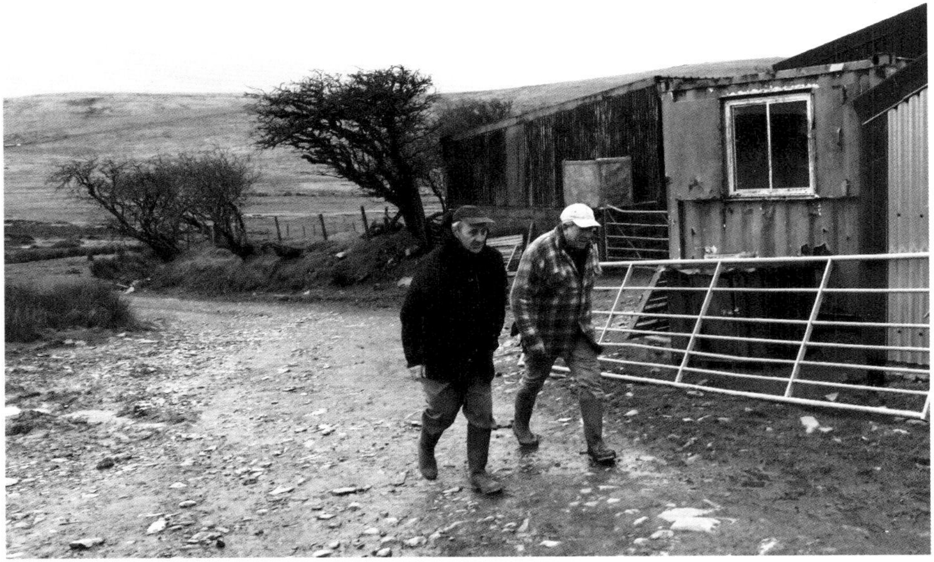

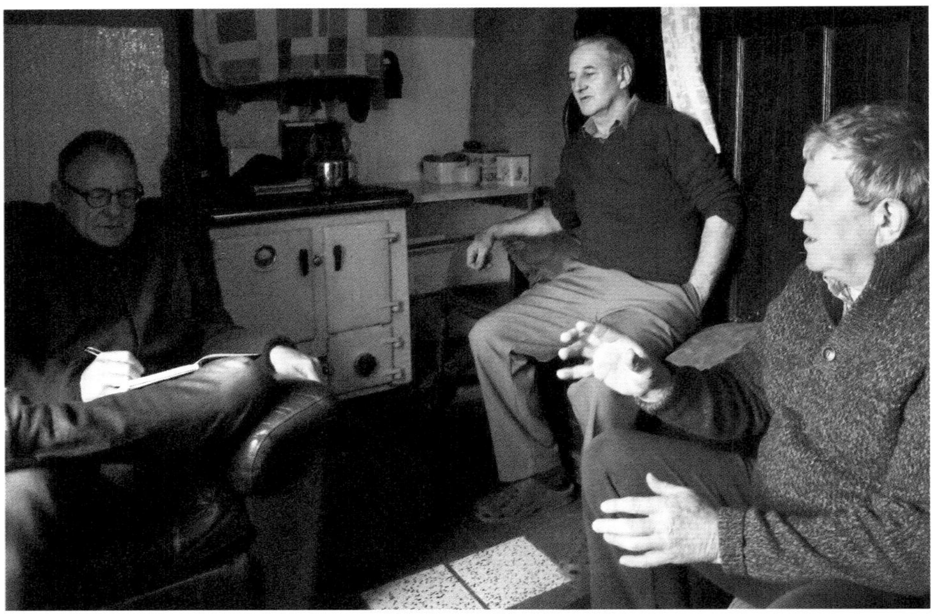

 Jamie Owen with Lynne and Gwyndaf Rees of Gernos Fach

when the market rejected small operations filling a few churns in favour of mass-producers. These days the farm runs to a hundred acres, with some 500 Welsh mountain ewes and 30 Charolais cattle to fatten up for market. The home fields close to the house, tamed from the bracken of the mountain, provide grazing and a watchful eye over the worst of winter.

If farming on this mountainside sounds challenging, the harsh upland conditions are supplemented with the use of lowland winter grazing at Castlemartin, in the south of the county. So when the weather conditions are just too difficult here the sheep are transported to kinder pastures over winter. Gernos Fach is a thousand feet above sea level and winter begins three weeks earlier than on the land kneeling below, while spring arrives later. If eking out a living here now seems hard, the brothers recount how their mother raised three boys on this farm a generation ago. They tell me she cooked on an open range nestled in the chimney where we drink our tea; she dug culm – coal dust – mixing it with water she drew from the well in the farmyard. She didn't drive. The boys agree that their mother was tougher than their father. Their father would come into the house for a break and a cup of tea, his lunch or dinner perhaps, but the boys couldn't ever recall their mother taking a break. Life was difficult here for the farmer, but for the farmer's wife it was doubly so.

There was no mains electricity in those early days, electric power came later from a petrol generator, bought second hand from a farm near Morvil. In those days, the cheque from shearing the wool would fund a substantial down payment on a new tractor and the task of shearing the flock would take a month. Now the wool cheque just about covers the cost of hiring the shearers and their work is completed in a few days. Times were different then – different expectations, different economics, different prices and a different world.

Mr Rees senior, the boys' father, liked to chat to walkers passing the farm. In isolation, curiosity grows. He would bring them back to the house and talk all day, delighted to meet like-minded worshippers of the place he called home.

The Preseli Hills are as land-locked as Pembrokeshire gets. Though you can see the coast in the distance from here, the walkers who visit do so to scale the mountains. Theirs is often a solitary countryside, with the mountains often overlooked by tourists in favour of the more popular Pembrokeshire Coast Path. We are drawn to the sea and leave the mountains behind us. Lynne loves going to Castlemartin to deliver or collect their flock of sheep and seeing the sea. When you live in the mountains, even among such breath-taking beauty, you can also crave another environment.

The Rees brothers are in their 60s. Who will take on the farm after their days? Their nephews tell a story of farming that is familiar across Wales: one of them is an animator who works for Aardman Animations in Bristol, the other a yacht master who skippers sailing voyages around the world. They came here to stay on their school holidays. Will they be seduced home by the hills and the peace? Perhaps they will return one day. Whatever Gernos Fach's future, its past is a landscape that is shaped by subsidy.

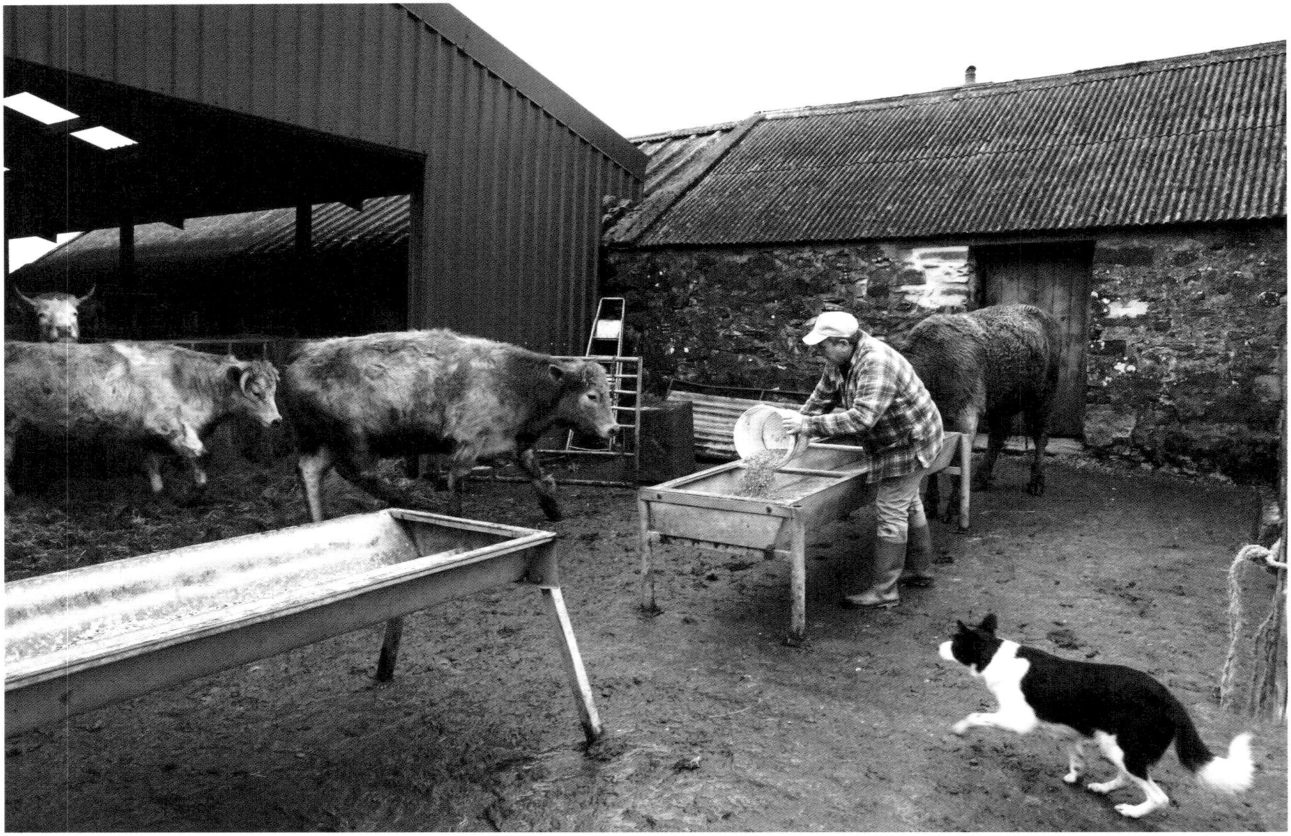

 Gernos Fach farm

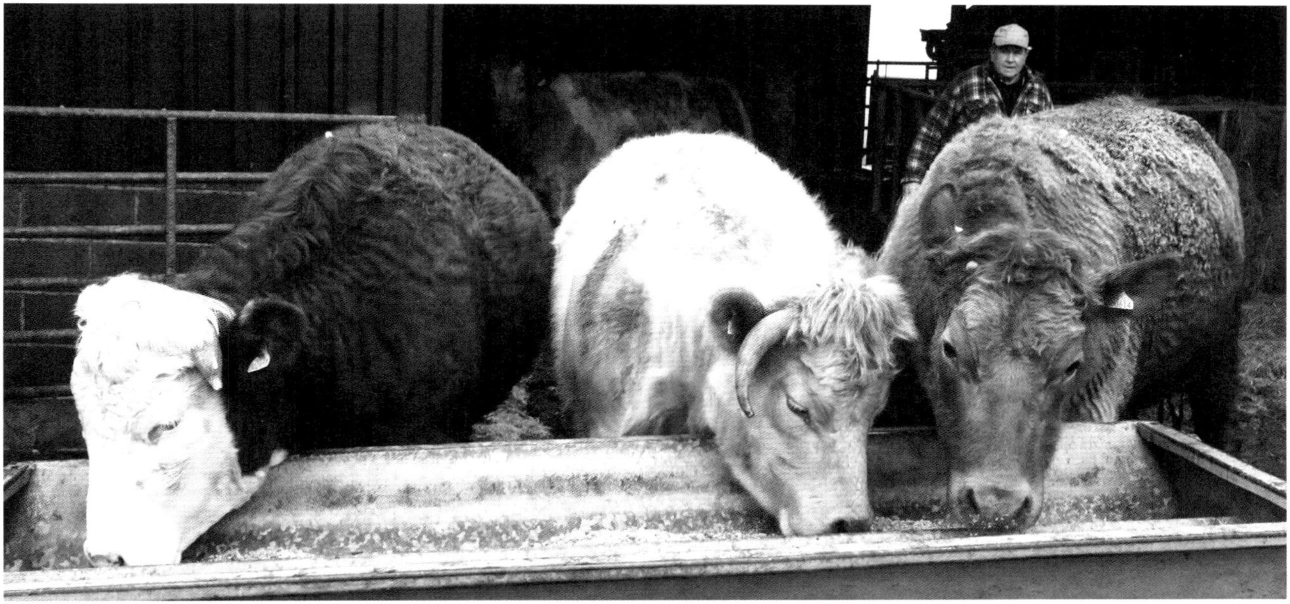

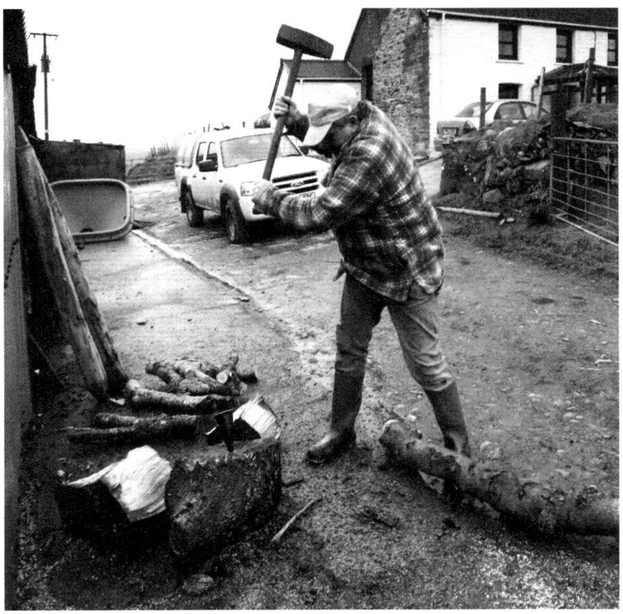

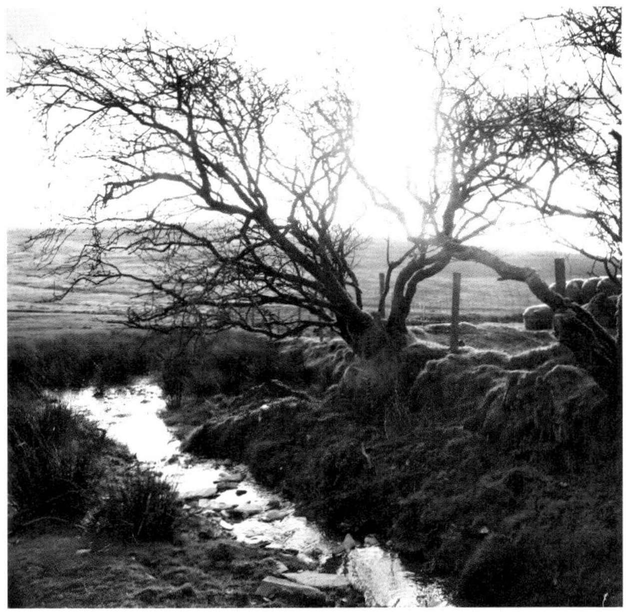

We pay farmers to keep going on smallholdings like this because generations of us accept that to prevent an exodus from the land we have to reward those who are custodians of a countryside we love. In doing so, we also accept that the economics of farming sheep in these snow-covered hills doesn't add up. But it is a price we must pay if we want these hills and their communities to endure.

The warmth of the Rayburn is enticing and the offer of more tea too, but it's time to set out to walk the hills that dominate the view from every window. The Golden Road, running along the top of the Preseli Hills, is one of the finest walks in Wales. The farm sits in a bowl surrounded by these hills and I will be able to see it throughout most of my walk – the shed's red roof and garish tractor will be visible from miles away. Lynne and Gwyndaf embody a shared memory of a way of life that is slowly fading and I feel recharged by listening to their stories. There is nothing wistful or romantic in their recollections, they are matter-of-fact, down to earth pragmatists. It takes a stranger to appreciate their home and its surroundings. For them, it's what they've always known.

Our walk is gentle, with time enough to catch our breath and admire the views across south Wales and to Newport and Cardigan Bay.

My walking companions for the rest of the day are two friends who both work for the Pembrokeshire Coast National Park. We meet at Bwlch Gwynt car park, which watches over north Pembrokeshire in one direction and the south in the other. The view here has passing motorists stopping in their cars to find their cameras. Colleagues Geraint Jones and Julie Garlick have made their life's work in this county's landscape. Geraint is from this part of north Pembrokeshire and Julie, like me, is from the south. Together, there is nothing they don't know about the people, the plants, the farming or the history of the Park. This is their parish and its people their congregation. Their god is nature and their religion is spreading the word of conserving the natural beauty of all we can see. Not all of the congregation wants to hear the word, but their ministry goes on undimmed. They are the latter day evangelists, winning over hearts and minds.

Leaning against cars, trying not to lose gloves blowing about in the wind, we pull on waterproof leggings, thick socks, fleeces, jackets, woollen hats and walking boots. The leggings flap like flags until they are zipped up and buttoned tight. It has started sleeting gently, as forecast, but the promise of bright, sunny conditions later makes us stick to our plan. On a dry day the path from the car park would usually be hard and dry, but days of wet weather have reduced our route to ankle-deep mud, that in places becomes calf-deep ponds.

You won't have to pant as much walking the Preseli Hills as you might in the Brecon Beacons or Snowdonia. Our walk is gentle, with time enough

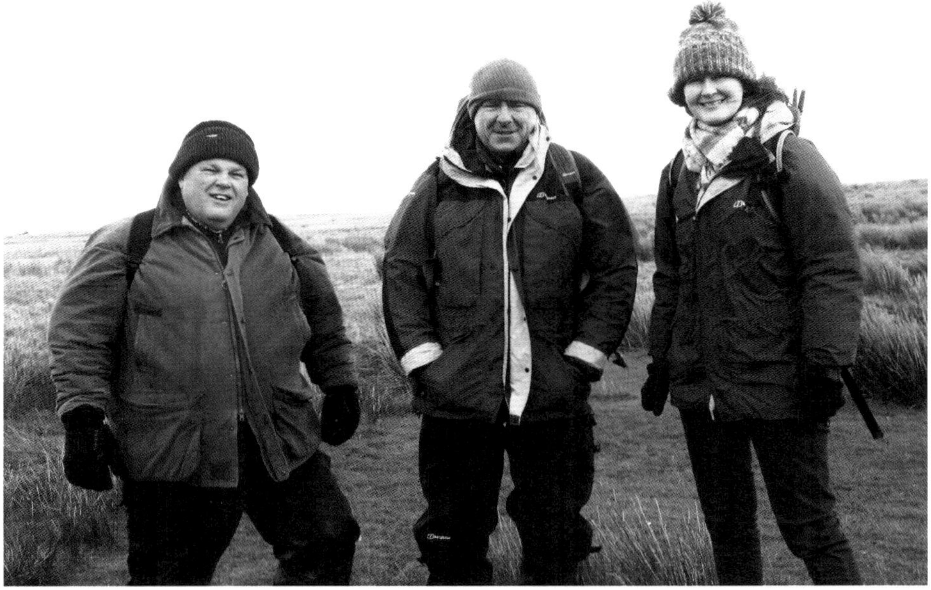

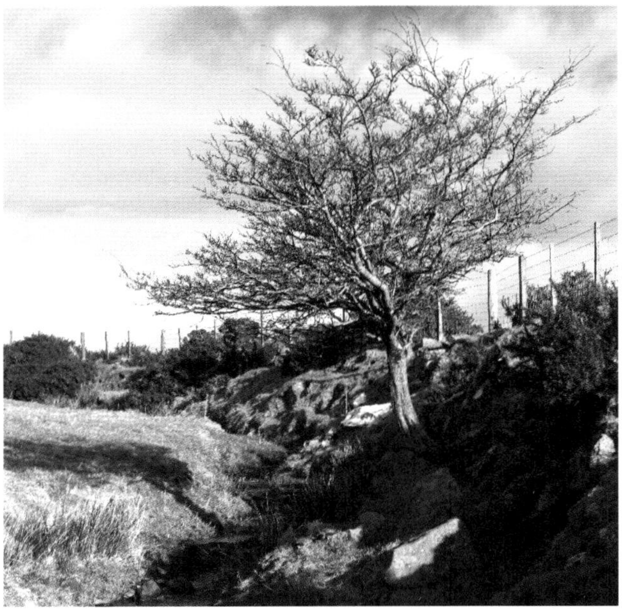

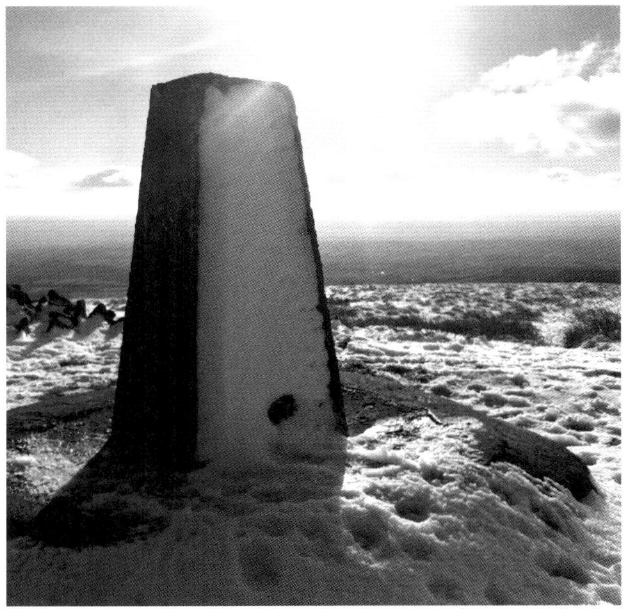

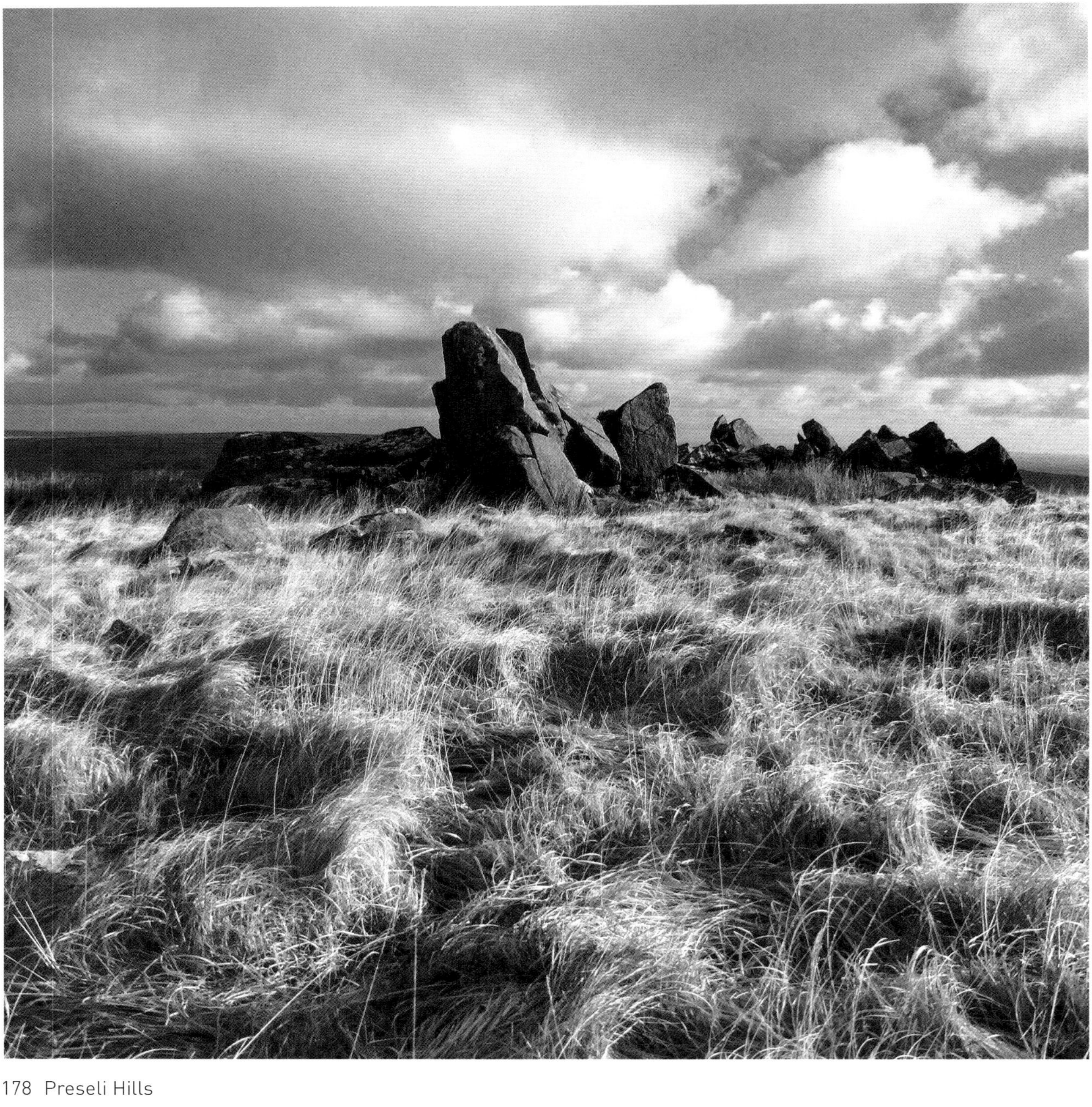

178 Preseli Hills

to catch our breath and admire the views across south Wales and to Newport and Cardigan Bay. We are about to enter a time capsule and journey to Pembrokeshire past. Over seven miles, we will walk through the story of Wales – from the land of myth to its first farmers and traders.

From the car park at Bwlch Gwynt, near Foel Eryr, we have a seven-mile walk ahead us of us to Llainbanal, near Crymych. Foel Eryr is a dramatic beginning; the 'Place of the Eagle', with a Bronze Age burial cairn at its summit. It is covered on its east face with a light dusting of snow. We won't see any eagles, but buzzards and red kites are common.

We pass Pantmaenog Forest. Growing timber is big business in the Preseli Hills. Julie explains our route on the top of the mountains was never thought to have been wooded, whereas the lower slopes might have seen widespread birch forests. The general consensus is that woodland covered most of the hills, except for the rocky tors poking through. The woodland would have been sparser on the tops though (and composed of pine, birch and juniper), making it easier to travel through. The lower slopes would have had denser woodland, composed of oak and hazel as the climate warmed. The dominant story of the timber trade of the last century here is the relatively quick-growing spruce and other evergreen softwoods, but their over-bearing dominance makes them a less environmentally preferable species. Today, the edges of the plantation have been harvested. The broken trunks, scattered bark and bare earth look like a man's face carelessly shaved.

The footpath leads to the highest point in the Preseli Hills – Foel Cwmcerwyn, 1,759 feet high. The marker on its summit is half covered by snow. Only the higher slopes are covered; some fields facing the sun have escaped, yet their adjacent pastures seem to have received double helpings. Here the weather is partial and random. When the snow comes, height and aspect can mean shelter or storm, even within the same farm.

We are alone on our walk. There are no other backpackers in any direction on the horizon. In green and white colours, the mountains take on an almost supernatural atmosphere that makes even a gentle walk dramatic.

The Mabinogion tells of King Arthur and his knights fighting a fierce battle below Foel Cwmcerwyn with a vicious boar, the Twrch Trwyth. Rocks at Cerrigmarchogion are supposedly the graves of some of Arthur's knights killed in that battle. Geraint stops us to point out a cottage on the distant lowlands. It's home to a British Geological Survey monitoring box that listens to the heartbeat of the earth. From there, the tremors of the world are recorded, each of the planet's judders and eruptions noted with the flicker of a measuring needle. North Korea's missile tests and the tide crashing onto Parrog beach in Newport are all faithfully captured in its daily diary. Stop here and listen and in the silence you will hear the earth.

We are high above Rosebush, once home to a thriving quarry whose slate was used to roof the Palace of Westminster. Exports from here were loaded onto the now disused railway and taken to boats in Fishguard, then shipped all over the empire. This wasn't a slate industry to rival north Wales, but nonetheless a significant operation by Pembrokeshire standards. Rosebush these days is perhaps better known for its worldwide appeal to save its pub, Tafarn Sinc. Few walkers miss the chance to plan their walk in the Preseli Hills around it. The sawdust floors, log fires, Welsh choirs on the sound system, steak and chips and a pint are fixtures for those in the know, a reward to eat and drink all those calories walked off on the hills. But it has faced a year of uncertainty.

Like so many rural businesses in Pembrokeshire – the post office, the shop, the garage, the bakery, Tafarn Sinc faced closure on the retirement of its owners. In this Welsh-speaking heartland of Pembrokeshire, the prospect of shutting shop was simply unacceptable to the community, who refused to countenance another totemic loss in their village. So an appeal to raise funds to purchase the pub as a community enterprise gathered support from as far away as Hollywood. The hostelry, built from timber and zinc sheets to serve quarry workers and tourists, will survive another century.

High above Mynachlog-ddu, the rocky tor of Carn Bica, with its large rock, overlooks Bedd Arthur, a ring of stones in the shape of an eye, one of many locations claimed to be the grave of King Arthur. There may well have been a burial mound inside the stones that has since eroded away, but the monument probably dates to Neolithic times, long before Arthur is believed to have lived. If he lies here, they chose well. He commands all he can see, though for a moment we can't see much at all. The sleet, which has threatened all morning, is now shooting horizontally into our faces. Not that you can see much flesh; our woollen hats and waterproof hoods are now pulled down even more tightly over our foreheads. All that is exposed to the elements are reddened noses and mouths. We trudge on in that very British fashion, hoping this will pass. The noise of the hail is too loud to speak or hear any conversation. I find myself humming the words of 'Blaenwern', the Welsh hymn tune: 'Love divine, all loves excelling'. I'm not usually taken to humming music, religious or otherwise, but given where we are, this hymn seems appropriate. William Penfro Rowlands, the composer of one of Britain's most popular hymn tunes, a feature at many weddings, must have been inspired by these towering hills, their soaring skies and racing clouds. He was born in 1860 at Llys-y-frân beneath us, near Maenclochog. The schoolteacher composed 'Blaenwern' in 1905. The tune is named after the farm near Tufton where Rowlands sent his son to stay with friends of the family to convalesce. It was thought the fresh air of the Preseli Hills would improve his health. Rowlands named the tune in honour of the family at Blaenwern.

Like climbing a mountain where the landscape reveals itself with each yard ascended, 'Blaenwern' starts gently in the musical foothills and gradually builds to a powerful climax:

Love divine, all loves excelling,
Joy of Heav'n to earth come down;
Fix in us thy humble dwelling;
All thy faithful mercies crown!

This was Rowlands' heaven on earth, his spiritual inspiration; these are the hills he saw from his window. The storm surges across the landscape

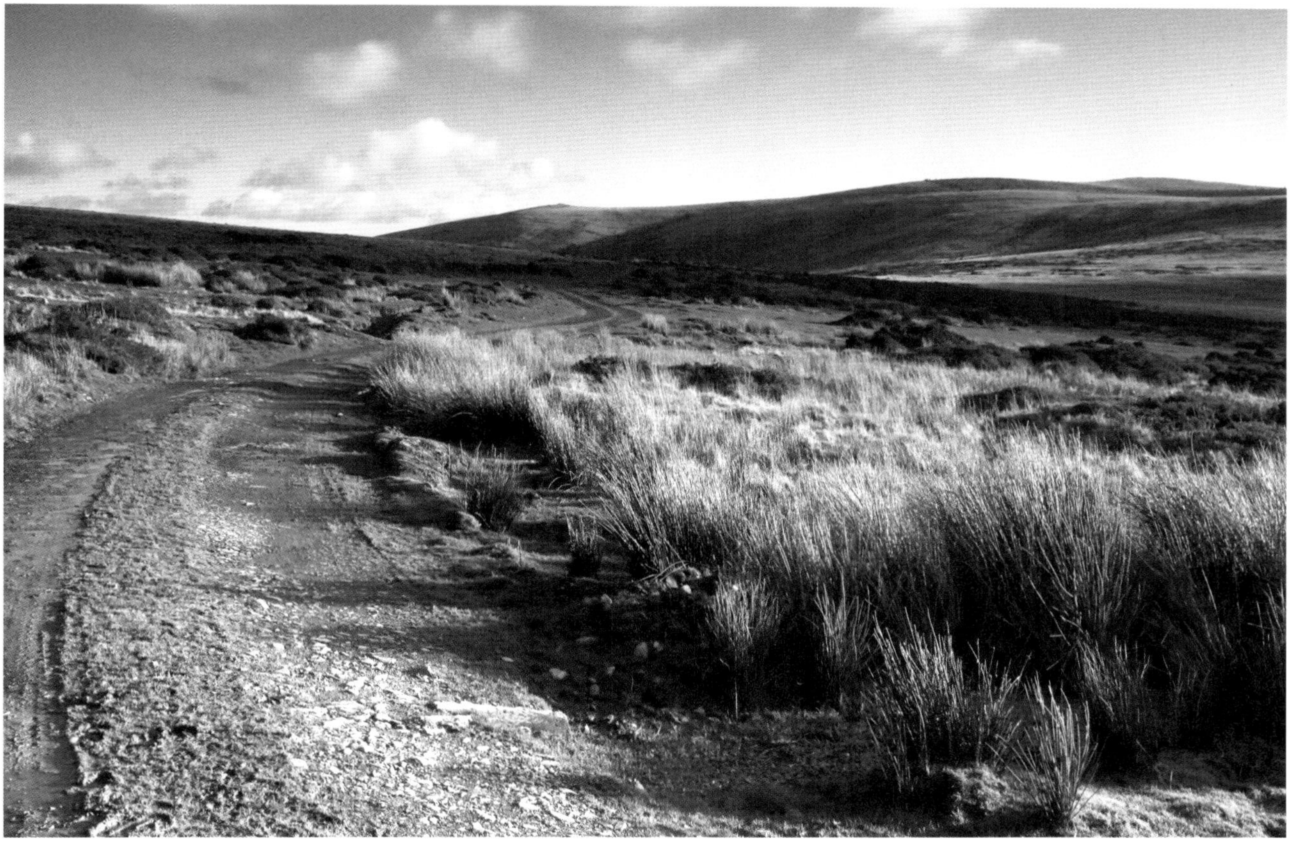

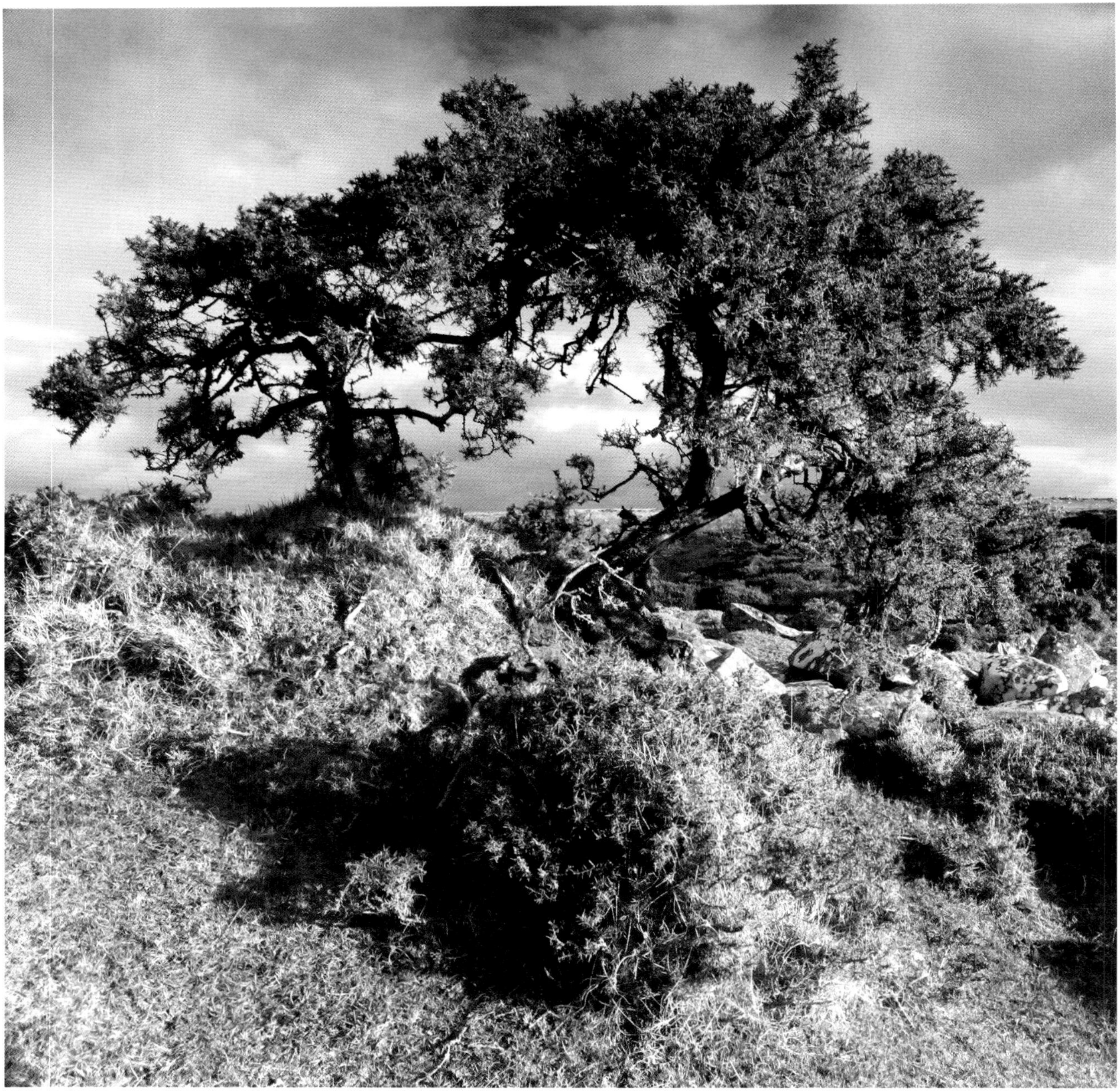

and the sprinting clouds shut out the daylight, on then off. First jet black sky, then bright again, as though someone has turned up the brilliance on the television remote control. Dark brown fields of stubble become bright golden and then almost purple before turning white, showered with hail. Four seasons in four minutes. Rowlands, living through the Welsh religious revival of the early 1900s, must have felt certain he was in the Promised Land. I stop humming. If Geraint and Julie heard me, they are too polite to say.

The hail stops as quickly as it began and we pause for sandwiches and tea. We stand to eat; the ground is too soaked to sit – even in waterproofs.

If the Preseli Hills inspired William Penfro Rowlands, the magic here also extended to poetry. Waldo Williams was born in Pembrokeshire the year before Rowlands published 'Blaenwern'. Williams would become one of Wales' leading poets of the 20th century. He was also a pacifist, a Christian and a Welsh nationalist. After university in Aberystwyth and a number of teaching posts across the country, he married in 1943. His wife, Linda Llewellyn, died just two years later. He never remarried.

Objecting to Britain's involvement in the Korean War, he refused to pay his income tax on the grounds of his deeply held pacifist views. It was a campaign that would see him sent to prison. He stood unsuccessfully as a parliamentary candidate for Plaid Cymru in the 1959 election. For Williams, politics and poetry were intimately bound. In Wales, the landscape defines who you are and what you believe in.

In later years he returned to the classroom, where he is said to have been a mesmeric teacher. But his greatest legacy is surely the words he left behind. Waldo was in a long line of Welsh folk poets who served their community by writing in verse about the people they knew. The interdependency of communities that were so much part of life in the Preseli Hills was a regular theme in his writing – the sense of knowing your neighbours, of belonging to a particular place, and a desire for peaceful coexistence. As he wrote in his poem *Preseli* composed after the end of the Second World War: 'The sick world's balm shall be brotherhood alone.' The sun comes out as we walk towards the Bronze Age burial cairn at Foel Feddau. No one suggests we turn back in the face of driving rain and low visibility, and our perseverance pays off as the white skies clear to blue and the horizon is revealed in every direction for miles. Soaked socks and mud-covered waterproofs have been a small price to pay for witnessing the clouds lifting off this magnificent landscape.

Like Tafarn Sinc and its regulars, the natural terrain of the Preseli Hills finds itself in the midst of great change. The grazing regimes that have shaped the area and its ecosystems for generations are now fragile. To keep the bracken and the grass in check, heavy animals have trodden down the growth, followed by sheep close grazing the vast acreages. Without their presence, the Preseli Hills would revert to scrub.

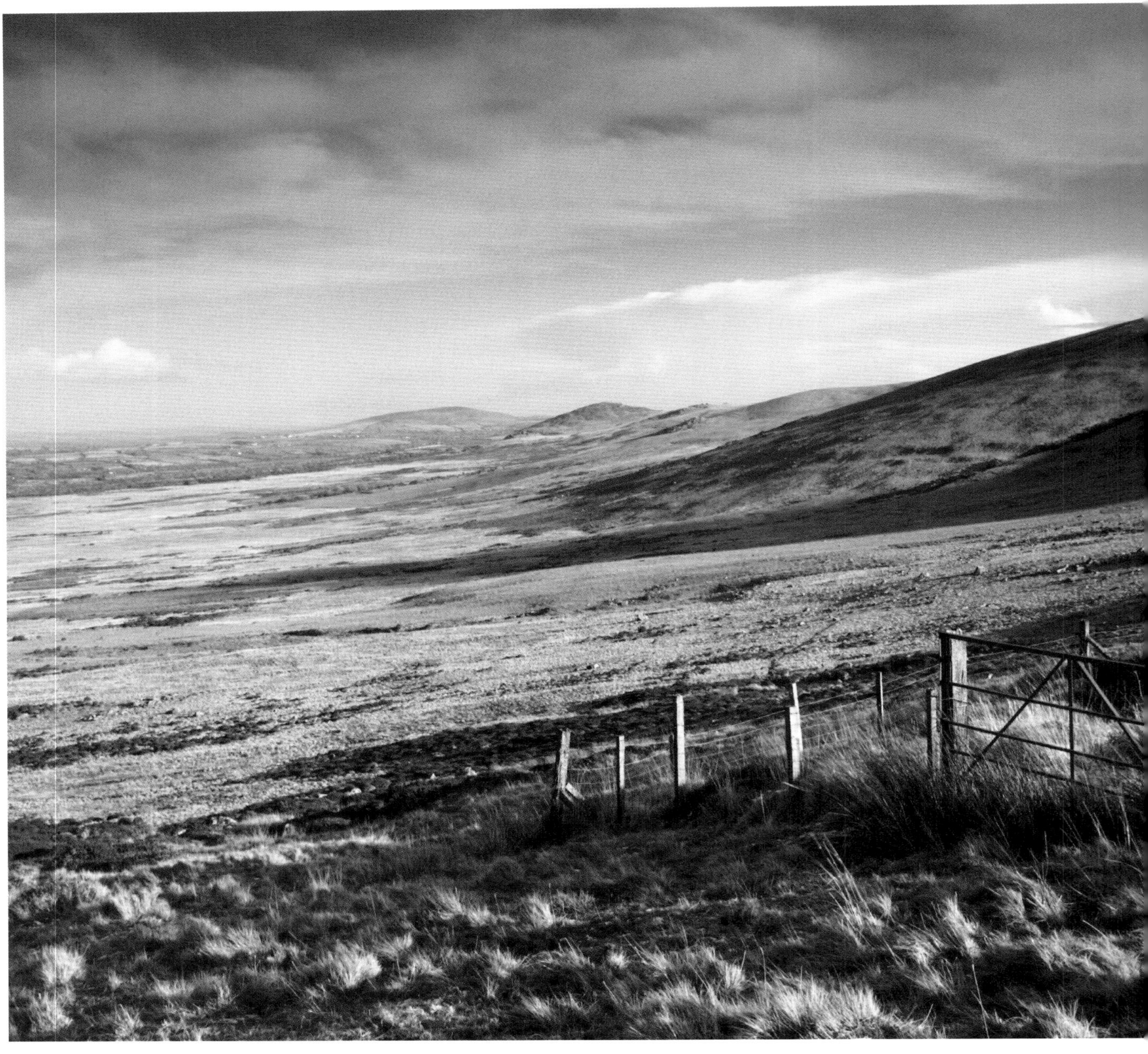

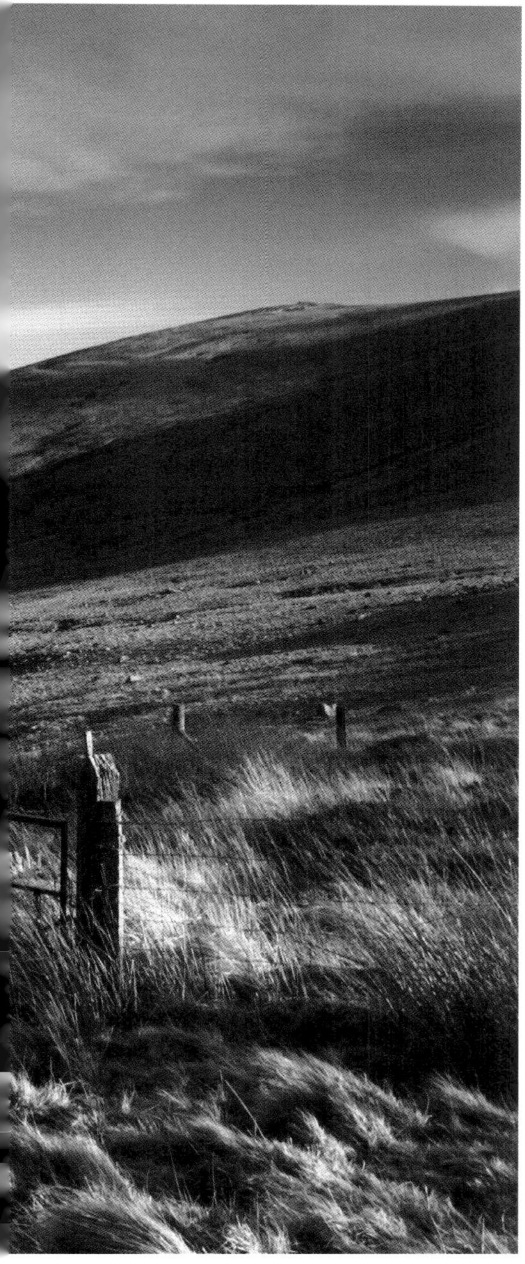

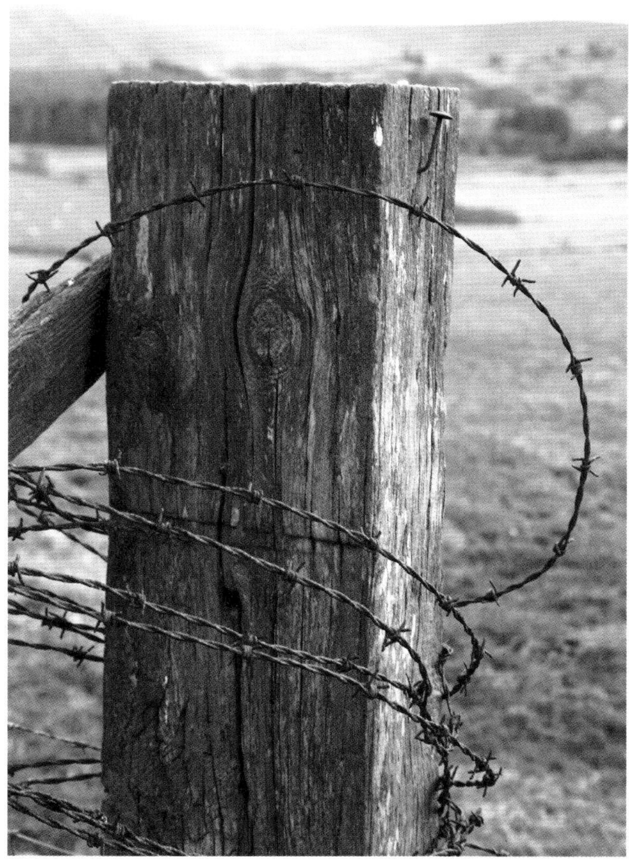

What we see around us today is not an entirely natural landscape – it is the product of generations of human intervention as foresters, farmers and quarrymen have made their mark. The heather-clad slopes, so familiar for a century, have been achieved by subsidy and the underwriting of struggling small farms. The truth is that bovine tuberculosis in cattle in west Wales has kept all but the ponies off the mountains and a stuttering market for lamb has also steadily reduced the quantity of small animals grazing. The hooves of large animals like cattle are good for the land; they break up bracken and till the soil. Without cattle barging down the bracken and sheep munching the grass, the area would become a different environment.

Some conservationists will point out that unmanaged wilderness is the natural order of things. But no one can be sure precisely what the implications would be for the wider environment if farming on these uplands were to beat a retreat.

On the cold windswept slopes, a number of rare plants thrive, untroubled by agricultural chemicals that have turned some of the flatter fields beneath us an unnatural green. Julie launches into her adoration for the pale butterwort – a small but striking carnivorous specimen with sticky olive-green leaves and a delicate lilac flower that grows well in big animal hoof marks. You might be lucky to find a bog orchid here too; it's only a few inches high and fiendishly difficult to stumble upon. March clubmoss is a rather primitive plant, only to be found here and in Snowdonia. But November is not the month to go on a plant hunting expedition in these hills.

We've walked a mile or so since stopping for a cuppa. It's slow and hard walking when your boots are caked in mud and you're navigating your path through deceptive bogs. Geraint stops us to look at the small marker stones placed on the boundary of the common with Pantmaenog. We're all grateful for an excuse for another breather. They have the letters TDLl carved into them. TDLl – Thomas Davies Lloyd was the Lord Marcher of Cemais – effectively the landowner of these parts during the 19th century. Our generation will add conservation to the long list of human activities which have taken place here.

Julie explains that the Pembrokeshire Coast National Park proposes to restore several streams within the common land of the Preseli Hills. Allowing nature to do its own thing isn't necessarily what might be seen as most beneficial to improving biodiversity. Sometimes nature needs a helping hand. Here, the plan is to improve the habitat for southern damselflies. For the damselfly to flourish, a mini digger will scoop out the existing choked stream channels that have become overgrown and create wide, shallow streams.

As you ask, the southern damselfly is a tiny insect, perhaps no more than 30mm in length and no, you won't see one on a winter's day like today, but come here in the summer from June to August and you might spot one. The National Park's efforts to look after them seem heroic, until you learn that two other members of the family of damselfly have become extinct in the last 40 years. The race for preservation is urgent. Little interventions in this vast wilderness might strengthen the southern damselfly's tenure for a little longer.

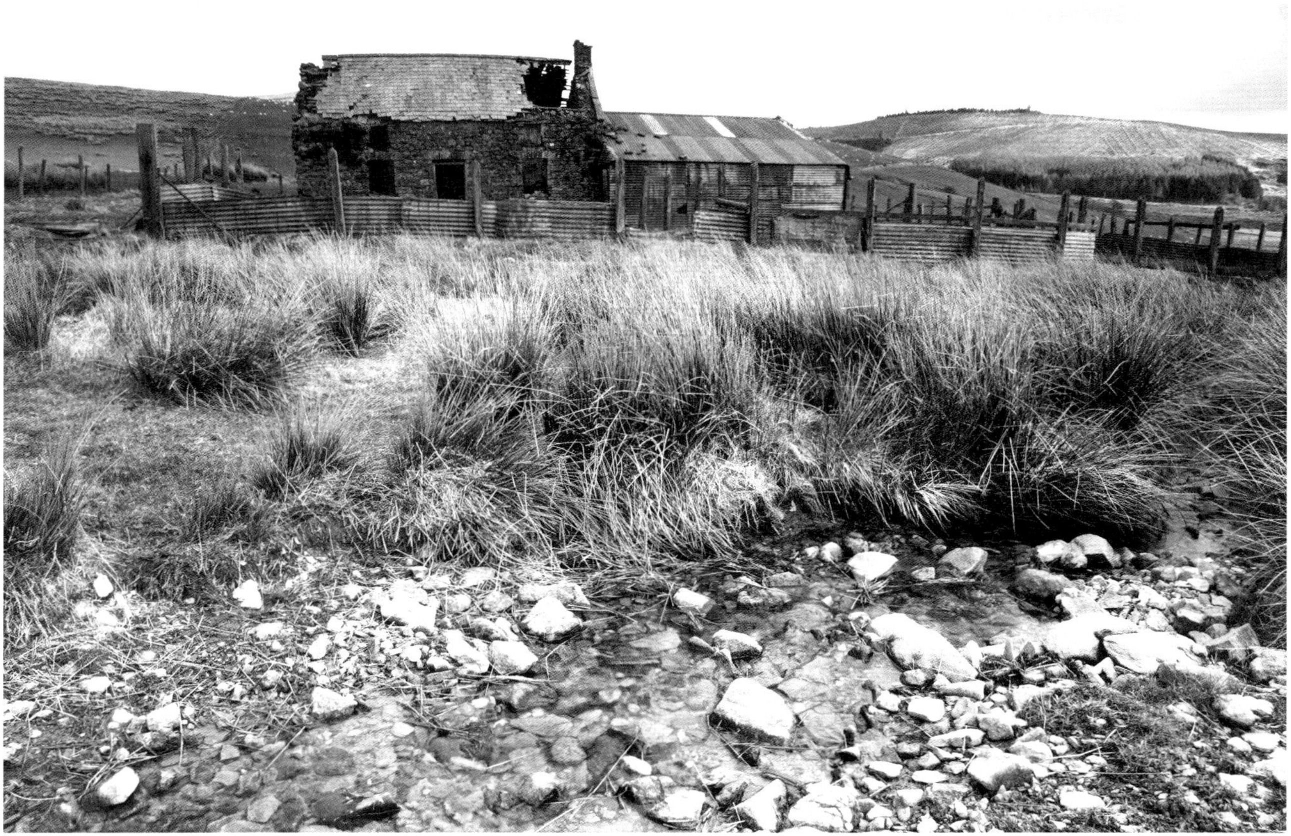

What happens here, high in the mountains, matters to a far wider region. If the biodiversity is damaged, the consequences extend much further than these hills alone.

Close to the end of our walk, Foel Drygarn's Iron Age fortress with its double ramparts and ditches glares down. The large flat stone is Bwrdd y Brenin, the King's Table. They say there's a pot of gold buried here somewhere. The walk to see it is reward enough. Just below is Carn Meini, its bluestone rock eroded into jagged boulders. For many years it was believed that the bluestones in the inner circle at Stonehenge were quarried here. Then, in 2013, new research suggested the stones might in fact come from another location in the Preseli Hills – the nearby Carn Goedog and Craig Rhos-y-Felin. The geologists and archaeologists are still engaged in a furious war of words, frantically rewriting the history books. Every generation writes its own Preseli story. But the lure of this location is surely its uncertain truths and unknowable legends, as much as its beguiling lanes and less-trodden hills.

The large flat stone is Bwrdd y Brenin, the King's Table.

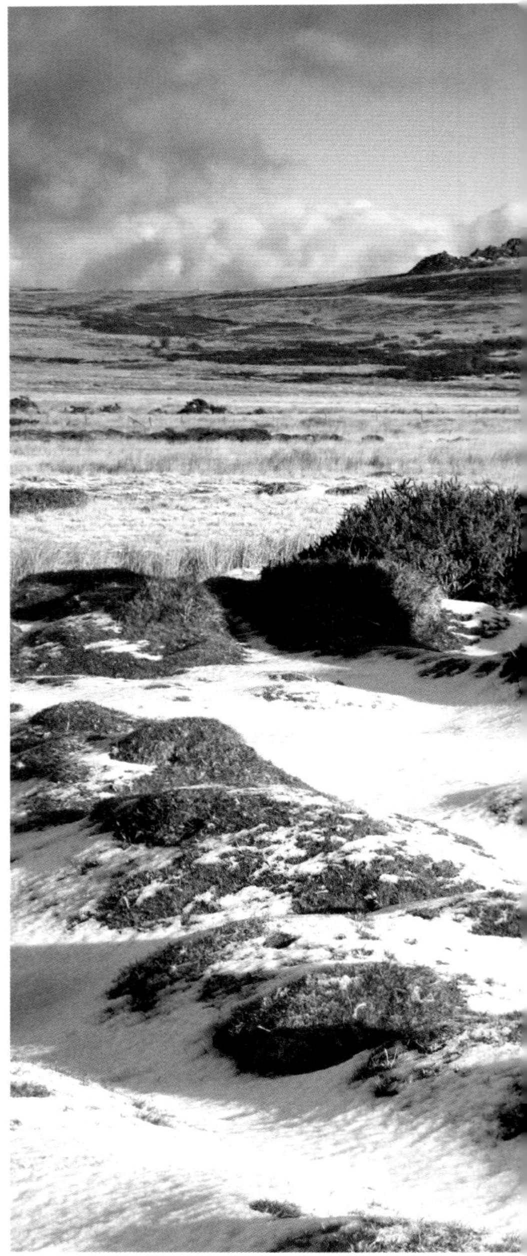

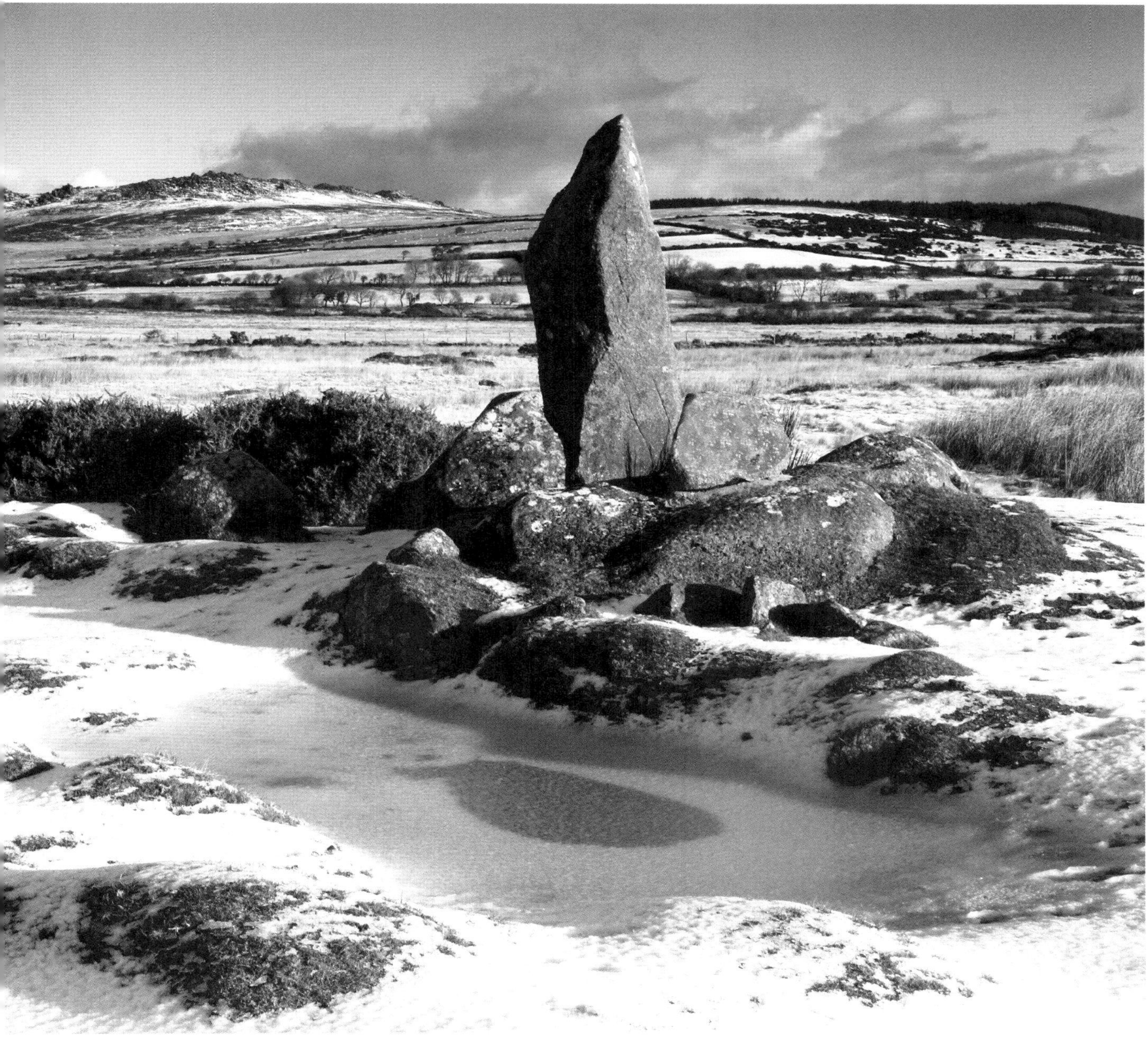

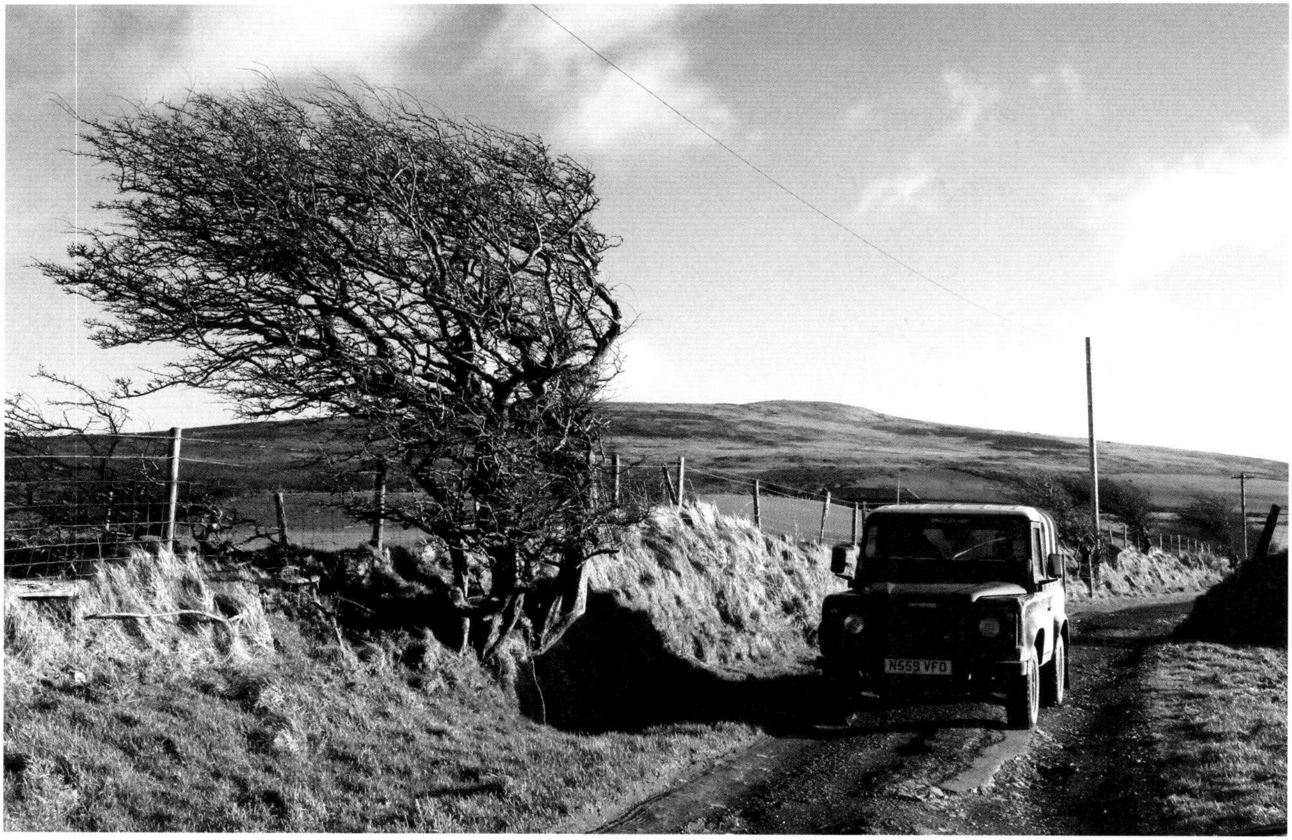
N559 VFO

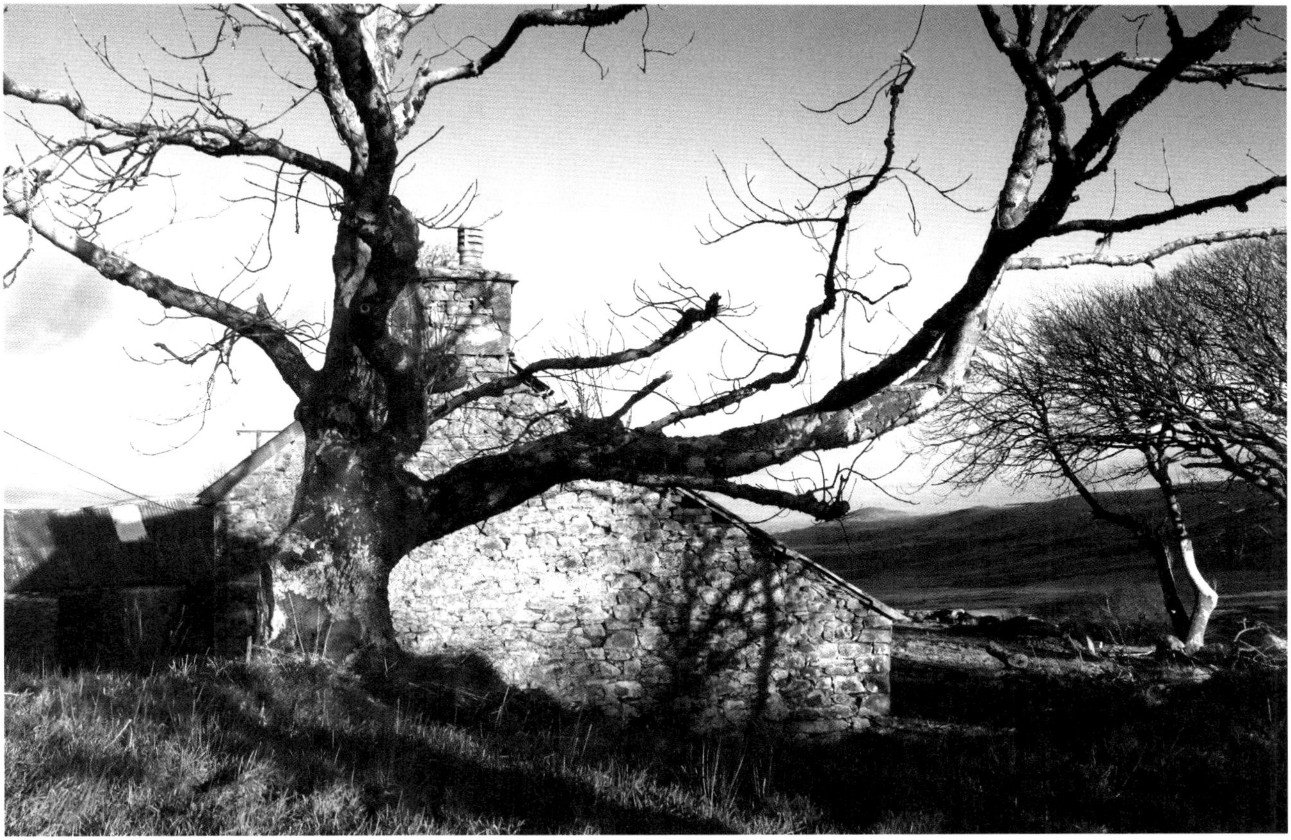

Bibliography

Evans, Revd. J. Wyn, and Turner, Rick, *St David's Bishop's Palace*, (Tretower: CADW, 1991)

Fenton, Richard, *A Historical Tour through Pembrokeshire*, (London: Longman, Hurst, Rees, Orme & Co., 1811)

Fitzgerald, Michael, and Knapp-Fisher, John, *Pembrokeshire Churches*, (Rosedale, 1996)

Gossage, John, *Some notes on the history of Coedcanlas*, (2001). Available at www.coedcanlas.co.uk/history.htm

John, Brian, *Pembrokeshire*, (Exeter: David & Charles, 1976)

Jones, Maj. Francis, *Historic Houses of Pembrokeshire and Their Families*, (Pembrokeshire: Brawdy Books, 1996)

Kelsall, Dennis and Kelsall, Jan, *Walking in Pembrokeshire*, (Milnthorpe: Cicerone Press, 2005)

Lockley, R.M., *Pembrokeshire*, (London: Robert Hale Limited, 1957)

Rees, Derek, *Rings and Rosettes*, (Llandysul: J.D. Lewis and Sons, 1977)

Seymour, John, *About Pembrokeshire*, (Pembrokeshire: Carningli Press, 1971)

Von Friesen, Hero, and Lloyd, Thomas, *The Families of Picton*, (Pembrokeshire: Picton Castle Trust, 2002)

Acknowledgements

Tony O'Shaughnessy for reading and improving the text, Suzanne Hay and Anna Wilson for corrections and comments and additional photography.
Peter Gill, Joana Rodrigues, Daniel Williams and all team at Graffeg.

Strumble Head: Pembrokeshire Coast National Park and Melin Tregwynt.

Hen Galan: Staff, pupils and parents at Ysgol Llanychllwydog, Mrs Bessie Davies, The Church in Wales, Bonnie and Vivien Davies and their grandson Llyr of Penlanwynt farm.

Castlemartin: David Devonald, Cerwyn Davies, the graziers of the Preseli Hills and Castlemartin, the British Army.

Sailing the Haven: Neyland Marina; Sam and Bob – crew of Sea Legs.

County Show: Jemma Owen, the staff of the Pembrokeshire County Show.

St Davids: RNLI, The choir and clergy of St Davids Cathedral.

Picton Castle and Gardens: Dai Evans Director. Head gardener Roddy Milne, staff and volunteers.

Tenby: Alan Thomas, the monastic and ley community of Caldey Island.

Preseli Hills: Geraint Jones and Julie Garlick, Pembrokeshire Coast National Park, Lynne & Gwyndaf Rees of Gernos Fach.